White Ship

Ship

Red

Crosses

Second Edition

A Nursing Memoir of The Falklands War

Nicci Pugh

Published by

MELROSE BOOKS

An Imprint of Melrose Press Limited
St Thomas Place, Ely. Cambridgeshire. CB7 4GG, UK
www.melrosebooks.com

SECOND EDITION
ISBN 978-1-907732-23-2

A percentage of the profits from the sale of this book will be donated to
The South Atlantic Medal Association
www.sama82.org.uk

Front Cover: Following her hasty conversion in Gibraltar Dockyard, Her Majesty's Hospital Ship Uganda
leaves The Mediterranean for the uncertainties of The South Atlantic. April 19th 1982.
Photograph: Author's private collection
Back Cover: The author with former patient and Welsh Guardsman Simon Weston O.B.E. at her home in
February 2007.
Photograph: David Fitzgerald

Typesetting, Cover design and Cartography by Matt Stephens

Printed and bound in Great Britain by:
CPI Antony Rowe, Chippenham, Wiltshire

FSC
www.fsc.org
MIX
Paper from
responsible sources
FSC® C013604

This book is dedicated to the three British Servicemen who died on board Her Majesty's Hospital Ship *Uganda* in June 1982:

Marine Paul Callan
Royal Marines
died June 10th 1982

Corporal Stephen Hope
Third Battalion The Parachute Regiment
died June 13th 1982

Private Richard Absolon MM
Third Battalion The Parachute Regiment
died June 13th 1982

MM = Military Medal

What is Dying?

What is dying? I am standing on the sea shore.
A ship sails to the morning breeze and starts for the ocean.
She is an object of beauty and I stand watching her until at last, she fades on the horizon.
And someone at my side says: 'She is gone'.
Gone where? Gone from my sight, that is all. She is just as large in the masts, hull and spars as she ever was when I saw her, and just as able to bear her load of living freight to her destination.
The diminished size and total loss of sight is in me, not in her.
And just at that moment when someone at my side says:
'She is gone'…there are others who are watching her coming.
And other voices take up the glad shout:
'There she comes'.
And that is dying.

Bishop Brent

CONTENTS

FOREWORD

One of the early key decisions made by the Ministry of Defence after the sailing of the Task Force to take the Falkland Islands back from the invading Argentines in April 1982, was to requisition a P&O cruise ship, the SS *Uganda*, as a hospital ship, and position her in the war zone. This was to save many lives.

Now, at last, the story of The Hospital Ship *Uganda*'s service in The Falklands War has been told by Nicci Pugh. Her portrayal of that episode, starting from the day of *Uganda*'s requisitioning by the Ministry of Defence right through to the ship's return home, makes great reading. The blend of poignancy, humour, fascinating medical detail, and personal narratives makes this a unique and very special book. Nicci, a Trauma Operating Theatre Sister in Queen Alexandra's Royal Naval Nursing Service, was working right in the centre of The Hospital Ship *Uganda*'s momentous experience down south, and no one is better qualified to tell the tale.

As the commander of the Commando Brigade of Royal Marines and Parachute soldiers during The Falklands War, I was responsible for the lives of over 5,000 fighting men. At the time it was very reassuring to know that we could send our wounded out to The Hospital Ship, where we knew that they would be in good hands, and safe under the protection of her big red crosses. When a planned battle was being fought, we would ask that the *Uganda* be moved to a position out at sea, reasonably close to the Falkland Islands, to allow helicopters to take the wounded out to her.

The conversion of a ship from floating classroom, which had spent years transporting children on educational cruises, to a fully operational hospital ship, in a matter of days was an achievement enough in itself. Modifications included the construction of a helicopter deck and refuelling point to allow The Hospital Ship to refuel at sea. Next the doctors and nurses had to train themselves to work in this unfamiliar environment. Having done that they had to put into practice their medical and surgical skills carrying out major surgery in a hospital afloat in the great southern ocean. Here, in latitude 50 degrees south, which old sailors called the 'filthy fifties', one encounters some of the roughest seas in the world. If this was not enough, to begin with, at the back of most of their minds was the question: will the Argentines respect the Red Cross, or will we be attacked and sunk? In the event this last worry proved groundless, but bearing in mind the track record of the ruling Argentine Junta, it was an understandable concern.

This is a great story, well told.

Major-General Julian Thompson CB OBE
Commander of 3rd Commando Brigade, Royal Marines, during
The Falklands War 1982.
London
JUNE 2009

ACKNOWLEDGEMENTS

When I left school in the sixties and the subject of a "career" came up, I told my parents I wanted to become a journalist and author. This was greeted by my father, a distinguished and forthright retired Royal Naval Captain, with the enthusiasm of a fly swat, and I was sent off to train as a nurse and "do something useful". I have never regretted my parents' pragmatic suggestion, as I found within the nursing profession a fulfilment and meaning to life of which I was formerly unaware. I had a natural empathy with all my patients, and felt they appreciated someone who seemed to quickly respond to their needs and requirements at the hospital bedside. When I moved into operating theatre specialisation my interest and knowledge in both surgery and anaesthetics rapidly increased, and I seemed to be destined for an acute trauma-related career centred principally within the operating theatres of both civilian and Royal Naval Hospitals.

So my first debt of gratitude must go to my late parents, Dick and Judy Pugh, who not only directed me towards the nursing profession, but who also gave up so much in their own married life, to ensure that all four of their children received the very best education they could afford for us at the time.

Secondly, to all the many teachers along the way, especially Miss Phyllis Dence, Miss Lidgate and Miss Bailey at Stover School in Devon, who helped ensure that my groundings in both History and English were as thorough and fundamental as they were enjoyable.

When, after 20 years or so at the sharp end of the nursing profession, I finally had the opportunity to widen my offshore sailing experience, I then became renowned for prodigious log and travel writing journals, my pencil and notebook recording in finite detail the many anchorages, harbours and cruising experiences as they unfolded over the years. I even approached the Yachtsman's bible, *Yachting Monthly,* to write articles for them, but a much more experienced lady writer and yachtswoman, Annie Hill, beat me to it.

So, when, following our Inaugural Hospital Ship *Uganda* Reunion in 2008, I was approached by so many attendees requesting someone to try to collate all the information that might otherwise fade with our memories, I had pause for thought. Could I combine the three fundamental interests and skills of my life: nursing, writing and my love of the sea and everything nautical, into one channel, and write the book myself?

Could I take on this prodigious task, or should I choose the slower and more research-oriented route, working with a professional author? I chose the former, and this book, with all its faults and failings, is the result.

Such a change of lifestyle and direction was, for a now middle-aged retired nursing sister, a huge undertaking, and indeed, at times often nearly defeated me.

But everything aside, I and others knew the tale needed to be told. The Royal Naval medical and nursing personnel who served on board The Hospital Ship *Uganda* during The Falklands War twenty-seven years ago have followed their professional traditions, and chosen to avoid any form of publication, or indeed media involvement, for all the right reasons. Military surgery in conflict is not a subject that sits easily with light conversation, particularly in a country that could be defined, today, as more "civilian" than "military" in its outlook. It was felt that perhaps now, twenty-seven years after The Falklands War, enough years have advanced for many of the wounds to have healed, and perhaps as good a time as any for this, as yet untold story, to be read.

Not only my colleagues, but many of our former patients have asked me to do this, and a huge privilege it has been for me to gather all the information and write this book on their behalf.

Initially, having made the decision to write the work myself, I was very much on my own, with only one "self-help writer's guide" by Michael Oke, published for *The Daily Telegraph*, to hand. It was a steep learning curve, and I would not have completed the complex process at all without much help as the project expanded and consolidated. Fortunately, when help did arrive, it was reliable, efficient and prompt.

My initial and most heartfelt thanks must go to Major-General Julian Thompson CB OBE, and Jane Thompson, not only for their reliable and professional editing help and advice, but also for their support and encouragement in the early stages. I felt they too both believed in the book's message. The Hospital Ship *Uganda* was included in the Imperial War Museum's Falklands 25th Anniversary Exhibition in London in 2007; this reintroduced former patient Bill Belcher MBE and myself again after 25 years, and may have been the catalyst we needed. What, perhaps, had been a distant glimmer on a hexi-stove was enough to warm the can, and the subsequent success of our 2008 and 2009 Hospital Ship Reunions the final cooking.

For "General Julian" (as all within the SAMA82 "family" respectfully call him) to then agree to write the Foreword for us was a huge accolade for us all. We thank you, Julian, for your invariably prompt and reliable advice throughout this long and challenging year, that has seen the book move from its early creation to final publication and production.

Particular thanks must also go to Rear Admiral Andy Gough CB RN, Doctor Peter Bull FRCA, Captain Grahame Burton FNI and Lt. Commander Mark Trasler MBE RN, all of whom helped at various stages with details and updates as required.

John Phillips DSC (Trustee, British Limbless Ex-Service Men's Association), Lt.Col. Tony Davies MBE (Chairman, South Atlantic Medal Association) and Denzil Connick (Trustee, South Atlantic Medal Association) provided prompt last-minute data as we approached publication in April 2010. Commodore Carolyn Stait CBE RN, a friend and colleague from our 1983 appointments in Gibraltar, provided much sound advice for the addendum on Military Females in Combat Today, and I am most grateful for her encouragement and support for this project overall. Angela Perry (Secretary, The Falkland Islands Memorial Chapel Trust, Pangbourne) kindly helped us in trying to contact the families of the three servicemen who died on board The Hospital Ship, to whom the book is dedicated. The Dedication can be read on page iii.

The lengthy publishing process was initially kicked off in May 2008 by fellow Falklands War veteran and publisher David Connett and his teams, based at Witney, Oxfordshire, and thanks must go to him for his help in the early stages. Also to his freelance editor Richard Walden, member of The Society for Editors and Proofreaders, who was immensely helpful at that time. Regrettably, this team had to withdraw from the project in October 2009. Melrose Books near Cambridge then took over the final and more demanding stages of publication, and my sincere thanks are extended to all their teams for their professionalism, efficiency and reliability throughout this most challenging time.

Others who have helped along the way are Lynn New, the poet and illustrator, for her delightful drawings of The Hospital Ship *Uganda* used throughout the work. Also, Dr Jo Stanley FRHS and Captain C.M. Taylor RRC QARNNS, both of whom helped with sound advice in the early days of planning the project.

Marion Browning, Secretary of the SS *Uganda* Trust, and the SS *Uganda* Trust itself, are also thanked for permission to include much material from their 1998 publication: "*UGANDA* The Story of a Very Special Ship" published by The SS *Uganda* Trust Registered Charity No. 1020247. The Society of Authors, as the literary representative of the estate of John Masefield, kindly gave permission for me to use the poem *Sea Fever* for the chapter titling, and to reproduce the poem at the beginning of the work. I also thank Philip Hemmings, then Editor of "The Nursing Times", for his agreement some years ago for me to copy "The Nursing Times" article on page 121 in publications, to help clarify the situation on board The Hospital Ship *Uganda*, with regard to the press, media and subsequent use of amateur photographs taken on board in 1982. Thanks must also go to The Imperial War Museum in London, who kindly gave me the actual exhibit picture of Her Majesty's Hospital Ship *Uganda* which had been displayed in their 25th Anniversary Exhibition of The Falklands War in 2007. I was able to present this personally to The Falkland Islands Museum in Stanley the following year, where it will remain on permanent display. The Imperial War Museum also gave permission to use the picture of former patients Corporal Roy Bassey with Lance Corporal Denzil Connick FKD797 (see pages 96 and 129). Royal British Legion member Trevor Johnson kindly gave us permission to use some of his photographs taken during our Royal British Legion Travel trip to The Falkland Islands for the 25th Anniversary of The Falklands War in November 2007.

In The Falkland Islands, my host in Stanley on my first return trip to The Islands in 2003 was Shirley Hirtle. Shirley has since helped enormously with research and contacts in The Falkland Islands that would have otherwise taken months to follow up and action.

Also, to Tim Miller and Don Bonner for their email inputs "from 52 south to 52 north", and especially to Don, who spoke so openly about events in 1982 when we talked on my last visit to The Islands in November 2008. The teams at both "Penguin News" (The Falkland Islands weekly newspaper) and The Falkland Islands Museum in Stanley have all supported the project loyally from the outset.

Above all, thanks must be made to all the contributors to the book, particularly the former patients whom we treated, cared for and looked after on board The Hospital Ship, during and after The Falklands War in 1982. They all had the belief and trust that I would fully respect their writings, and carry the detail forward, on their behalf, to present to our publishing teams to the best of my ability. I hope I have achieved that objective, and I owe them all a deep debt of gratitude. It was an enormous privilege to help them on board our Hospital Ship in 1982, and I much appreciate their prompt and frank contributions more than twenty-six years on, the majority of which were sent to me almost by return of post. I know that much of what they have conveyed must have been difficult to write, and I take this opportunity to thank each and every one of them from the bottom of my heart.

Two of the most significant factors that are frequently referred to, by those who participated in the British Task Force in 1982, are both the teamwork and the comradeship that ensued. The success of any mission has to be a sum of all those who participate in it, and this element has undoubtedly contributed to both the readability and candour of this work. All who have helped in so many different ways to get the book into print hope, by the frank revelations written here twenty-seven years after the events of 1982, that this will help and encourage other injured servicemen and women today, who follow so closely with similar problems and setbacks.

* * *

The author is most grateful for all the contributions for inclusion in this book. The majority have been divided to flow into the relevant periods as the timescale of The Falklands War unfolds. Of necessity some amendments have had to be made, but overall, the style and writings of each individual author have been retained.

* * *

The information in this book has been obtained from a variety of sources, the majority of which are listed in the Select Bibliography on page 200. Wherever possible the author has made reasonable efforts to check the validity of the information. Mention of current conflicts is all in the public domain. However, the author is unable to guarantee the accuracy or completeness of the information published in this book, and the author shall not be held responsible for any errors, omissions or damages arising from this information.

INTRODUCTION

This little book is an account of The 1982 Falklands War from a military nursing point of view. In simple terms, it tells the unique story of the role of The Hospital Ship *Uganda* within the complex but highly successful chain of treatment and care of casualties, as they were evacuated from ship, battlefield and site of injury, through the Regimental Aid Posts and Dressing Stations to The Hospital Ship, and thence back to UK. It is not a detailed military historical record, nor indeed a medical textbook. It could easily be called "The Nurse's Tale".

It is not the intention in any way to overshadow or even compete with the invaluable work done by our forebears in former wars, campaigns and conflicts, many of whom had to deal with casualties on a much greater and indeed almost unimaginable scale, in far more arduous and dangerous conditions than ourselves. Of particular note are the Nursing Sisters of Queen Alexandra's Imperial Military Nursing Service whose stories of unbelievable bravery, courage and fortitude over prolonged periods are well told in Nicola Tyrer's "Sisters In Arms" published by Weidenfeld and Nicolson in 2008, which I would commend to all who have an interest in this subject.

As injured servicemen continue to return to our shores today from battles being fought in similarly harsh and difficult terrain, our thoughts and support should be with them. For the majority, being severely injured at the peak of their military career is a triple edged sword. Not only will they have lost close friends and comrades in arms with whom they will have shared much difficulty and danger over many years, but they may well be having to come to terms with a future encompassing some form of physical disablement, and this may also preclude them from active military service again.

The underlying purpose of this book is to raise awareness of these issues, as injured servicemen and women continue to return to this country from active fronts on an all-too-regular basis.

There have been rapid advances and many improvements in the medical treatment and care of trauma victims since the end of The Second World War. Consequently, the simple statistic in battlefield injuries, in The Falklands War and today, is that behind the tragedy of every soldier killed in action, it is likely that at least three of those injured in zone, who may not have survived in previous wars, can and almost certainly will now be saved. Some of that group of survivors may well be severely injured, and a number will then have to face some level of disability for the rest of their lives. The models for our current casualty evacuations are based on all wars and conflicts subsequent to the availability of rotary wing aircraft (i.e. helicopters) within the battle zone, which include Borneo, Vietnam, Northern Ireland, Korea, Belize and The Falklands War.

It is hoped that this short but as yet untold story will help others understand the principles of battlefield surgery, and the requirement even now for Hospital Ships and/or Military Hospitals to be available in zone, and in UK, for these vital stages in the treatment and care of servicemen and women injured in battle today.

BACKGROUND

When The Falkland Islands were invaded by Argentina in 1982, a complex British amphibious assault plan, referred to by the military as Operation Corporate, was swiftly put in place to re-take The Islands. This would use a Task Force involving some 30,000 British servicemen who would be operating 8,000 miles from UK, with only Ascension Island approximately halfway as a staging point, to support the ships and fighting units.

Within the fighting elements of the Task Force, preparations had to be made for the evacuation of casualties from all areas within the battle zone – from land, sea and aviation incidents. A chain of medical evacuation was put in place that would require a fully equipped and operational Hospital Ship that could work for an indefinite period within the Combat Zone. The initial plan was that this role would be served by SS *Canberra*, a P&O ship requisitioned by The Ministry of Defence, working as a floating Main Dressing Station (MDS), following her earlier troop-carrying role. When this original idea had to be abandoned as the ships headed south, another P&O ship requisitioned by the Ministry of Defence, The Hospital Ship *Uganda*, was then required to move much closer to hostilities than had been originally foreseen.

In principle, the three elements of medical evacuation of casualties in War can be simplified into: Regimental Aid Posts, Dressing Stations/Main Dressing Stations and Field Hospitals/Hospital Ships. They are all part of the complex life-saving chain of Casualty Evacuation, and their specific different roles will emerge as this tale unfolds.

Speed of evacuation of casualties is one of the key principles in this demanding process. Today, we often refer to "the golden hour" in which emergency and resuscitative treatments can be put in place which greatly increase survival rates. In The Falklands War the helicopter was crucial within this process, ideally suited for the unforgiving terrain of The Falkland Islands, and the relatively short distances from ship to ship, and ship to shore.

During The Falklands War, battlefield casualties would initially be assessed and given "first line treatments" at Regimental Aid Posts (RAPs) located with fighting units. At the earliest opportunity they would be swiftly moved to Dressing Stations (often referred to as Field Hospitals) some distance from the advancing troops. From The Dressing Stations, where further resuscitative treatments and surgery could be carried out, wounded men were transferred, again by helicopter, to The Hospital Ship *Uganda*. Here, ongoing surgery, further treatment, care and eventual stabilisation could be effected, before onward transfer by sea and air to military hospitals in UK. Similarly, injured sailors could be flown directly by helicopter to The Hospital Ship, or amongst the Naval fleet as required.

With long-haul flights such an integral part of our lives today, it is difficult to appreciate that there was no direct air link from The Falkland Islands back to UK in 1982. The only way for servicemen injured within the Combat Zone to return to UK military hospitals was via this network as described. Likewise, at the end of hostilities, troops had to return to UK on board the troop-carrying liners and vessels.

At that time, all three British Military Services ran their own Military Hospitals, Medical and Nursing Services, and trained their own medical, nursing and support personnel and specialised teams within that framework. The Military Hospitals in UK in 1982 included The Royal Naval Hospital Haslar in Gosport, Hampshire and The Royal Naval Hospital Stonehouse in Plymouth, both run by The Royal Naval Medical Services and Queen Alexandra's Royal Naval Nursing Service personnel, known as QARNNS. The Queen Elizabeth Military Hospital at Woolwich was run by The Royal Army Medical Corps (RAMC) and Queen Alexandra's Royal Army Nursing Corps (QARANC). Royal Air Force Hospitals at Wroughton and Halton were run by The Royal Air Force Medical Service and Princess Mary's Royal Air Force Nursing Service (PMRAFNS).

These UK military hospitals, all with approximately 300 to 400 bed capacities, would accept civilian (National Health Service) patients for treatment and care in peacetime. This was a sensible arrangement that suited all concerned by helping to reduce National Health Service waiting lists, while maintaining a priority for injured servicemen and women.

The Military Hospitals abroad also treated and cared for servicemen's families, so there was also a requirement for midwifery and gynaecological specialities within both the medical and nursing military framework and professions.

Since the nineteen fifties (1950s) there had been a considerable tri-service element to all our work, particularly in exercise and training in UK and abroad.

Nursing training in the United Kingdom in the seventies and eighties was principally a national two-tiered system that ran throughout the National Health Service and military hospitals across the country. A three-year hospital and classroom based training programme led to State Registration, a State Registered Nurse, Staff Nurse or "SRN". A two-year, more practically oriented training programme, led to the State Enrolment, a State Enrolled Nurse, or "SEN". All three British Services, The Navy, Army and Royal Air Force, ran their own Nurse Training Schools and supported both these training structures within their frameworks. On the whole, QARNNS Nursing Officers of all ranks held some additional post-registration qualification, specialising for instance in Intensive Care Therapy, Operating Theatre Technique, Orthopaedics, Ophthalmology, etc.

The majority of the Nursing Officers who served on board The Hospital Ship *Uganda* in 1982 were selected because they held one or more of these extra qualifications. The QARNNS Naval Nurses were Senior and Junior Ratings, some SRNs (Staff Nurses) and some SENs (Enrolled Nurses) of all different QARNNS ratings (a combination of both "Junior Ratings" and "Senior Ratings").

At that time there were no male QARNNS personnel. In 1982 an integrated nursing service was being established to allow male nurses to serve as officers and ratings within QARNNS, but this had not been implemented by the outbreak of The Falklands War. So, on board The Hospital Ship, Royal Navy male Staff Nurses (SRNs) and Medical Assistants completed the teams. A simplified explanation of QARNNS/Royal Naval Ranks and ratings appears later in the book.

As soon as the country was at war in 1982, civilian in-patient numbers within the military hospitals were rapidly reduced to prepare for war casualties (injured servicemen) on a considerable scale. A number of civilian hospitals were also put on an alert/standby state of readiness, should casualty figures reach even higher levels than anticipated. During the planning stages of conflict casualty numbers, to some extent, can be predicted; mercifully, as things turned out, they were lighter than early estimations.

It is to the credit of all those involved – the medical and military planners and senior officers who worked so hard in the early stages, and those within The Task Force who carried out their duties so efficiently at the "sharp end" of this complex chain – that casualty figures during The Falklands War were not higher.

Our hearts, of course, will always be with the families of those servicemen who, so bravely and unselfishly, gave their lives in that harsh environment so far from their homes and families.

Fortunately, as this book will reveal, for those hundreds of men injured on land, at sea or in aircraft during the short but vicious days of fighting in 1982, there was a reliable lifeline of evacuation, care and treatment available to them at every stage following their injury. This strong and highly professional medical chain of casualty evacuation during The Falklands War owes much to the careful forward planning by all three military medical directorships: The Royal Navy Medical Services, The Royal Army Medical Corps and The Royal Air Force Medical Services.

This little book covers one small link in that successful chain; the conversion, preparation, the work carried out, and the treatment and care of patients on board The Hospital Ship *Uganda* from April to August 1982.

Medical care is an aspect of warfare that receives little or no acknowledgment in the overall scheme of things. This is understandable. Safe at home, we hear of those injured in battle, and are thankful that they have survived. But for many of those injured servicemen (and now today, women), their battle is only just beginning. They have to come to terms with and face up to many issues, as has been covered in the Introduction.

Nobody wants fighting, conflict or wars; we all know they leave a nasty legacy on people, places and things. But as they seem to crop up with such monotonous regularity, we must continue to ensure that those fighting them are given the very best chances of survival which our country can offer.

Assuredly, within the harsh terrain and bitter weather of The Falkland Islands War, we can be safe in the knowledge that everything that could possibly be done for our injured servicemen in their hour of need was indeed made available for them.

This book is about one small group of the extraordinarily dedicated professionals who, in 1982, helped in that challenging and difficult process.

SEA FEVER

I must go down to the seas again, to the lonely sea and the sky,
And all I ask is a tall ship and a star to steer her by,
And the wheel's kick and the wind's song and the white sails shaking,
And a grey mist on the sea's face and a grey dawn breaking.

I must go down to the seas again, for the call of the running tide
Is a wild call and a clear call that may not be denied;
And all I ask is a windy day with the white clouds flying,
And the flung spray and the blown spume, and the sea-gulls crying.

I must go down to the seas again, to the vagrant gypsy life,
To the gull's way and the whale's way where the wind's like a whetted knife;
And all I ask is a merry yarn from a laughing fellow-rover,
And a quiet sleep and a sweet dream when the long trick's over.

John Masefield

CHAPTER ONE

"A GREY DAWN BREAKING"

Her Majesty's Hospital Ship *Uganda* at anchor,
Port William, Falkland Islands.
July 13th 1982

For some reason I woke early that morning. Perhaps the ship had turned during the night; I often heard the anchor chain pulling as we usually anchored from the bows only, so she would tend to swing more should the wind increase. I could see a few flakes of snow falling, outboard, through the salt stained porthole. I lay in my bunk, slightly shivering with cold, watching some drips of sea-water fall into the little tray positioned for that purpose under the glass.

It was a great privilege to have been allocated a single cabin, particularly one on the port outboard side of the ship, but if we were steaming for long periods into heavy weather, this tray would fill with salt water remarkably quickly. The porthole would not open… but neither would it close! Over the months, I had devised a system for keeping the tray emptied, as the rusty sea-water splashes would stain any uniform or papers within range. The tray slopped some water, so I shot out of my bunk and dealt with the spillage, thus saving several hours of uniform cleaning later in the week. I dressed in haste, with my breath steaming even inside the cabin, in the cold early morning air of The South Atlantic. With our personal washing water permanently restricted while on board The Hospital Ship *Uganda*, washing was a cold flannel and a tiny drop of fresh water for teeth cleaning. A quick hair comb and I was off at speed for a hasty breakfast. I had much to organise and do that day, but little realised at 0730 quite how much that was to be.

A month ago, June 14th 1982, had seen The Official Surrender of Argentinian troops who had invaded The Falkland Islands on April 2nd that year. I was working as a Queen Alexandra's Royal Naval Nursing Service (QARNNS) Senior Nursing Officer on board Her Majesty's Hospital Ship *Uganda*. My specific job as a Trauma Operating Theatre Sister was to lead one of three small teams of QARNNS Naval Nurses and Royal Navy (RN)

1

medical technicians through surgical procedures within our operating theatres. We had been at sea since we left Gibraltar on April 19th, and now, a month after cessation of hostilities, were looking forward to our casualty levels finally dropping. We all hoped to hear within the next few days that we would be returning northwards from the rigours of The South Atlantic Ocean, as the Austral winter months rapidly approached and the weather continued to deteriorate.

It was a strange sort of "time in limbo". Officially, we were still operational as Her Majesty's Hospital Ship *Uganda*, yet work had already begun to de-commission parts of The Hospital. After The Surrender on June 14th our casualties had continued to rise for some time, so we were not quite out of the woods yet… but we still hoped to hear soon that our Army colleagues, now installed at King Edward VII Hospital in Stanley, would finally be ready to take over from us ashore.

I made my way through the myriad of ship's corridors to the operating theatres, where our three teams of Queen Alexandra's Royal Naval Nursing Service (QARNNS) Naval Nurses were all reporting for duty that morning at 0800. This was luxury indeed, not to be working in 24 hour Naval watch-keeping routines as we had all through the days of War.

Having assembled our military hospital from the 750 crates and boxes of medical stores piled on the Gibraltar dockside some months ago in April, our task now was to continue to de-commission all this complicated technology and equipment, starting today with our friend "Vesuvius", our nickname for the vital porous loading steam autoclave installed at one side of our Operating Theatre areas. This noisy but trustworthy belcher of heated steam had sterilised all the instruments for our operating theatres for the last three months, as well as providing all the sterilised dressings, bandages and other clinical requirements for our floating hospital, Her Majesty's Hospital Ship *Uganda*, currently anchored in Port William, a deeper bay just to the north of Stanley Harbour.

Even today, 26 years onwards, I remember the next few hours quite vividly. We all worked together during the early morning "watch", rationalising and sorting equipment, and were just about to start to de-commission the last of our three portable Boyle's machines which had served as our anaesthetic tables throughout the Conflict. I was leaning on this anaesthetic machine, talking with our Consultant Anaesthetist, Surgeon Commander Peter Bull RN, when the all too-familiar sound of incoming "casevac" helicopters clattered from the sky towards us. Without a backward glance we all instantly shot to our "Action Stations" again. Doctor Bull moved with his usual speed and efficiency to our Casualty Reception Area (CRA), calling backwards 'Leave everything in place until I get back to you…' as we watched his fast-disappearing back move towards the CRA. The CRA and our high-dependency Sea View Ward were located directly underneath our specially constructed helicopter landing pad at the stern of the ship. We all glanced glumly at each other, and swung into our well-rehearsed preparation routine for commencing surgery as required.

We didn't have long to wait. News soon reached us in the operating theatres that there had been a tragic accident at The Stanley Airfield ashore that morning. Some Welsh Guardsmen had been clearing snow at the airfield, and a Sidewinder missile had inadvertently been discharged. Eleven soldiers had been seriously injured, the majority being transferred to us in haste by helicopter.

Within a few minutes we were anaesthetising the first of eight Welsh Guardsmen that we treated and operated on that day.

It was a very sad and harrowing day for us all, as in those short few hours we had to amputate five limbs between four soldiers, as well as start treatment and care for the other four injured soldiers. I made a point of staying with the guardsmen until each one was well awake from his anaesthetic and safe in a bed in our Intensive Care Unit (ICU), adjacent to the operating theatres (OT). I would then carefully hand over to one of my QARNNS colleagues working in this high-dependency unit the details of the surgical and anaesthetic procedures that had been carried out, before returning to theatres. As soon as one operation was complete we simply continued with the next soldier's wounds.

That evening, I met my close friend and colleague Sister Margaret Kerr in her cabin. Margaret, the other Trauma Operating Theatre Sister on board, was well trained in dealing with acute trauma from her many years working at The Royal Victoria Hospital, Belfast all through the notorious carnage of the seventies. She was a true friend and ally in these difficult times. Before leaving theatres earlier we had both talked the day through with our teams of Naval Nurses, who were much younger and less experienced than ourselves; Margaret and I were friends with them all, and knew the continual emotional drain was hurting them all too much. But for us both, now was a bit of "us time". Outwardly, we had to always be as strong, tough and unemotional as it got, but quietly, in private, Margaret and I would often meet after our Operating Lists were finished, and would support and help each other as time permitted. Today was no exception. I well remember saying to her, 'I'm not sure how much longer I can go on at this level, Margaret.' She was a much calmer and outwardly less emotional character than me, and I valued her strength and maturity immensely after that particularly gruelling day for our OT teams. 'Come on, Nicci,' she said, in her familiar Irish brogue… 'You've been through worse than that in the last few months, and before we ever set foot on this Hospital Ship… let's go and find Roger.' It was exactly the right suggestion to cover the wobbly moment, cementing once again the need throughout the Ship for true and reliable friendships. For us all, from time to time, the going got a bit too tough.

So we toddled off to find Surgeon Lieutenant Commander Roger Leicester RN, our Head of Surgery and immediate "boss". Roger, too, was feeling a bit glum, so we cheered ourselves up with some traditional Irish fluid, of which Margaret seemed to always have supplies in her "emergency medicine cupboard".

Throughout our time on board The Hospital Ship, Roger was a complete tower of professional and emotional strength. As well as being an excellent, safe and reliable surgeon, he was a strong character who was always there for us, "his Operating Theatre Teams". A tough man doing a very tough job; just the sort of person you need in the unpredictability and hardship of war-torn surgery on board a Hospital Ship working in the most inhospitable and unforgiving ocean on earth. 'I know this is hard on you all, girls,' he assured us. 'I know we may not have saved all their limbs... but we sure as hell saved their lives.' Feeling a bit stronger from this firm reassurance, we all finally disappeared off to our separate cabins just before midnight.

The porthole "drip tray" was not overflowing! Perhaps the wind had relented later in the day. So I emptied the tray for the night hours, and drifted off to an exhausted but not entirely restful sleep.

Just another day in The South Atlantic? Well, we all hoped it would not be for much longer. Why were we there? What were we doing, 40 female Naval Nursing personnel, bobbing about at sea in the middle of a Combat Zone, more than 8,000 miles from the safe and familiar world of Royal Naval, and indeed civilian hospitals, near to our homes and families?

We hope, in the contents of this short but lively tale, that these and many other questions will be answered, explaining why, from time to time "White Ships with Red Crosses" must be on hand, in even the most inhospitable corners of the globe...

CHAPTER TWO

"A TALL SHIP"

Converging on Gibraltar
April 13th – April 19th 1982

The P&O Educational Cruise Ship SS *Uganda* was on her routine Alexandria and Egyptian pyramids' trip in the Mediterranean, when she was requisitioned by the Ministry of Defence on April 10th 1982 for conversion to a Hospital Ship to serve in The Falklands War. The 940 students and 300 adult passengers were disembarked at Naples from where they were flown back to UK. Teams of P&O Engineers, Royal Naval constructors and our Royal Naval Surgeon, Lt. Commander Roger Leicester, joined the ship at Naples to commence the advance planning of the conversion while underway to Gibraltar, where she entered Number 2 Dry Dock in The Royal Naval Dockyard at 1600 on Friday April 16th 1982.

Uganda, built in 1952 and weighing 17,500 tons, was considered most suitable for conversion for use as a Hospital Ship, operating 8,000 miles from UK, in the desolate and windswept South Atlantic Ocean. Her patient carrying capacity could, if necessary, be augmented to just over 1,000 beds, because she already had a dormitory sleeping system with shower areas for the students in place. The Royal Yacht *Britannia* had been an earlier suggested possibility to serve as a Hospital Ship, but her lower bed capacity, and reliance on a heavier diesel fuel eventually ruled her out of the planning equation.

The Naval personnel selected to work on board The Hospital Ship *Uganda* were flown out to Gibraltar during the night of April 15th/16th from RAF Lyneham in a C130 Hercules transport plane. We were to make up the main contingent of what was to become Naval Party 1830, and had travelled to RAF Lyneham in military buses in two separate groups from The Royal Naval Hospital at Stonehouse (Plymouth, Devon) and The Royal Naval Hospital Haslar (Gosport, Hants.). Some of us, myself included, were already part of what were called Surgical Support Teams within those Hospitals. These teams were, in effect, "short notice to move" teams of Royal Naval Medical and QARNNS Nursing personnel, who could travel at short notice as required around the globe in the event of national or international emergencies. Thus, in early 1982, just before The Falklands War, QARNNS female personnel within the British military were already being introduced to the principles of administering medical care to troops in battle zones.

One of my colleagues, then Senior Nursing Officer Elizabeth Law, was an ICU trained Nursing Sister. In the adjacent inset she describes briefly her own early nurse training with QARNNS in the seventies, working at both The Royal Naval Hospitals in UK, before meeting up with the rest of Naval Party 1830 at RAF Lyneham on April 15th. Her then boyfriend, Howard Ormerod, later becomes an integral part of this tale, which is why he is mentioned at this stage.

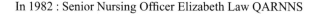

In 1982 : Senior Nursing Officer Elizabeth Law QARNNS

Photograph: Elizabeth Ormerod

I joined QARNNS in May 1972 to train as a State Registered Nurse. Initially at RNH Haslar, I spent a year in RNH Stonehouse before returning to Haslar in 1974 to complete my training and sit my State finals in 1975. Following qualification as a State Registered (Staff) Nurse I gained experience in various clinical areas, spending a considerable amount of time in Casualty. By now I had been promoted to Head Naval Nurse (CPO). In 1980 I was commissioned as a Nursing Officer which necessitated my moving to RNH Stonehouse. Early in 1981 I undertook the Coronary Care Course at the London Chest Hospital and, following successful completion, returned to the Naval Hospital in Plymouth as Senior Nursing Officer and began working on B2 Ward which was a joint Intensive Care/Coronary Care Unit. I had met Howard Ormerod by then. However, he was serving on the Royal Fleet Auxiliary vessel *Fort Grange* and spent a good deal of time at sea. As a result, our courtship was long distance.

Here Elizabeth Law describes joining Naval Party 1830:

> When I received the call to go to The Falkland Islands I had just completed a week on night duty and was expecting to have a week off duty. Instead, that week was spent attending lectures on treatment of gunshot wounds, bomb blast injuries, burns and anything else it was felt we may encounter. Once we had been kitted out with camouflage clothing, it all began to become rather real and frightening. Eventually, after several false starts, we were sent by coach to RAF Lyneham, where we joined up with the team from RNH Haslar and all flew to Gibraltar to join the SS *Uganda*. As we prepared to set up the Hospital Ship we were equipped with seamen's working uniform which seemed very practical.
>
> By now, my boyfriend Howard Ormerod was back in UK and working in the dockyard for the Royal Naval Supply and Transport Services. Having spent a relatively short period together at home it was particularly poignant to have to say Goodbye on that last morning. We had agreed that, eventually, we would marry but I had been reluctant to set a date. This was something that I almost missed the opportunity to rectify.

Other members of Naval Party 1830 (NP1830) were selected for their considerable experience and varied skill mixes, the majority of levels proving, in time, to be a sensible and evenly balanced combination of inter-related medical professionals. Our Medical-Officer-in-Charge (MOIC) was Surgeon Captain Andrew Rintoul FRCS, an ophthalmic eye surgeon from The Royal Naval Hospital Haslar, Gosport. Other Royal Naval Consultants specialising in anaesthetics, burns and plastics, orthopaedic, and facio-maxillary surgery were complemented by specialists in radiology and psychiatry.

The Queen Alexandra's Royal Naval Nursing Service (QARNNS) teams were similarly selected for their post-Registration qualifications. They included specially trained personnel with sub-specialty experience in ICU therapy, burns treatment, Accident and Emergency care, and Operating Theatre (OT) qualifications and skills. As an experienced Trauma Operating Theatre Sister, with post-RGN registration qualifications under my belt, I was to help run one of the three small surgical teams within the operating theatres.

Royal Naval Medical Assistants (the RN equivalent of today's civilian Paramedics) of differing skills, ranks, rates and experience completed the clinical teams.

Our Senior Anaesthetist, Surgeon Commander Peter Bull, was to lead our Operating Theatre and Intensive Care Teams. In the adjacent inset he describes his background from when he joined the Royal Navy in 1965 to joining The Hospital Ship *Uganda* in April 1982.

In 1982: Surgeon Commander Peter Bull RN.
Consultant and Senior Anaesthetist to The Task Force

Photograph: Author's private collection

I joined the Royal Navy as a medical student cadet in 1965 and did initial training during my elective period in Gibraltar in 1966. After house jobs in Liverpool Hospitals, I commenced a five year Commission in 1967 with appointments to HMS *Victory*, *Vernon* and *Dolphin* before joining my first ship HMS *Exmouth* on Arctic Fisheries patrol. Further appointments followed in HMS *Hampshire*, HMS *Phoebe* and Singapore before commencing anaesthetic training at Haslar in 1974.

I then signed on for a Full Career Commission in the Royal Navy to specialise in Anaesthesia. As well as serving at RNH Haslar and RNH Stonehouse, I underwent an NHS secondment to The Radcliffe Infirmary, Oxford in 1976. After attaining my Fellowship in 1977 (whilst serving in the last fixed wing aircraft carrier HMS *Ark Royal*), I spent 12 months at Addenbrooke's Hospital Cambridge in 1978, to obtain the necessary extra experience to qualify as a Specialist. In 1979, I was loaned to the RAF to serve in Belize and experienced my first war zone. I was appointed Consultant Anaesthetist later in 1979 and promoted Commander in 1980, returning to RNH Haslar until appointed to Her Majesty's Hospital Ship *Uganda* in April 1982.

* * *

Where there are hospitals there need to be ambulances, even in the remote sea areas where we would be working. Three Royal Navy Ocean Surveying Ships, HMS *Hydra*, HMS *Herald* and HMS *Hecla,* were chosen to converge with The Hospital Ship *Uganda* on our route south to Ascension Island. Their role would be to transfer recovering injured service personnel from The Hospital Ship to a suitable port, from where they could be flown back to UK by RAF VC10s fitted as air ambulances. All three ambulance ships carried RN Wasp helicopters for casualty transfers, which had been partly painted white with red crosses for easier identification.

So the Survey Ships' conversions and preparations for war continued apace in tandem with *Uganda*'s timescale in Gibraltar. HMS *Hydra* and HMS *Herald* were in UK waters at the time of the Argentinian invasion of The Falkland Islands, so their conversions to Ambulance Ships took place in Portsmouth Dockyard. HMS *Hecla*, commanded by Royal Navy Captain Geoff Hope, was already in Gibraltar, so her conversion from Survey Ship to Ambulance Ship commenced there from Wednesday April 14th onwards.

In UK we had all been given a couple of days' "shore-leave" as we call it, before our departure from UK from RAF Lyneham. Like many of my colleagues I was a single working lady with an elderly Mum, so couldn't really leave her with lists of chores to do on my behalf. I closed up my cottage in Cornwall, left a set of keys with a former colleague at The Royal Cornwall Hospital, and left my car and keys at the Sisters' Mess, Royal Naval Hospital Haslar.

In the adjacent inset our QARNNS Head Naval Nurse Maggie Freer writes about how she and her husband David Freer were both selected to head south with The Task Force:

In 1982: QARNNS Head Naval Nurse Maggie Freer

Photograph: Maggie Freer

I was a 28-year-old HNN QARNNS Staff Nurse (Senior Rate/Chief Petty Officer), second in charge of General Outpatients at The Royal Naval Hospital (RNH) Haslar when we became aware of the Falkland Island Invasion during the day of Friday 2nd April 1982. Although we didn't really pay very much attention to it at the time, we followed the news bulletins through the next day. In the evening David, my husband, also a State Registered Nurse, Chief Petty Officer/Senior Rate Medical Technician One (MT1 in the Royal Navy), was contacted to say he was to join a team of up to eight medics on board HMS *Intrepid* as MT1 (N) of the sick bay. On the Monday I went to the Allocating Office to volunteer should any QARNNS Naval Nurses be needed and on Tuesday 6th April I was detailed "to stand by". The team attended a one day Advanced Casualty Care Course in the Training Division at RNH Haslar.

At the time I don't think either of us gave a thought as to how we would cope with us both being in a possible war zone at the same time, or as to what it might mean for our families. I was in the QARNNS, nursing was my job and as David was going anyway it would save disrupting another family's life. At one point there was an announcement that no husbands and wives would be deployed to the South Atlantic. That rule didn't seem to apply to the Freer household!

David and I left our home on the morning of 15th April, – he to HMS *Intrepid* to sail at 1700 from Portsmouth Dockyard to Portland for sea trials before leaving for the South Atlantic – and me to RNH Haslar for a briefing at 0830 in the Conference Room prior to travelling to RAF Lyneham for a flight in a Hercules to Gibraltar at 1700 the same evening. After a briefing in HMS *Rooke* we boarded Her Majesty's Hospital Ship (HMHS) *Uganda* and sailed from Gibraltar on 19th April.

At the same time QARNNS Naval Nurse Karen Dawson and her friend Marilyn (Maz) Gay had been called from night-duty at RNH Haslar to join the medical and nursing teams travelling to Gibraltar.

In the adjacent inset Karen describes from when she started training for State Enrolment within QARNNS, to when we arrived at Gibraltar on April 16th:

In 1982: QARNNS Naval Nurse Karen Dawson

Photograph: Karen Harwood

I joined Queen Alexandra's Royal Naval Nursing Service in June 1979 to train as a State Enrolled Nurse at Royal Naval Hospital Haslar and qualified when I was 20 in 1981.

So I wasn't qualified for that long before I was called on to serve aboard The Hospital Ship *Uganda* in The Falklands War. Myself and Marilyn (Maz) Gay were both on night-duty at RNH Haslar working on the Orthopaedic wards. We were given 48 hours' notice telling us we were on stand-by to go to the

Conflict after being taken off nights. My mother came home from work to find me sitting there in a daze. My Mum had forgotten I was in the Navy, she was expecting my brother who was also in the Navy to go, but he hadn't finished his training on submarines. My poor Nan wanted to write to Maggie Thatcher to say I couldn't go, as she thought I was too young, bless her.

I had not flown before, so my first experience of flying was the RAF Hercules flying us to Gibraltar. Ironically I had been waiting for months to get a draft to The Royal Naval Hospital in Gibraltar, but it was always so popular you were very unlikely to be drafted there. I even thought the Falklands was somewhere in Scotland which shows how much I learnt in geography at school.

* * *

On board the RAF Hercules in those early days of April all we were thinking about was wishing this flight to Gibraltar, on such a stormy night, was behind us!

This early entry in the diary I started that day, April 16th 1982, written in the Hercules transport plane, reads:

> We are sitting in the Herc. waiting for take-off. No
> stewardesses or trolley service here! They are troop-carrying
> planes, that's what they do. We sit facing each other across
> the body of the plane… about 100 of us in all; the girls
> seem to be nearer the front. Looking at their faces they
> are all calm and reserved and I feel we will be a united
> and wonderful team. I am so pleased my dear friend Chris
> Asendorf (who started at Haslar on the same day as me in
> 1980) is with us; a close friend in this sort of set-up will
> be invaluable. So, at last, after ten days of uncertainty and
> conflicting tales we are finally on our way. What awaits us
> we just don't know; the only certain prospect is the next five
> hours on board this Herc. to Gib…

A long flight and a difficult landing at Gibraltar ensued. Most of us were billeted at The Naval Base at HMS *Rooke*, but as there was "not room at The Inn" for us all, some of us, randomly selected, had to stay at The Rock Hotel in Gibraltar. Chris Asendorf, the burns specialist Senior Nursing Officer, and I were two of those. Our cabins looked directly over Gibraltar Dockyard below, so we had the privilege of being able to see SS *Uganda* arrive from Naples and berth into No 2 Dock on April 16th; those who had cameras took photos as she manoeuvred gently into the dry dock on a clear and still April afternoon.

The Conversion of SS *Uganda* to a Hospital Ship took place in a frenzy of enthusiastic activity by all concerned. The main structural task was the fitting of a forty-ton helicopter landing platform at the stern of the ship. The steel platform had been shipped out from UK the previous week, and had to be strong enough to take a fully-laden Sea King helicopter, or a 10-ton point load. This required the strengthening of the deck with steel pillars in what was to become a ward area underneath. From the platform a ramp was created by cutting through the deck, thus allowing speedy transfer of battle-injured casualties to the emergency reception area below. A satellite communication unit was fitted on the port side of the flying bridge, electrical power supplies were augmented, and a myriad of other essential work carried out in the three short days we had in hand. The black British India funnel was painted out, along with other non-white markings such as the black line along the hull. Red Crosses, in compliance with Geneva Convention regulations, were then painted on both sides of the hull, the funnel and the lifeboats. Modifications for refuelling at sea (RAS-ing), store-ing * and water transfer also had to be installed. (* see Glossary)

P&O Captain Grahame Burton was the Chief Officer on board *Uganda* in 1982. Grahame also held the rank of Lieutenant Commander in The Royal Naval Reserve (RNR).

In the adjacent inset he describes *Uganda*'s early years:

In 1982: P&O Chief Officer Grahame Burton RNR

Photograph: Grahame Burton

Uganda was a unit of the P&O Cruises fleet, in a section called British India (B.I.) Discovery Cruises, which had, until 1975, also included the SS *Nevasa*. *Uganda* had started her life as a passenger vessel in the large British India fleet, and was commissioned into their East African service in 1952. Surplus to requirements in 1967 with the advent of modern jet travel, she was withdrawn and converted into an Educational Cruising ship, a market that BI had entered in 1961. Accommodation was provided for 920 students as well as about 300 Party Leaders and Independent Cabin Passengers.

April 1982 found *Uganda* carrying out her normal winter itinerary of fly cruises in the Mediterranean. There was much interest on board when it was announced that the P&O ship *Canberra* had been requisitioned for service as a troopship in the developing Falklands conflict, although none of us thought it likely that this would happen to *Uganda*, and most thought that the conflict would be quickly resolved by diplomatic means.

One of the more popular ports of call on this itinerary was Alexandria, Egypt, where tours were run to Cairo and the Pyramids. One of the features of Educational Cruising was that the cost of all shore excursions was included in the fare, so that the whole ship would nearly empty each port day. The tours to Cairo involved a long drive across the desert, and did not return before dark. The entrance channel to Alexandria was narrow and quite shallow, and had been the location of a previous *Uganda* grounding, so passage was normally arranged for daylight hours only, and the ship would stay in port overnight and sail next morning.

Grahame's account continues with *Uganda*'s official requisition in Alexandria on April 10th, the voyage to Gibraltar via Naples, and the start of the re-fit in Gibraltar Dockyard:

I had rejoined SS *Uganda* in Malta in March 1982, in my appointed role as Chief Officer. This is the senior P&O Deck Officer position, and as such I was not a Bridge watch keeper, although I had Bridge duties on entering or leaving harbour. My principal task was the running of the deck crew and supervision of the deck tradesmen, the carpenters, shipwrights, and plumbers, as well as the Masters-at-Arms, who provided the safety and security for our floating School Ship.

On 10th April 1982, *Uganda* arrived alongside in Alexandria at 0800 and students and passengers departed on their tours as normal, returning at about 8pm for a late evening meal. Staff Captain Jeff Clark was accompanying the tour along with a Medical Staff member, in the chauffeured Mercedes provided by the tour operator, which provided back-up should the need arise. On board ship things settled into the normal in-port routine of attending to maintenance tasks that were difficult to accomplish whilst there were too many people around. Preparations were also underway for an Officers Wardroom BBQ that was planned for 2130 that evening.

That afternoon at about 1500 I was in my cabin, when our local Egyptian port agent burst through the curtain with a telex message for the Captain. It must be remembered that before the days of satellite radio communications, ships received their signal traffic by HF or MF radio, and these transmitters and receivers were not allowed to be used in port, thus the Radio Room on board was shut down. Any urgent traffic therefore had to be passed to the ship via the local port agent's office.

The Port Agent was savvy enough to know that it was more than his job was worth to go barging into the Captain's cabin in mid afternoon, hence his sudden arrival in my cabin instead. 'Secret message for the Captain,' said the Egyptian. 'Ship been requisitioned.' No doubt he had been the one to take the message off the Telex machine, and had obviously read it and understood the significance. The message said that the ship was forthwith to be placed at the disposal of the Secretary of State for Trade. She was to proceed immediately to Naples, there to disembark her passengers, then proceed to Gibraltar. Once there, the Master was to report to the Flag Officer Gibraltar, regarding the future destination and employment of the said vessel. It is my subsequent understanding that there had been prior discussion between the Department of Trade and P&O head office regarding the repatriation of the passengers and that Naples, the original termination port of the cruise, was seen as the best option, as it was also en route to Gibraltar.

I thanked the agent, reminded him of the secrecy of the message, then immediately informed the Captain, Brian Biddick. Permission was granted for us to sail during the hours of darkness, in view of favourable conditions, and sailing time was advanced to midnight, no reason being given to the passengers, although many "put two and two together". In the event, with all passengers and crew back on board, the ship sailed for Naples at 2300. No Wardroom BBQ that evening.

```
SS UGANDA                                              CRUISE 276

At Sea
11 April 1982

TRANSCRIPT OF CAPTAIN's BROADCAST

Good Morning Ladies and Gentlemen.
Good Morning Boys and Girls.
This is the Captain speaking.
I have to tell you that UGANDA has been requisitioned by the Government. I have been
instructed to proceed direct to Naples where the cruise will be terminated.
Homeward flight details and travel arrangements are still being co-ordinated in
London and I will promulgate this information when it is received on board.
I expect to arrive in Naples at 4.00 pm on Tuesday 13 April and anticipate that
disembarkation will take place shortly after.
Both the Company and all of us here in UGANDA truly appreciate your disappointment
but these circumstances are beyond our control.
A transcript of this broadcast will be available from the Purser's Bureau shortly.

CAPTAIN BRIAN BIDDICK
```

Transcript of Captain Biddick's broadcast to the ship when SS Uganda was requisitioned by the Government on April 10th 1982.

Photograph: Author's private collection

After the ship had cleared the harbour, Captain Biddick made a broadcast informing everyone that the ship had been requisitioned and that the cruise would end in Naples on Tuesday 13th April. The next day was Easter Sunday, church was held and chocolate Easter eggs were distributed. Meetings between the ship's senior officers were held on board, but nobody really knew what to expect. More information would be forthcoming when David Monument, the P&O hull superintendent, joined in Naples. He had just attended refitting discussions with MOD personnel in Bath, England. Also joining would be Gibraltar dockyard personnel and Surgeon Lt. Commander Roger Leicester, an RN General Surgeon, who made plans for the layout of the new hospital on the Promenade Deck.

Arrival into Naples was made at 1430 on 13th April. The BBC and Kate Adie were there to witness our arrival and, to the strains of the children singing "Rule Britannia", disembarkation was completed in record time. Wednesday 14th April was taken up with removing surplus equipment, some of which I arranged to store in the forecastle (Foc'sle). There was a Captains' meeting at 1130 at which more information was disseminated, and where the shipboard senior officers could express their concerns. Time was taken to offload baggage and to load stores and equipment, before *Uganda* sailed at 0200 from Naples for Gibraltar.

One of my responsibilities was the management of all the water on board; washing, drinking and ballast. SS *Uganda* did not have fin stabilisers, as is common on most modern ships, but employed "Flume Tanks" which endeavoured, usually unsuccessfully, to provide stabilisation by means of water flow through two large transverse tanks. These, however, had significant "free surface effect" and were somewhat detrimental to the ship's stability. Due to this impact on the ship's stability, the tanks were fitted with emergency dump valves, designed to quickly empty the tanks in situations where stability needed to be increased. Unfortunately these dump valves were also prone to leak.

Uganda had no means of producing her own fresh water, except for a small, engine-room evaporator used to top up the boiler water tanks. This was not normally a problem, as the ship was alongside in port every few days and could easily replenish supplies. The forthcoming deployment south would, however be different, with no "alongside port" envisaged once we left Gibraltar. We had therefore filled the ship's tanks to capacity with fresh water in Naples, as fresh water is very scarce in Gibraltar. I had also decided I would fill these stabilising tanks with fresh water as an additional resource, hoping that the valves would not let in too much sea water. This water would be used for washing only, as there was a separate tap in each cabin for drinking water, which came from a separate tank. This way we saved several days of water consumption from our wash water tanks once the ship left Gibraltar.

Plans were made for entering dry dock in Gibraltar, and for the crew changes that would then be taking place. An agreement had been made with the seamen's unions involved, that the 130 Indian hotel crew would remain, but that the deck and engine Asian crews and some of the galley staff would be replaced by British seafarers, almost all of whom would be new to passenger ships. There was much to do to ensure a smooth transition. On the morning of 16th April as the ship neared Gibraltar, a Sea King helicopter came out to the ship to lift off hull superintendent David Monument and two dockyard personnel, in order that they might make preparations for the ship's arrival later that day.

Uganda arrived in Gibraltar at 1600 on 16th April and entered No 2 dry dock in the Naval Base. This was obviously going to be no ordinary dry-dock situation, where the ship had control over the work at hand. Bridge watches were stood down and each Deck Officer was assigned a specific work area to be the contact person. The only shore telephone line was placed in my office, and I can remember getting some unusual calls from the dockyard, one warning me to secure all ammunition due to an expected thunderstorm. Work proceeded 24 hours a day fitting the helicopter pad, which had been prefabricated in the UK and shipped out. Work was also undertaken fitting out the ship for underway refuelling, satellite communications and cutting access holes in the deck to facilitate the transfer of patients. Throughout all this there was still the feeling that it could all be called off at any moment if the conflict was resolved.

Some hectic days followed. We now had the ship and most of the personnel assembled. The next thing was the arrival of 90 tons of stores… the contents of a complete military hospital, all of which had to be sorted and stowed on board before our planned departure in two days. This equipment was, in effect, a mobile tri-service Field Hospital consisting of an Intensive Therapy Unit, resuscitation and reception areas, Operating Theatre, X-Ray, laboratories, beds, mattresses and everything in between. This had all been offloaded from 22 4-ton trucks at H.M Dockyard Portsmouth, and transported to Gibraltar in The Royal Maritime Auxiliary Service (RMAS) *Throsk*. She and her vital cargo arrived at Gibraltar on Saturday April 17th.

On the same day arrived our much-needed stretcher-bearers, the wartime role of Royal Marine Bandsmen. These were Flag Officer Portsmouth 3rd Flotilla (FOF3) under the command of WO2 Trevor Attwood; they too had flown from RAF Lyneham to Gibraltar, also arriving on April 17th.

My next diary entry written April 17th reads:

The first day was hectic, hectic! What seemed like a million tons of stores had to be moved on board. In time, these will become the basis of our floating Hospital.

There will be facilities for Laboratory/Pathology/X-Ray/ Intensive Care/Burns unit and Operating Theatre (x three tables) a blood transfusion unit and several hundred beds. Some of the mattresses were horsehair; we had to ditch those: 'hospital care has moved on a bit since The Crimea,' one of the nurses was heard to say! Even if none of it is used it will be a more than useful exercise just setting the whole thing up; things like that keep cropping up. There don't seem to be any accompanying lists of what the cases and containers hold; this is making things interesting, and we are feeling the time pressure. Roger (Surgeon Lt. Commander Roger Leicester, who had joined the advance planning team on board SS Uganda *in Naples) has done a great job, though, visualising our requirements and setting the whole thing up in such haste.*

S.S. Uganda *will now be known as Her Majesty's Hospital Ship* Uganda *– there are red crosses on the funnel and sides… (Let's hope The Argies know what they mean…!) There are many protocols we have to undertake to comply with The Geneva Convention, including being fully illuminated at night. The three RN "survey ships, converted to Ambulance Ships" will be in same colour scheme. One of them is also store-ing and converting alongside us,* HMS Hecla. *There is a problem with the strengthening of* Uganda's *stern helicopter landing pad, so we may not make our Monday 19th ETD…*

The P&O Captains, Officers and the majority of supporting staff and crew remained on board *Uganda* on a voluntary basis. They were led by Captain Brian Biddick, Captain Jeff Clark and Chief Officer Grahame Burton.

A Team of Royal Navy Communications and Flight Deck specialists completed the remainder of what was to be Naval Party 1830 (NP 1830). Commander Andy Gough RN was the Senior Naval Officer of SS *Uganda* and the Commanding Officer of Naval Party 1830. He and Lieutenant Commander Keith Tatman RN led those teams and were already starting their work-up to operational use, which they were aiming for by the time we approached Ascension Island; some ten days away, steaming south.

We moved on board *Uganda* during the morning of Saturday April 18th. Cabins had

L.to R: P&O Captains Jeff Clark and Brian Biddick, P&O Chief Officer Grahame Burton. March 1982.
Photograph: Grahame Burton

been allocated by The P&O Accommodation Officer Derek Houghton, in conjunction with Surgeon Lt. Commander Roger Leicester and other NP 1830 and P&O Team members. I was allocated an outboard cabin on the port side, and my friends Sister Margaret Kerr (Operating Theatres) and Sister Christine Asendorf (Burns Unit) were in nearby adjacent cabins. These cabins had a small shower, basin, lavatory (heads) table/desk and bunk. I noticed an ominous looking pool of rusty water which had collected in a little brass tray positioned underneath the porthole. This porthole became both a friend and an enemy over the next few months that we spent at sea. It wouldn't open… but neither would it close! In fact, steaming south through the tropics, the fresh air was a refreshing bonus, and friends with inboard cabins used to come and enjoy a breath of fresh sea air when time permitted. Not so as we headed south to The South Atlantic Ocean! Hard as I might try I could never secure the thing. The little tray would constantly overflow, spraying rust-stained seawater onto any available surface and uniform that happened to be in its path.

The diary I quote from in this book still retains an air of salt-stained deterioration to this day! Still, heading back up north again in August I could once again enjoy a few friends calling round for a bit of breezy sea air, so I guess it balanced itself out in the end.

On board *Uganda* everyone quickly formed into appropriate teams based on our specialist areas. Meetings, planning and final arrangements were going on at higher levels at a frantic pace to try to get us away for our deadline departure on Monday morning.

QARNNS Naval Nurse Karen Dawson recalls the one evening we were allowed ashore in Gibraltar:

When we arrived in Gibraltar we were billeted in the RN shore Establishment in Gibraltar, HMS *Rooke*, while we were waiting for *Uganda* to come into the harbour to have the flight deck fitted and all the other bits they had to do before we could leave.

We were allowed some "shore-leave" and I met a chef from HMS *Rooke* in a pub called The Horseshoe on the "run ashore". He rescued me from a confrontation between a Gibraltarian and one of the bandies, which I was attempting to stop, quite funny really considering how tall they both were. The chef came from near my own parents in Hayling Island, so he said he would visit them when he was next on leave in UK, to say I was safe and well. We have remained great friends ever since, and he is now the godfather of both my teenage children.

Whilst the re-fit was happening we had to be kitted out with uniforms of "naval blues" from HMS *Rooke,* as personnel from RNH Haslar were not fully equipped; unlike the Stonehouse lot who had already been issued with khaki shirts and trousers and even all made their Wills before they left Plymouth.

By Sunday midday all the stores had been loaded and the framework for the hospital structure was in place. Although looking somewhat chaotic, things seemed to be coming together well, and our planned Monday departure was now looking more optimistic.

CHAPTER THREE

"WHITE CLOUDS FLYING"

Gibraltar to Ascension
April 19th – April 28th 1982

Finally, some 60 hours after *Uganda*'s arrival in Gibraltar on Friday April 16th, we were considered, in traditional Royal Naval terms, "in all respects ready for sea".

This amazing and little recognised feat of conversion from cruise/educational ship to hospital ship in such a short time was due, in the main, to the magnificent skills, hard work and professionalism of all levels of dockyard personnel within The Royal Naval Dockyard, Gibraltar. The Officer-in-Charge, Captain Alan Cooper, Mr Bill Thames, Dockyard General Manager, and their teams are due some long overdue thanks and gratitude, which all on board would join in now, albeit so many years after 1982. Even as we left harbour some of the dockyard personnel were to remain on board completing last-minute work; they were collected by tender later that day.

All ranks and rates within Naval Party 1830, as we were now officially called, had pulled together and helped with the massive store-ing from dockside to ship; human chains of all ranks and rates of nurses, stretcher-bearers, doctors and technicians had worked ceaselessly for the two days, and our original departure deadline could now be realised.

On a bright and sunny morning, April 19th 1982, Her Majesty's Hospital Ship *Uganda* left Number 2 dry dock at 0900. Her white hull gleamed in the sun, her red crosses stood proudly declaring our aim and objectives; to help and heal injured servicemen irrespective of nationality, faith or creed.

QARNNS Naval Nurse Karen Dawson wrote of her first moments on board a ship at sea:

> I had never been on the water in anything bigger than the Gosport ferry, before joining The Hospital Ship *Uganda* and, as it turned out, living on board for four months; thankfully I did not suffer from seasickness. I will always remember seeing the dolphins in the ship's bow wave soon after

we left Gibraltar Harbour, and the feeling of not so much fear, but worry, as we headed south from The Mediterranean.

Few on board could not have been moved, at the start of such uncertainty for what lay ahead. I feel sure we all hoped that the appearance of The Task Force and accompanying support vessels might have encouraged the Argentine Forces occupying The Falkland Islands to withdraw and return to their own country… but of course history reveals otherwise. From local news broadcasts in Gibraltar it seemed that the Argentine forces were in fact reinforcing and strengthening their troops around Port Stanley, and early hopes of their withdrawal seemed less and less likely with the passage of time.

The signal from The Medical Officer-in-Charge Royal Naval Hospital Gibraltar read:

"HEAL NAVY – YOU LOOK BEAUTIFUL – WISH WE WERE THERE"

We liked the signal, especially "Heal Navy". At that time there were many self-adhesive RN logos stuck on all the Ships and Establishment notice boards, car stickers, etc with things like: "Dive Navy", "Sail Navy", "Fly Navy", etc., printed on them. So inventing a new one for the Royal Navy and QARNNS Medical Teams seemed an appropriately timed touch, at what would subsequently turn into quite a historical moment.

Staff from The Royal Naval Hospital Gibraltar stood on the hospital roof and waved us off. The hospital has always been quite a distinctive feature from the sea, with its high elevation towards Europa Point and distinctive white colonnades, so we could see them waving for some time as we steamed away from the Naval Dockyard towards the Straits of Gibraltar. They had all helped in so many ways supporting us, and supplying us with many specific surgical needs, particularly for the operating theatres, at very short notice.

My diary for Tuesday April 20th reads:

> *Well, we made it! What an amazing and wonderful effort on behalf of all the dockyard staff in Gibraltar, to have worked SO hard to enable us to leave in such style yesterday morning.*
>
> *Over the last few days we have started building the basics of our floating hospital. Our Operating Theatre will be positioned in a central area that was known as The Veranda. It has wooden floors and we have already set up three operating tables with most of the necessary back-up and equipment. In one corner we have set up a large and noisy porous loading autoclave which we have christened "Vesuvius" that belches out much steam, but is going to be*

essential in the months ahead. The secondary role of the Operating Theatre Teams will be to produce and manage a mini "Theatre Sterilising Supply Unit" (TSSU) sterilising all our Theatre instruments and linen drapes, as well as all dressings, bandages and other items that require sterilising for the whole hospital.

Our working capacity will be in the region of 250 – 300 beds, with a 20-bed intensive care unit next to our Operating Theatres. Uganda's original ship's hospital has been designated as a high-dependency burns unit, and on the same deck more than 400 dormitory bunks will be suitable for low dependency casualties as required. Laboratories, which include the blood transfusion unit, are located between the ICU and our theatres, where some existing cold cabinets show promise for cold storage of blood at the correct temperature. The Casualty Reception Area (CRA) at the base of the helicopter landing pad is nearly ready. Rev David Barlow, our RN Anglican padre, is going to set up a patient identification system at the CRA entrance area.

It's all a massive undertaking and will take more than a week for us to implement all the plans that are in place.

From Gibraltar we steamed south at approximately 12 knots, our estimated time for arrival north of The Falklands being between two and three weeks, with some days off Ascension Island to water and store. Our first "dry-run" to refuel at sea (RAS) from the Royal Fleet Auxiliary (RFA) *Olna* was timed about 60 miles south of Gibraltar during our first day at sea and seemed to go well and without incident. Another essential milestone crossed, although in the rougher waters of The South Atlantic this operation would prove to be more hazardous.

P&O Chief Officer Grahame Burton noted the completion of this procedure with some relief:

Being a Hospital Ship and protected under the Geneva Convention was very reassuring, but there were a few disadvantages, as our Naval Party Officers soon found out. Suddenly they had no access to classified signals and had to listen to the BBC World Service for news of the conflict. As all warships were operating under radio silence, it was interesting to see our RN officers keen to talk on the phone line that was rigged between us and our replenishing tanker, to find out from their crew what was really happening down south.

The Royal Fleet Auxiliary (RFA) Service is a civilian manned fleet, owned and operated by The Ministry of Defence. Their purpose is to supply ships of The Royal Navy with fuel, stores, and ammunition so that the Naval warships can remain operational at sea for long periods. In war, this role extends to include the ships taken up from trade (STUFT), of which there were about 50 requisitioned during the campaign, The Hospital Ship *Uganda* being one of those. RFAs *Olna, Olmeda, Alvega, Apple Leaf, Tidespring, Fort Austin, Fort Grange* and *Toronto* were some of the RFAs who were to help with our fuel and water as the next few months unfolded. This is another group of unsung heroes. Without the RFAs' reliable presence in southern latitudes, supplying all the ships in The Task Force with essential fuel and other supplies, the outcome of Operation Corporate could have been very different.

We thank you, RFAs, and all your dedicated personnel for your reassuring presence month after month working in those wild grey seas all those years ago.

P&O Chief Officer Grahame Burton describes the transition time from leaving Gibraltar to starting the new shipboard routines as we headed south:

> The people of Gibraltar were very supportive; T shirts appeared with logos such as "Hands off the Falklands, They're ours"., Several of our Officers were invited for food and drinks at lunchtime on Saturday in the Wardroom of HMS *Rooke*, and the "Gibraltar Chronicle" published a large front page article about our Hospital Ship the day after we sailed. Shore leave was posted as expiring at 2359 on 18th April and at 0900 the next day we sailed into unfamiliar waters. All our merchant crew members who sailed south were volunteers, and what made it different for many of the crew of *Uganda* was that, compared with most of those who deployed south, we never got to see our families in the UK before we left, or to say goodbye to them in person.
>
> Normal sea watches were set on departure, with 1st Officer Peter Harris, Jnr, 1st Officer Paul Dilks, 2nd Officer Glyn Wintle and 3rd Officer Richard Bowler being the bridge watch keepers. The Engine Room team was headed up by Chief Engineer Officer David King, 2nd Engineers Peter Johnson and Chris Freeman, plus Alex Jamison as 1st Electrician. Bruce Cooper was our ship's own P&O Doctor, assisted by two P&O (civilian) Nursing Sisters. One new addition to our normal complement was Jimmy Dean, (James Buntin) as Entertainments Officer. Whilst it was normal to sail with a full entertainments staff on most cruise ships, entertainment functions on board *Uganda* were traditionally provided by the Staff Officer and his team of Cadets. The Staff Officer position was often filled in rotation by one of the deck 1st Officers.
>
> Strange though it may sound now more than 25 years on (when one thinks nothing of having a Global Positioning System [GPS] in your

boat or car), up until our arrival at Gibraltar in April 1982, *Uganda* was navigated without the aid of satellite navigation. Positions were fixed using visual objects when in sight of land, and sun and star sights when on ocean passages. Decca Navigators could be used when around Northern Europe. A passage to the South Atlantic, out of sight of land for days on end, with frequent overcast skies, would have meant that we would only have had an approximate idea of what our position might have been. This would not have satisfied the Geneva Convention, under which we were to operate as a Hospital Ship. We needed to be either in a fixed position, or to be able to advise others of our exact location, which should then provide us with immunity from the combat forces. We therefore happily welcomed the small, black box-like Satellite Navigator that was positioned above the chartroom table, and displayed an LED one-line latitude and longitude position. (LED – Light Emitting Diode)

In addition to the Royal Navy Medical and QARNNS teams who embarked at Gibraltar, there were a number of other important additions on the operational complement. First was Naval Party 1830 (NP1830), with Commander Andy Gough as the Senior Naval Officer of *Uganda* and Commanding Officer of Naval Party 1830, Lt. Commander Keith Tatman as First Lieutenant/Aviation Officer, and Lt. Commander David Porteous as Supply Officer, to work with our Purser, Barry Mulder. There were also two embarked Royal Fleet Auxiliary (RFA) Officers: First Officer Chris McKenzie as Replenishment at Sea (RAS) Officer and Senior Radio Officer Bruce Barnes, to assist in NP1830 communications using the new satellite dish and to work with our Chief Radio Officer Ken Gibson.

For many on board it was a new experience to be working with the Royal Navy. However I was fortunate to have been commissioned into the Royal Naval Reserve in 1967, and to have completed many training courses as well as serving time on several RN ships prior to 1982. At the time I was a Lieutenant Commander in List One of the RNR specialising in Naval Control of Shipping and in Amphibious Warfare. As such I was able to provide a valuable link between the two services, while we grew accustomed to each other's routines and terminology.

There was much to do in preparing ourselves for our new role. The afternoon we departed from Gibraltar, we exercised refuelling at sea (RAS) and flight deck landings with RFA *Olna*. The replacement deck and engine ratings needed to settle into their new surroundings, and realise that life on board a passenger ship with several hundred souls aboard was very different from the small cargo ships and tankers that most had come from. Some were motivated by a sense of duty to their country, but many I believe were more motivated by the potential monetary "war bonus" of 150% of earnings, that was to be paid each day the ship was south of Latitude 7°S. Jimmy Dean the Entertainment Officer did a difficult job in trying to keep them occupied in their off duty time, when the "default thought" for many of them was to head for the crew bar and stay there.

* * *

As we headed south away from Gibraltar, the first essential for the nursing personnel was to start our thorough cleaning of the hospital areas, in preparation for unpacking and sorting of the 700 or so crates and boxes that now comprised our floating, as yet uncommissioned, hospital. We organised ourselves into teams relating to our skill mixes and forthcoming work areas; thus the Intensive Care Unit teams worked in that area, our own Operating Theatre teams next door, and so on round the entire working hospital. Bear in mind that our "hospital", as we left Gibraltar, had looked more like an abandoned garage under construction!

We armed ourselves with mops and cleaning equipment and soon had the place looking and indeed smelling more like the basis for an efficient hospital.

The sorting and subsequent unpacking of the hundreds of crates and boxes then commenced. The lack of any sort of outside labelling in the system did have its problems. A crate of, say, 100 litres of intravenous solution would weigh in at 100 kgs, so no one wanted to lug these around the ship unnecessarily. We could have worked much faster and more efficiently if we had not had to open every single case to discover what lurked inside. Still, we plodded on assiduously and soon the makings of clinical areas started to appear. As the medical equipment began to emerge we were back in familiar territory; syringes, needles and intravenous equipment were and always will remain the tools of our trade.

In our operating theatres, our surgical instruments and mounds of other related material were all familiar friends, and we set to with enthusiasm on the long process of cleaning and preparing them, to eventually emerge processed as sterilised packs of instruments for all types of surgery.

Likewise anaesthetic and respiratory equipment had to be carefully checked and tested meticulously before use. Everyone pulled together helping to fix the field hospital operating table bases to the floor, securing electrical equipment, suction apparatus, lighting and all the other essential items that make up our hidden world of surgery and anaesthetics.

We had already assessed that supplies of fresh water were going to be a problem, and water usage was strictly rationed from departure. Hospitals require much fresh water to function efficiently, and this initial concern was finally resolved some 3 weeks later when some desalinators, which could convert seawater into fresh water, arrived from HMS *Intrepid*.

The surgical "gels" and spirit hand cleaners in such common hospital use today had not long been available commercially in 1982. Fortunately they were included in the operating theatre kit supplied, which was a huge bonus and proved to be a vast fresh water saving benefit, over the many months we remained operational. A traditional "scrub-up" for surgery under running water would use well over a gallon of fresh water for each routine scrub process, so the hand-rub gels provided were a much valued treasure within the OT kit.

Theatres were then always damp-dusted several times a day, and floors cleaned and sterilised to the best of our ability. These essential routines all helped to maintain our low infection levels, which remained notably minimal throughout the entire deployment.

Here, QARNNS Head Naval Nurse Maggie Freer describes her progress south as she and the teams were setting up Sea View Ward, a high-dependency unit underneath the helicopter landing pad:

> During the journey to the South Atlantic we stored ship, set up the various hospital areas and improved our skills through a variety of lectures and doing casualty handling and medical exercises.
>
> I'm not a good sailor at the best of times, and felt very seasick and had to resort to taking an anti-emetic Stugeron, especially as Sea View Ward was at the stern of the ship and seemed to travel in the vertical as well as the horizontal line in rough weather!
>
> In spite of there being 37 (augmented to 40 later in the conflict) military females serving with QARNNS on board we wore men's "number eights" most of the time due to a lack of suitable female uniform being available. We felt very isolated from the international news until it was regularly broadcast through the tannoy system.

Overall storage of the pre-packed sterile items that had to be readily available was, initially, going to be an issue. But we quickly saw that the clean inner cardboard boxes within the outer packing cases could readily adapt with some careful cutting and labelling, to become little storage lockers that we could lash in place as appropriate. We called this our "patent *Uganda* storage system"…it worked!

Our Heads of Departments and Medical-Officer-In-Charge (MOIC) were facing similar problems with lack of instructions and manifests at every level. Commander Gough's "Book of Instructions" for working up a Hospital Ship was an official Ministry of Defence publication which had the words: "Disestablished, Disused and Not to Be Used In Action" stamped all over the cover. This was an inauspicious start. It was very much a case of: "Here's a ship… convert her into a hospital". Well, we did just that and even at this early stage of proceedings it was becoming clear that improvisation and adaptability, combined with practical and inventive skills, were going to be key to the success of this venture.

QARNNS Senior Nursing Officer Liz Law continues her side of the tale here, as she describes some aspects of how she and the Intensive Care Unit teams set up their working area adjacent to the operating theatres:

The Intensive Care Unit (ICU) was to be located in what had been a cocktail lounge. It was mid-ship and therefore relatively stable. It was also quite close to the Casualty Reception Area, Operating Theatres, X-Ray and Laboratory facilities.

The team detailed to work on the unit included Surgeon Commander Peter Bull, Superintending Nursing Officer Jane Marshall, Head Naval Nurse Rosemary Lake, Senior Naval Nurse Sally Middleton and myself as Senior Nursing Officer, together with other QARNNS Naval Nurses and RN Medical Assistants with varying degrees of experience. Senior Nursing Officer Jean Kidd (now Adley) was in charge in the Casualty Reception Area but, once we had stopped receiving casualties for the day, she would come to the Unit to lend a hand. We planned to have 20 beds on the Unit with capacity for four ventilators (external breathing apparatus) and spent the transit time travelling from Gibraltar to Ascension Island setting up the beds and trying to find convenient storage for all the ancillary equipment required in such a unit. We utilised cupboard space normally housing cocktail glasses for IV fluids, and drawer space for syringes, needles etc. Empty cardboard boxes were re-used on every available surface to house easily accessible dressings, infusion equipment and emergency plastic airways.

The carpet was retained partly to prevent slippage in rough sea, and also for clinical and practical reasons. We also had to give consideration to the securing of the large glass bottles used for the chest drains required by many of the troops sustaining chest wounds. The infusion stands we used were secured to the metal-framed beds by screws which had the uncanny knack of loosening by themselves! On several occasions staff had to do a mad dash from one side of the unit to the other to tighten up the stand and prevent the infusion falling.

We had to ensure that we got the best from the equipment that we had as it was unclear how long we would be required to be operational. It was also uncertain how easily more supplies could be accessed. To this end we used CIDEX (a liquid glutaraldehyde solution) to re-sterilise disposable suction catheters, syringes etc. that would otherwise have been discarded.

Each bed had a life-jacket underneath which subsequently proved useful either as a back-rest for the patients or to elevate the foot of the bed if required.

During these early days heading south everyone started to find their sea legs, getting into the sea-going watches, and settling in to this new and for many, strange environment. Although coincidentally some friends had joined the ship together, few of us had worked together before, so in some ways it was a good time to get to know each other; part of the ship's "shake-down" routine, as we call it in the Navy. A series of very useful lectures were set up in the ship's cinema area which was an ideal place for what in those days were projector screen and slide talks. They helped to prepare us all for what we hoped would not lie ahead. But the further April progressed, with no sign of Argentinian withdrawal or a diplomatic solution emerging, the more likely began to seem the possibility of casualties from the Combat Zone requiring hospital facilities.

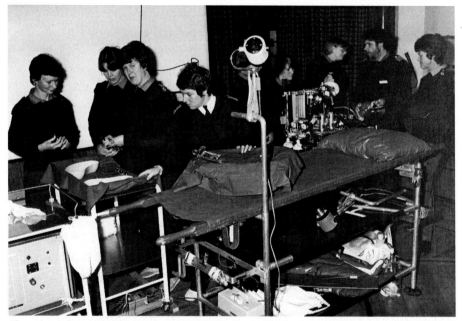

The author (white shirt and tie) sets up a Teaching Session in The Operating Theatre as the ship heads south from Gibraltar. Late April 1982.
Photograph: Author's private collection

Royal Naval Surgeon Commander Peter Bull (Consultant Anaesthetist for The Task Force) assesses our anaesthetic situation at this early stage of proceedings here:

> As will be reported elsewhere the P&O cruise liner SS *Canberra* had also been requisitioned, and was originally designated to be the Main Dressing Station/Hospital Ship for the campaign. Unfortunately, by carrying troops and armaments as she travelled south, she would have been breaking the Geneva Convention, and therefore a different Hospital Ship was needed.
>
> At very short notice, as a relatively junior Anaesthetic Consultant, I was asked to be the senior of two Royal Navy Anaesthetists for The Hospital Ship *Uganda*, and therefore had to plan my requirements

28

carefully, bearing in mind that the designated War Stores were already in *Canberra*. These could not be recovered as she would need to undertake some hospital functions herself, if involved in the re-taking of the islands (this was the case) – albeit without the protection of the Red Cross.

I had already decided that Ether, though a most suitable agent for wartime and for the less experienced, should not be taken because of its flammability, so general anaesthesia would be based on Halothane and Trilene via a Tri-service machine. I determined we would utilise soda lime for closed circuitry as much as possible to save valuable resources and contamination of theatre staff. We would intensively practise using this system, in case we lost our oxygen supply or had cause to use field anaesthesia which is, of course, what did happen ashore.

Furthermore the muscle relaxant of choice would have to be Alcuronium, rather than Suxamethonium, as we could not rely on keeping this refrigerated, especially if new supplies were to follow. Any equipment and drugs I requested would be flown out as soon as possible from the start of the conversion in Gibraltar. The "Stand-by War Stores" were to be made available to me (as *Canberra* now had the designated War Stores) and I was given a list of the expected items. Most unfortunately this list was not accurate and many expected items were not present or beyond use. In particular, there were no anaesthetic machines, no tracheostomy tubes, urinary catheters, naso-gastric tubes or indeed bedpans. My own selection of items had to take into consideration the length of our deployment and number of casualties, as well as their complexity – all in all, an almost impossible scenario. Also, I did not realise then that I would be the re-supply depot for casualty stations elsewhere (e.g. Ajax Bay), nor for the Army (e.g. at Fitzroy). Until the *QE2* arrived and brought us some supplies, including blood units, in mid May, I was not aware the Army had medical units to assist us. By late May we did obtain a re-supply route via Montevideo when our ambulance ships transported recovered casualties for repatriation.

On April 20th the P&O Captain, Brian Biddick, fell seriously ill. We operated on him in the ship's own theatres as ours were not yet in commission. Post-operatively, it was decided the best course of action was for him to be airlifted back to UK, so we diverted into Freetown, the capital of Sierra Leone, where we berthed alongside the Queen Elizabeth the Second quay during the early morning of April 25th. Captain Jeff Clark took over command of the ship, and Captain Roger Knight was flown out from Gatwick as the relief Deputy Captain. No shore leave was granted at Freetown. We took on fuel, water and some fresh stores and left at 1900 that evening. All the ship's company had to take malarial preventative medication for a month over this period.

P&O Chief Officer Grahame Burton said of P&O Captain Biddick's illness:

> Captain Biddick had appeared tired even before the ship was requisitioned and I was therefore relieved when, in Gibraltar, Dr. Tom Poole the P&O Medical Superintendent, and Peter Motion our Fleet Director, were able to talk with him. There was obviously no undue concern, as Captain Biddick did sail south with us. However, I remember him telling me the afternoon we had completed our refuelling-at-sea with RFA *Olna*, that he was going to take it easy and rest for a few days. That was the last time I saw him, until I helped carry him down the gangway on a stretcher at Freetown, Sierra Leone. It had been planned to divert the ship to Dakar in Senegal to casevac Captain Biddick, but this did not prove possible. In the event Captain Biddick was flown back to UK at low altitude in an RAF VC10 sent out especially for the purpose.

We were all saddened to hear some weeks later on May 12th that Captain Biddick had died in his home county of Cornwall. He was only 47 years old, a very special Cornishman who got his P&O command in 1972. We all contributed to a memorial fund which was distributed to various maritime charities.

* * *

Here, QARNNS Naval Nurse Karen Dawson describes how she helped set up The Intensive Care Unit with Sister Law and the teams as we headed south towards Ascension, and a few incidents she remembers from that time:

> I was to work on the Intensive Care Unit (ICU) on board and considering I had only just qualified it was a bit scary, but a challenge. We found when fitting the ICU out we could only find one bedpan and one urinal bottle, that would have been between 20 or so patients, and they were made of papier-mâché which was funny as we had nowhere to dispose of them… other than the obvious, i.e. over the side of the ship! I laugh now but, at the time, we had to keep moving boxes and boxes of intravenous fluids from one place to another till somebody changed their mind and we had to move them all again. We used to have a chain of people of all different ranks and rates, including all the Nursing Officers and a few doctors, to help move them around the ship and they were very heavy.
>
> The Junior Rates showers were timed, with people outside on watch to check that you didn't go over the couple of minutes allowed. We didn't

have the water converter on board so we couldn't make our own fresh from seawater and needed to ration as much fresh water as possible until the equipment arrived.

When we arrived at Freetown it was so hot, you could not even stand on the Flight Deck it was so hot to the touch. Somebody fried an egg on it to see how quickly it would cook! Little boats with locals came out from the shore to sell their goods and I wanted a carved elephant but didn't have anything to barter with. After we had sailed I was upset I hadn't got one, but one of the merchant crew had heard me and he got one for me. I still have that elephant today, even with his chipped eye that he got coming down the gangway back in Southampton.

I slept in a 3-bedded cabin with another Enrolled Nurse called Annie Blocke. I had the bottom bunk as I don't do ladders and I was bound to fall out. Annie worked in the Operating Theatres with Jo Scade, Denise (Fred) Bassett, Jim Lacey, and the Nursing Officers Sister Gauld, Nicci Pugh and Margaret Kerr.

We arrived off Ascension on April 28th 1400, having crossed The Equator the previous day. Ascension was a hive of activity, as the assembled Naval warships were making their final preparations for the passage south. Our Matron Edith Meikeljohn ARRC (Principal Nursing Officer, Queen Alexandra's Royal Naval Nursing Service) transferred from *Canberra* which was anchored nearby.

We continued to practise our Casualty Evacuation Exercises (CASEXs) improving times from Flight Deck to the Casualty Reception Area (CRA), and adjusting routines accordingly. Intense sea and air activity continued; more stores and fuel were transferred with flying activity continuing apace.

My diary entry for that evening reads:

> *Ascension was a magnificent and dramatic landfall… a positive hive of activity here, the bay is full of "grey-funnel ships" with dozens of airborne helicopters store-ing and delivering people and things in every direction. The whole extent of the campaign is now beginning to expose itself and helps to make one realise what a very small cog in such an enormous wheel we are.*
>
> *I received 18 letters from UK in Ascension! Most people received something; it was a great morale booster. I'm still waiting for a new pair of white gym shoes though; maybe someone will send them with our next "mailies".'*

On April 29th a signal was sent to Commander in Chief, Fleet, informing them The Hospital Ship was now fully equipped and ready for action. Deprived under the Geneva Convention of direct links with other ships or units of The Task Force, official news of the impending conflict came to us from the BBC World Service broadcasts alone. We had heard that South Georgia had been retaken by British Forces by April 26th.

By this stage the Relief P&O Chief Officer for *Uganda*, Tony Chadwick, had been called to Active Service on April 19th, although he was required to remain in UK.

P&O Chief Officer Grahame Burton describes Tony's role at HMS *Warrior*, C in C Fleet HQ in Northwood, Middlesex:

> Unknown to me and to everyone else on board *Uganda* at this time, was the fact that Tony Chadwick, the relief Chief Officer for *Uganda*, also a List 1 Lt.Cdr. RNR, and currently home on leave, had been called to "Active Service" on 19th April, joining the staff of C in C Fleet at HMS *Warrior*, in Northwood, just outside London. It was from this location that Admiral Fieldhouse directed his forces in the South Atlantic, and one of Tony Chadwick's main tasks was to watch over Her Majesty's Hospital Ship *Uganda*. Later in the conflict, on 28th May 1982, P&O received the following letter from Admiral Fieldhouse:

> > **"I should like to express my appreciation for the willing manner in which your company has released Lieutenant Commander Chadwick RNR for duty at my headquarters. His advice and experience has been invaluable to my staff in their dealings with Ships Taken up from Trade and in many other matters associated with the Mercantile Marine.**
> >
> > **From the very outset of the Falklands Crisis the cooperation and willing assistance from the Merchant Navy and, in particular P&O Cruises, has been in the best traditions of our long association. I am most grateful to you."**

Grahame Burton also goes on to describe our departure from Ascension on April 30th:

> The P&O Deputy Captain, Jeff Clark, took over command of *Uganda* from Brian Biddick, and a replacement P&O Officer, Roger Knight, was called back from leave to rejoin as Deputy Captain, which he did in Freetown. Having refuelled and topped off with water, we left Freetown

at 1900 on 25th April for Ascension Island. Life settled into a mixture of military regime and cruise ship routine. Part of The First Lieutenants' Temporary Memorandum No.2/82 stated that: "Whilst *Uganda* is under Naval control, it is intended to allow the ship to operate as a cruise ship until casualties arrive on board, this meaning that meals, recreation spaces and facilities will be controlled in a manner compatible with a passenger ship. Once patients are received, the Navy will dictate routines more stringently."

As Chief Officer of *Uganda* it was also my duty to be President of the P&O Officers' Wardroom. From a review of my diary for this period, I see that social life still continued, with most evenings having one or more of the P&O Officers hosting a cocktail party. During our time at Ascension, we were anchored in view of P&O *Canberra*, loaded with her troops and their equipment, waiting to be deployed south. Whilst the fleet and its attendant merchant ships were under radio silence, we did manage to exchange messages with our colleagues on *Canberra*, which somehow did not seem to make us feel quite so far from home. Much equipment and personnel were transferred during this time by helicopter, and the Naval Medical personnel continued steadily building the hospital facilities as all the equipment continued to arrive on board.

As fresh water was a big concern for us, especially once we became a fully functioning hospital, the RN was arranging for a new type of desalination plant to be sent out to us. Unfortunately it did not arrive before we were ordered to leave Ascension, and on the evening of Friday 30th April we were suddenly ordered to replenish fresh water to capacity from *Stena Seaspread*. As I was required to oversee this operation, I was not too impressed at having to leave the Wardroom "Banquet Dinner" which had promised to be something special. At 2345 we received orders to sail south and by 0030 that night we were on our way to The South Atlantic.

During those days at Ascension our role within the Conflict had now changed. *Canberra* could no longer be used as a Main Dressing Station/Hospital Ship since she was carrying fighting troops, so could be regarded as a legitimate target by Argentine/enemy forces.

So Her Majesty's Hospital Ship *Uganda* now became the main British hospital ship "in-zone", and she would be moving closer to hostilities in time.

CHAPTER FOUR

"A CLEAR CALL"

Ascension to The Falkland Islands
April 30th – May 25th 1982

On Friday April 30th we received a signal to proceed south from Ascension, initially to a position about 1,000 nautical miles north of The Falkland Islands. We raised anchor and left Ascension Island immediately.

By May 5th the Argentinian cruiser General *Belgrano* had been sunk. HMS *Sheffield* was attacked on May 4th, and news of this reached us on the morning of May 5th. We were the nearest ship with suitable facilities for treating and caring for burns patients, so we were then to proceed further south at all speed to receive casualties.

Our next allocated "sea area" at that stage was outlined by the co-ordinates 49S-51S and 52W-54W. This northerly Red Cross Box (RCB) was located in the north-west corner of, and just inside, the Total Exclusion Zone (TEZ). The TEZ was a circular sea area of some 400 nautical miles in diameter centred on The Falkland Islands. As this position was some 150 to 200 nautical miles from The Falkland Islands this was obviously too deep for the Hospital Ship to anchor. So the ship would steam slowly and continuously around the RCB to maintain steerage; receiving casualties, RAS-ing and store-ing as required.

Thus, whilst in this sea area, from May 12th onwards we started receiving casualties by helicopter on a regular basis. Chapter Five reveals how this initial plan was quickly modified, and subsequently The Hospital Ship was working from anchorages located within Falkland Sound.

Between May 12th and July 14th, a period of nine weeks, a total of 730 cases were to be treated on board The Hospital Ship *Uganda*. This is the period covered in detail in the next four chapters. More than 500 surgical cases were carried out in our operating theatres, and more than 550 patients transferred safely back to UK. For this ongoing journey from The Hospital Ship back to UK we used the ingenious transfer system previously described of the three ambulance ships HMS *Hydra*, *Herald* and *Hecla* (all converted from RN survey

34

ships). They would transfer recovering patients by sea to Montevideo in neutral Uruguay and onwards by RAF VC10 to UK.

The first casualties from HMS *Sheffield* were transferred to The Hospital Ship by Sea King helicopter from HMS *Hermes* on May 12th, where they had been awaiting our arrival. We were well within the Total Exclusion Zone (TEZ) at 51S when the transfer took place. These casualties included Chief Petty Officer John Strange, Petty Officer Radio Electrician Richard Wood, Marine Engineering Mechanic David Harrington and Radio Operator Mark Bagnall.

The adjacent inset describes John Strange's time leading up to the conflict:

In 1982: Chief Petty Officer John Strange RN

Photograph: John Strange

As a Chief Petty Officer Marine Engineering Artificer (CPOMEA) I joined HMS *Sheffield*, a Type 42 Destroyer, in Portsmouth Dockyard on the 10th November 1981 but little did I know what the next 15 months would hold in store for me. The following week the ship sailed for a five month tour of duty in the Persian Gulf. The journey east took us to Gibraltar, through the Mediterranean Sea, the Red Sea and into the Gulf of Oman.

With Christmas over and into 1982 the time passed quickly and we soon found ourselves making the return journey home with Gibraltar being the final port of call before we were due back at Portsmouth on the 6th April 1982. However, between leaving Gibraltar and arriving in Portsmouth we were to take part in a Naval exercise in the North Atlantic. It was during this exercise period on the 2nd April that the Argentinians invaded the Falkland Islands, a British dependency for almost 150 years.

John Strange describes events leading to his escape from the burning *Sheffield* and up to his arrival on board The Hospital Ship:

CPO MEA   John Strange RN working in HMS Sheffield's *engine room in 1981.*
Photograph: John Strange

On 4th April, and only two days' steaming distance from UK and home, HMS *Sheffield* was diverted to head south as part of an advance task force. We sailed steadily southwards across the Equator, stopped for essential supplies at Ascension Island, and into the cold waters of the South Atlantic Ocean.

Daily we would listen to the BBC World Service hoping that Argentina would withdraw its troops and that we would be able to head back to Portsmouth and our families. It was not to be and, with a number of other ships, we took up station inside the 200 mile (radius) exclusion zone. Then came the waiting; the dawn action stations, the broadcasts of enemy aircraft and submarines in the vicinity, and reports of how the war was progressing ashore on the Falkland Islands.

After some of the rough weather we had been through recently, Tuesday the 4th May was quite a calm pleasant day but before it was over it was to become a nightmare, not only for the crew of HMS *Sheffield*, but also for the many relatives waiting patiently at home in the United Kingdom.

Just after fourteen hundred hours (2.15 pm local time) while patrolling off West Falkland near Pebble Island, an Argentine plane came over the horizon and found a British warship directly in its path. The pilot released two Exocet missiles, one of which hit HMS *Sheffield* amidships just above the waterline on the starboard side. The explosion and fire which followed were to kill 20 crew members and injure a number of others. (Seven days later whilst being towed towards safety, HMS *Sheffield* sank in mid Atlantic.)

I was working in the Forward Machinery Space close to where the missile hit and was one of the seriously wounded. I remembered a bang and the next thing I was recovering consciousness and finding myself in a dark, smoke filled compartment, my escape route to the main exit cut off by a wall of fire. I could see that the port side of the machinery space was reasonably clear so I covered my face with my hands and ran through the flames to relative safety. The skin peeled from my fingers and hands as I climbed the vertical ladder to the escape hatch which would lead me along the port passageway on No2 deck. Later I was to find out that, as well as numerous shrapnel wounds, I had received 46% burns to various parts of my body.

On leaving the escape hatch I was helped from the already smoke filled ship onto the upper deck, given morphine injections and lifted by helicopter onto HMS *Arrow* which had come to our rescue. After initial first aid by the ship's Medical Officer, who almost certainly saved my life, I was transferred to HMS *Hermes* which had a better equipped ship's hospital and was carrying extra medical staff. Onboard *Hermes* I was kept alive by Surgeon Commander Soul and his expert staff. I was later told that I hadn't been given much chance of survival and had been measured up for the canvas bag which I'd be put in to be dropped over the ship's side in the event of death. However, I did survive and eight days later on the 12th May I was well enough to be transferred by helicopter, yet again, this time to the converted Hospital Ship *Uganda* which had just arrived on station.

On board The Hospital Ship there was much relief, as all our careful planning and preparations seemed to have paid off. The incoming casualties were swiftly and safely carried from the flight deck to the CRA and thence onward to the appropriate hospital areas. It all seemed to be working!

My diary entry from May 25th reads:

> *In the last few weeks we have completed building our*
> *floating hospital, the teaching programme and more than*
> *a dozen emergency station procedures. Now it's all being*
> *put to good effect. We have over a dozen patients on board,*
> *including some of the worst burnt from HMS Sheffield. She*
> *finally sank some days ago after several valiant attempts to*
> *save her. HMS Ardent (May 22nd) and HMS Antelope (May*
> *23rd) have also been attacked by the Argentinians and sunk.*

QARNNS Senior Nursing Officer Liz Law (ICU) continues telling her aspect of things at this time:

We received our first casualties on May 12th following the attack on HMS *Sheffield*. They were flown to us from HMS *Hermes*. Among them was

CPO John Strange suffering severe burns. We were still experiencing water rationing at this time and this made the job of ensuring adequate hygiene quite taxing. The situation wasn't resolved until the arrival of a desalination plant in late May.

From late May onwards we were kept busy with casualties from both sides. It was difficult at times as we had only three staff per watch.

It was decided that we would work sea-going watches, four hours on, four hours off with two dog watches of two hours each between 1600 and 2000. This ensured the shift pattern rotated through the three teams which we named Red, White and Blue Watch. A similar system operated throughout the Hospital while we were operational. Staff were also supplemented during busy periods with the invaluable help of the Royal Marine Bandsmen (whose wartime role is to act as stretcher-bearers) and the P&O crew, both nursing staff and stewards. The inclusion of the two Royal Naval Chaplains proved useful both to the staff and patients. Father Chris Bester summoned his best Spanish to be able to converse with the Argentine casualties when the language skills from the rest of us were sadly lacking.

As the numbers of casualties increased from this stage of the war onwards they could only be helicoptered to us during the short daylight hours. This meant that we were often required to get up from bed to assist with initial assessment and treatment of arriving casualties when we should have been off watch. The situation was eased when we received additional staff from HMS *Hermes*, and later from *Canberra*. Inevitably at such times, close relationships are forged and I feel we were fortunate to enjoy good teamwork to enable us to work efficiently and effectively.

By mid-May The Hospital Ship *Uganda* had been authorised by The International Red Cross to co-ordinate the movements of all three of the RN Ambulance/Survey ships HMS *Hydra*, *Hecla* and *Herald*, and the three Argentinian Hospital Ships, the *Bahia Paraiso*, *Almirante Irizar* and the *Puerto Deseado*. The *Bahia Paraiso* and the *Almirante Irizar*, at over 10,000 tons each, were former polar transport vessels, the *Puerto Deseado* smaller at 2,133 tons displacement. They supported white-painted Puma and Alouette helicopters between their own Argentinian Hospital Ship fleet.

P&O Chief Officer Grahame Burton was continuing to monitor the fresh water situation at this stage as closely as we were! This is his assessment of the situation at the time, and then describing his role on the Flight Deck as casualties started to arrive:

Two of the converted from Survey to Ambulance ships in The South Atlantic during The Falklands War in 1982. Above: HMS Herald. *Below: HMS* Hydra *with WASP helicopter astern.*
Photograph: Terry Beddoes

From my records the following were our fresh water details. The ship's capacity was a total of 2,400 tons of wash water plus 200 tons of drinking water. Consumption had been reduced to 10/15 tons of drinking water per day and about 70 tons of wash water; this whilst operating in a stand by mode, with a total compliment of 390 on board. Obviously once the ship started accepting patients, the consumption would increase considerably and many of the water saving measures would have to be abandoned. We thus sailed south, independently, with about three weeks' supply of fresh water on board. Fortunately our two reverse osmosis plants had been placed on board HMS *Intrepid*, and they were eventually transferred to us on 18th May by 22 "vertrep" (under slung helicopter transfer) loads in position 49°S 51°W. In the interim we had been able to obtain some water during a "RAS" (refuelling-at sea) with RFA *Tidespring* and later with RFA *Appleleaf*. It took some time to assemble the desalination plants; however everyone on board was relieved that this vital equipment had finally reached us, as casualties had been arriving since 12th May, when we had entered the Total Exclusion Zone.

Once casualties started to arrive, one was constantly listening for the announcement over the ship's speakers, which preceded every helicopter landing astern:

"Hands to flying stations, hands to flying stations... The upper deck aft of the assembly hall is out of bounds... No more gash to be ditched... No smoking on the upper deck... Close all weather doors and scuttles in Zone 5... Crash boat crew close up".

My position was on the flight deck with Lieutenant Commander Keith Tatman RN, the Aviation Officer, CPO (Chief Petty Officer) "Kipper" Heron as Flight Deck Officer assisted by CPO Doran. One of my tasks was to liaise between the P&O Captain, or Deputy Captain, on the Bridge, especially regarding courses steered to provide a suitable cross-deck wind for helicopter landing. I was also in place should there be a crash on deck, as I was in charge of fire fighting, and had a team of fire fighters closed up each time we went to flying stations.

As Grahame Burton has mentioned above, on May 18th the two much-needed desalination plants arrived from HMS *Intrepid* by helicopter. They arrived in 22 shipments over several hours without manuals or instructions. After some days of intense engineering the RN and P&O engineering skills paid off. Sighs of relief went round the whole ship that we could now supplement fresh water supplies with these trusty friends, whom we christened "Niagara" and "Kariba". Eventually they were producing well over half the ship's total requirement of fresh water during the commission.

Head Naval Nurse Maggie Freer recalls of the fresh water shortage:

Initially fresh water was rationed, there being periods of time where the water was turned off, and showers had to be completed in three minutes, fine for people with short hair! I would finish a night watch at 0400 and then have an egg and bacon sarnie in the canteen. Before going to bed I'd fill a hot water bottle from a hot tap near Derek Houghton's office. When I woke before the next watch I would pour the hottie water into my sink for a wash before going on watch, & then use the same water later to wash some undies! So that water was recycled three times!! We became adept at little ways like that of saving fresh water, but still keeping our kit and ourselves clean.

The situation was eased later in May when two desalination units were brought to us from Ascension on board HMS *Intrepid*. We nicknamed them Niagara and Kariba. David (Maggie's husband, serving on board HMS *Intrepid*) came over with the first load and stayed for about two hours, which was a real bonus to see him so many miles away from home.

This is Maggie's account of the mid-May casualties:

On 4th May we heard from the ship's carpenter about HMS *Sheffield* being hit by an Exocet. He had been on the radio phone to his wife and the news was on as they were speaking; she relayed this to him and he immediately came to our mess (The Senior Rates Mess) to tell us.

The worst day for me was 21st May when five of our ships were hit in San Carlos Water. Ships' names were not mentioned but I knew HMS *Intrepid* was anchored there. Some of the casualties that came to us had been on HMS *Intrepid* and my husband David (one of the medics on board HMS *Intrepid*) had treated them. Some of the patients brought letters for me from him. His initial letters to me had gone back to the UK to come back to Ascension Island and the *Intrepid* actually brought some of his letters to *Uganda* from Ascension. Eventually we arranged for our mail to be delivered whenever a helicopter was going to or from our ships, the quickest delivery being 15 minutes, a real privilege. This made up for me being unable to book a ship to ship radio phone call to speak to David, even though I could [book a call] to speak to our parents in UK. Obviously there were no email, internet or mobile telephones in 1982! I have kept all our letters from that time, and treasure them carefully, as I would like our children and future generations to have them. Getting them out to refresh on these dates, etc makes you realise that freedom sometimes comes at a price.

On board we had to be very inventive at times as there was a shortage of equipment. We used squash bottles filled with water to the

QARNNS HNN Maggie Freer (Sea View Ward) hugs husband CPO David Freer RN (HMS Intrepid*) May 18th 1982. This was the date the vital de-salination plants were flown over from HMS* Intrepid*. HMS* Intrepid *in background.*
Photograph: Maggie Freer

correct weight for patients who needed orthopaedic traction. We allocated syringes for intramuscular or intravenous injections of antibiotics to individual patients. Drawing up the injections could take two staff up to an hour to prepare, which gives an idea how many disposable syringes we saved that we would otherwise have ditched; certainly several hundred a day just from our high dependency ward.

(Author's note: At our busiest times I would assess that more than a thousand disposable syringes were saved daily throughout the hospital in this way.)

A P&O Purser, Zak Coombs, used to come to the ward most mornings to help wash the patients and get them ready for the day; he was an invaluable help. The two P&O civilian nursing sisters helped on the ICU when their own shifts permitted.

The "watch bill", or rota/shift system was quite intricate. I worked on Sea View Ward with a capacity for 44 high-dependency beds, and a team of 15 QARNNS Naval Nurses and RN paramedics split into three watches. The watch bill was described as "naval watches with split dogs" and it took some time to get used to working 4-hour shifts with a maximum of six hours off at a time. It was especially difficult to sleep at times with the tannoy and bells going for "hands to flying stations" but eventually we got used to the routine.

By May 20th we had 31 casualties on board, some of them Argentinian personnel from the fishing/intelligence vessel *Narwhal* which had been bombed and captured by the British on May 9th.

One of the survivors from HMS *Sheffield*, POWEM (R) (Petty Officer Weapons and Radio Electrician RN) Richard Wood had now made sufficient recovery to make a much longed-for telephone call home via our satellite (Satcom) telephone system.

Richard Wood wrote of this uplifting experience:

> As Chief Petty Officer John Strange has mentioned, HMS *Sheffield* had already been deployed in The Gulf from November 1981, and many of us had been serving on board together for over a year, which makes for closely knit camaraderie at all levels. Although we were all immensely thankful to have survived, we felt a great underlying sadness for our lost colleagues and our ship, one of the first Royal Navy ships to be sunk in action since the end of the Second World War. The news that I could telephone home (by satellite phone) and speak with my wife was a huge boost to morale. We had all been through so much having lost many of our friends and shipmates in the attack, and dealt with our severely burnt colleagues in the aftermath. And of course we had lost most of our possessions and clothes. Speaking with my wife was the best tonic of all. As it happened John Strange's wife Hannah was with my wife when the call came through, so I spoke with her as well. I was the first person to tell her John had survived, so although it was all very emotional, I was able to leave them both in a much happier frame of mind.

Richard had been temporarily blinded in the *Sheffield* attack, and had severe head and eye injuries. Here, he continues to tell us more about his time on board The Hospital Ship, and the various people on board who helped him in practical ways:

> The reception on board The Hospital Ship was phenomenal. We were greeted by the warm and cheery smile of Commander Gough (The RN Commander of Naval Party 1830), Superintending Nursing Officers Miss Massey and Miss Poole, together with Naval Staff Nurse Maggie Freer, Senior Naval Nurse Marion Stock and a small group of other QARNNS junior nurses, one of whom I remember as Naval Nurse Gay, a delightful ebony skinned girl who was always smiling. We were escorted to our new home, Sea View Ward, a huge area filled with traditional hospital beds at the stern of the ship.

The ward was light and airy, and although we were still in the war zone, the clean atmosphere on board was comforting. I suppose we were something of a novelty for the first day or so, as we were visited by countless medics and nurses from all over the ship. Although I find it hard to recall all their names, I can honestly say that they were all brilliant, and I thank them for their kindness, care and understanding. None of us were to know at that time how soon they would be fully tested as the battles unfolded and more and more casualties started arriving.

We were given pyjamas to wear, and washing materials to tide us over until we were able to purchase some of our own. I wondered where John Strange and David Harrington were, and was told by HNN Maggie Freer they were both safe on board, but both needing more treatment. I should be able to visit John when he's stronger, came the advice. I looked forward to that, as I wanted to reassure him that his friends were there for him. I don't know why or where it comes from, but there is a certain bond that unites service people when they are in need of help and reassurance.

Over the following twenty days, I received treatment for my eyes from Surgeon Captain Rintoul RN, who examined them with a multitude of instruments. I had my eyes dyed bright orange on several occasions, until one day when he drew a picture of my eyes in front of me and then rained down on this drawing with the pencil with lots of dots – hundreds of them – to represent the shards of shrapnel that had become embedded in my eyes, some quite large whilst others were miniscule. The larger of these fragments were pressing on the optic nerves which had caused me to lose my sight, and although they would attempt to flush out my eyes, it was likely that they would have to take nature's course. Occasionally I would feel grittiness in my eyes as a fragment worked its way to the surface, and then it could easily be removed, on other occasions my eyes would become bloodshot as a tiny artery was severed by the movement of one of these particles. Over the days and weeks, with care, my eyesight began to improve and I began to see more and more colours instead of varying shades of grey. I would require regular eye tests and eye drops for the rest of my life to lubricate my eyes as the tear ducts had been damaged by the flash.

I also required treatment for the stress and trauma of the attack on my ship and the loss of close friends and colleagues. The worrying and unanswerable question of "Why did I survive?" became a constant topic of discussion with Naval Psychiatrist Surgeon Commander Scott-Brown RN as he tried to reassure me that it must have been God's Will, and that I should not persecute myself because my friends had perished. The shock of what had happened would not affect me deeply until I arrived back in

UK much later on. It was good to be able to talk openly about my feelings and experience, and to receive encouragement, although it was extremely difficult to relax and I don't remember smiling much if at all. I really felt sad, lonely and almost helpless.

There were other people too who played their part in helping me to recover from the ordeal that my colleagues and I had endured. The RN Padre, Rev David Barlow, would come and visit us in the ward each day, and say prayers for our recovery and for our families back home.

The Supply Officer Lt. Commander Porteous RN also visited and gave us the news that, as we had all lost our Naval Uniforms, they would be replaced with a Survivor's Kit to tide us through until we were repatriated. Of course the big headache was that, because all of our records had been lost, there was no way of knowing how much money we should receive; we had all lost that too. The decision was made to pay us a subsidy from *Uganda's* pay account and that it would be recovered upon our return to UK in due course. We were also given temporary Identity Cards to replace those lost with the ship, as we had had to hand them in for security on board HMS *Sheffield*, just in case of our capture. These had been replaced by Geneva Convention Identity Cards which were coloured buff, and dog tags which we had to wear around our necks.

The Naval Dental Surgeon Commander Keeble also played his part in examining our teeth. I was pleased to have my denture replaced, which had jettisoned from my mouth when we were hit, and fractures to some of my lower teeth attended to.

The Ship's Welfare Staff also helped enormously in providing entertainment for the crew and patients. We had almost constant BBC World Service coverage provided in the wards to keep us abreast of the events unfolding in the war. For those who were able to attend, there were recreational films shown daily in the ship's cinema, although with my vision and head problems I couldn't stay there for long.

One bonus I will never forget was the wonderful opportunity we had to speak to our loved ones back home via the Ship's Radio Telephone. I was quite emotional as I spoke firstly to my wife Elaine to reassure her that I was on the mend, albeit slowly, and then to Hannah Strange, who happened to be visiting my wife. Up to this time she was not aware of John's situation or whereabouts. 'Is he still alive?' I remember her asking me, followed by many questions about his health and nursing care. I had not realised that she had not been informed that John had been so badly burned in the missile attack on HMS *Sheffield*. Of course there were no mobile telephones, emails, or, normally, phone communications from RN ships to families ashore in those days. But I was pleased that I had been able to lift her spirits enough for her to know that he was safe and receiving the best possible treatment and to look forward to his homecoming.

I went to see John immediately afterwards in The Special Care Burns Unit and, having dressed in a protective gown and face mask to prevent infection, I was able to tell him that Hannah loved him so very much, and that she would be strong for him. I am certain that there were tears beneath the bandages, as I passed on Hannah's best wishes to him.

By this time, of course, we were not the only patients aboard the *Uganda* being so lovingly cared for by the fantastic QARNNS nurses and the RN medical teams. Soon afterwards, the beds began to fill as casualties from HMS *Coventry*, *Atlantic Conveyor* and the other ships and aircraft that were being attacked, and then the injured from the Army and Royal Marine units ashore started to arrive on board.

All the casualties' injuries seemed very varied, some so severe it was hard to imagine how they would pull through, but with the camaraderie which spread through the ship, new friends were made, each affording strength and encouragement to one another in the greatest tradition of our British Services. This spirit of everyone trying to help each other, coupled with the tremendous, and possibly never to be repeated efforts of the nursing staff in what seemed an impossible situation, seemed to ensure the mountainous task was conquered.

As the days passed I, along with several other patients, were deemed well enough to leave Sea View Ward, and I was transferred to the dormitories, which were laid out like typical mess-decks with two tier bunk beds. We didn't really need lockers, as we had nothing much to place in them. We were allowed a little more freedom to visit the ship's amenities, which in my case included being invited into the Senior Rates Mess where, I am afraid to admit, I outstayed my welcome on one occasion!

(Richard's tale continues in Chapter Five.)

* * *

The main British troop landings ashore at San Carlos Water on May 21st were swiftly followed by the bridgehead being established. Fierce air attacks were to follow. *Canberra* was ordered to leave San Carlos Water out of the immediate danger. A medical team from *Canberra* led by Surgeon Commander Rick Jolly RN then set up The Main Dressing Station (MDS) ashore at the deserted refrigeration plant at Ajax Bay, a desolate spot on the western side of San Carlos Water. The exemplary record of the teams, who treated over 650 casualties, carried out 210 operations and survived direct bombing by enemy aircraft, is well documented in Surgeon Commander Rick Jolly's "The Red and Green Life Machine", reprinted in 2007.

Thereafter, The Hospital Ship started taking casualties at high levels, usually at least a dozen a day, so I had no time to write my diary until June 1st. As our communications were restricted, we could not be told in advance of the numbers arriving, or the severity of injuries; some days 30 or 40 casualties were admitted in one day, occasionally less than ten or so. The majority were critically or very severely wounded and many were treated in our operating theatres as soon as, or within hours of, arriving on board.

One of these was Chief Petty Officer Terry Bullingham, Royal Navy, who was severely injured and blinded working on the Flight Deck of HMS *Antrim* on May 21st.

This is Terry Bullingham's story up to when he reached The Hospital Ship *Uganda*:

CPO Terry Bullingham RN at RNAS Yeovilton, August 1983.
Photograph: St. Dunstan's

Spring 1982 saw me in my second year as part of the Fleet Air Arm helicopter-maintenance team of the RN County class destroyer, HMS *Antrim*. Our "raison d'etre" was to keep "Humphrey", the Ship's venerable Wessex HAS-3 helicopter, serviceable. After playing a significant role in Operation "Paraquat" off South Georgia in April, *Antrim* was one of six warships protecting the *Canberra* as she started to disembark the troops in San Carlos Water on 21st May ("Bomb Alley Day"). A flight of four Argentine Skyhawk fighter-bombers passed over the ship dropping a pattern of eight 1,000 lb bombs. One of the bombs came inboard through the Sea-Slug missile launcher and came to rest unexploded in the after heads. Immediately above on the flight deck we were preoccupied deploying the fire hoses and failed to notice the follow-up attack by a pair of "Dagger" (Argentine Mirage-3s) who strafed the upper deck with their 30mm cannon. I saw the splashes in the water coming towards me followed by a sickening impact and I found myself on the deck, conscious but unable to see anything! The Ship's Doctor (Surgeon-Lieutenant Alisdair Maclean) reached me fairly quickly and after a spell lying on the Wardroom floor with other casualties, we were transferred to the *Canberra*, courtesy of a Sea King aircraft. This was a bit hairy as the aircraft only had room to put one wheel on our somewhat restricted flight deck.

I passed a delightful spell in a stretcher on *Canberra* listening to the massed small-arms fire of the 1,000 or so soldiers still on board, as they repelled the air attacks. Apparently, I was the first casualty the medical team operated on and I recall Surgeon-Commander Omrish Chakraverty talking over me to colleagues about "patella tap" *(a diagnostic medical test being discussed as Terry's right knee had also been injured)*, and Surgeon-Captain Roger Wilkes informing me that I was to be transferred to *Uganda* when circumstances permitted.

I was transferred, after a night on HMS *Hydra*, by the Ship's Wasp Helicopter to The Hospital Ship *Uganda* and was welcomed on board by Royal Naval Chaplain Chris Bester. I joined other patients in "Sea View" ward – slightly ironic considering both my eyes were bandaged! I was situated next to Colour-Sergeant Barry Howell (ex-RFA *Sir Lancelot*). Barry, together with First Officer Paul Dilks, looked after my non-medical needs, Barry lighting my cigarettes and Paul feeding me and bringing me up to date with the latest "buzzes". I recall two trips to the operating theatre; for the enucleation of my left eye (Surgeon-Captain Andrew Rintoul) and for skin grafts (Surgeon-Commander Charles Chapman).

* HMS *Antrim*'s Wessex helicopter was affectionately known as "Humphrey" throughout the Royal Navy, and particularly the Fleet Air Arm world. Humphrey had been instrumental in the recapture of South Georgia (referred to by Terry as Operation Paraquat) from the Argentinians and successfully put their submarine the *Santa Fe* out of action much earlier in the Conflict (April 25th).

* * *

Chapter Five will cover the treatment and care given at all levels on board The Hospital Ship during hostilities in more detail. The reader would be asked to respect our medical-in-confidence guidelines. Even 26 years after The Falklands War no personal or inappropriate details will be covered in these pages, and patients will only be mentioned by name with their given consent. The vast majority of our former patients are still very much alive, doing extraordinarily well, and they and their families deserve all our continued respect for their privacy, and indeed continued good health for their future days.

All through the following chapters you will be able to read in full some of our former patients' "own stories" like John Strange's and Terry Bullingham's, which have started in this chapter. Most have written about their time in the Services before joining The South Atlantic Task Force, how and where within the Combat Zone they were injured in 1982, and how they reached The Hospital Ship following their action or trauma. All these former servicemen have volunteered to make these contributions, and all have written them themselves, many taking this opportunity to write how they felt for the first time. They are written from the heart of the British soldier, sailor and airman who has survived injury at war, casualty evacuation, much subsequent surgery and ongoing treatments. These accounts also cover their eventual recovery and rehabilitation, and resumption of totally fulfilling and successful lives.

At the end of the book I have collated the conclusions of many of our stories into one final chapter. The chapter is dedicated to those who have helped in this way, and to all the other injured servicemen from The Falklands War in 1982. The former patients have then described, many in some detail, how they adapted to their "new", and certainly altered life after their return to UK. We have much to learn from their frank and compelling tales, which is why they are included in such detail.

We all hope that by including these candid, revealing, sometimes humorous and at times emotional stories in this book, other injured servicemen returning to our shores today, and many others who have been through similar circumstances, will be encouraged by the bravery and courage of those who were injured during The Falklands War, at sea, on land and in aircraft, fighting for freedom so far from their homes.

CHAPTER FIVE

"A WHETTED KNIFE"

Casualty Treatments within the Combat Zone
May 24th – June 8th 1982

The Hospital Ship was now receiving and treating patients at high levels, and continued to do so until well after cessation of hostilities. This chapter deals with the logistics of how we all coped with events as they arose, some of the problems and shortages encountered, and how, like everyone else within The Task Force, our own adaptability and improvisation helped us in so many situations.

The main logistics problem up to May 24th was our enforced lack of access to classified signals within the Fleet. Due to Geneva Convention restrictions, we were severely limited in our communications between other ships and indeed the Field Dressing Stations ashore. Also, as treated casualties were recovering from their first lines of treatment at the Ajax Bay Main Dressing Station, they needed to be transferred to The Hospital Ship with all speed. However, this was becoming increasingly difficult as the ship was in our northerly station (Red Cross Box) some 150 nautical miles north west of Cape Dolphin, and out of range for convenient helicopter transfer.

This was, in the main, resolved from May 24th when we were ordered to leave our Northerly Red Cross Box (a sea area located within the North Westerly corner of The Total Exclusion Zone as described above, and in Chapter Four) and proceed further south to Middle Bay, just north-east of the entrance to Falkland Sound which is the channel between East and West Falkland Islands.

At 2130 we entered the bay, our first sight of land since leaving Ascension, where we surprised HMS *Coventry* who was at anchor nearby. Crew from HMS *Coventry* have since related to me how close they were to attacking us as they, of course, had no idea The Hospital Ship was within the Combat Zone, and assumed we were an Argentinian attacking vessel. Sadly, HMS *Coventry* was attacked and sunk the following day and we were subsequently embarking casualties from her in haste.

The next day, May 25th was Argentinian Independence Day. At 0924 we were buzzed by two Argentinian Skyhawks in fighting formation, but they pulled away when they saw visually we were a Hospital Ship. (Our MOIC learned much later at a de-briefing at Northwood that the Argentinian pilot had radioed his HQ at Port Stanley for permission to attack us. The request was denied.) We were unaware for some hours that the destroyer HMS *Coventry* and the Cunard container ship *Atlantic Conveyor* were attacked and sunk on that day.

Here, QARNNS Senior Nursing Officer Liz Law describes how events unfolded for her on that fateful day:

> Shortly after leaving Gibraltar I heard that Howard (my then boyfriend) had volunteered to serve on board the requisitioned MV *Atlantic Conveyor* as their Supply Officer. It was during one of our busiest times on board The Hospital Ship on 26th May that I was taken aside by the two Chaplains and told that his ship had been sunk. I feared the worst and felt distraught that I might not now have the chance to set that date for a wedding. I remain most grateful to the Senior Naval Officer Commander Andy Gough who speedily sent a signal back to the UK to clarify the situation. It took some 18 hours before the reply was received that Howard was known to be a survivor and that he would be transported back home. At the earliest opportunity when I was able to speak to him we finally set that date – 2nd October 1982.

Casualties arrived from HMS *Broadsword*, and from ashore, in the next couple of days.

On May 28th we carried out our first casualty disembarkation to HMS *Hecla*. Forty-two casualties, including the survivors from the MV *Narwhal* were transferred, and arrived in Montevideo on June 2nd. On the same day we were buzzed by five Argentinian Skyhawks; we had 112 casualties on board at the time.

On May 29th, after several days of strong south-westerly gales had abated, we were able to proceed to anchor in Grantham Sound, a sheltered bay further into Falkland Sound, just a few nautical miles south west of San Carlos Water. Our distance steamed from Ascension to Grantham Sound was 6,929 nautical miles at an average speed of just under 10 knots. Steaming time was six hundred and ninety seven and a half hours.

P&O Chief Officer Grahame Burton recalls a small but significant moment during that week:

> During the early part of the land battle, *Uganda* went into Middle Bay at the northern entrance to Falkland Sound. However, with our brightly illuminated hull and funnel and big red crosses, we were thought to provide too much of a beacon to enemy forces. Thus on 29th May we

were ordered to proceed to Grantham Sound, which was on the west coast of East Falkland just south of San Carlos Water, and close to the field hospital (Main Dressing Station) at Ajax Bay. To this day I still have a small piece of rock from the beach, brought out to the ship in one of the first boats that night, which to me symbolised the fact that re-taking The Falkland Islands was now in our sights. For the next three weeks our normal routine centred on being anchored in Grantham Sound during the day, then out to sea to a "new" "Red Cross Box" at night. (By now we had been allocated a new "Red Cross Box" in an open sea area just twelve nautical miles north of Cape Dolphin, the most northerly point of East Falkland.) We also transferred recovering patients for onward move to Montevideo aboard the three RN survey ships, *Hydra*, *Hecla* and *Herald*, and transferred patients to two of the Argentinian hospital ships, *Bahia Paraiso* and *Almirante Irizar*.

Thereafter, a pattern of receiving incoming casualties and returning those who had recovered sufficiently for the onward sea/air voyage to UK evolved. By day we would proceed into Grantham Sound, a bay just a couple of nautical miles south west of San Carlos Water, to receive casualties by helicopter onto the specially constructed helo-pad astern. At night we would steam north-eastwards out of Falkland Sound as we were required to remain fully illuminated in hours of darkness to comply with the Geneva Convention. It was imperative that we departed every evening, as any ship illuminated in this way would act as an excellent "fix" for enemy aircraft seeking targets at sea and ashore.

Although some of the communications' problems seemed to be resolved, we were now experiencing difficulties with actual patient transfers from our higher decks, to the lower decks of the ambulance ships, with the two ships plunging up and down in the heavy winds and seas. It was decided to abandon this cross-deck routine in favour of helicopter transfers in stronger winds. Fortunately, each ambulance ship now carried RN Wasp helicopters astern, so they were used for all "heavy weather" patient transfers from then on; but the Wasps could only carry one stretcher case at a time, so this made for lengthy transfers. With such severe helicopter shortages ashore since the loss of *Atlantic Conveyor* on May 25th, we tried to cope as independently as we could, and in fairer weather, patients continued to be "stretchered" across to the ambulance ships which would position alongside *Uganda* when weather permitted. This enabled a brief medical handover to take place as the patients were settled into their new quarters for the ongoing sea voyage to Uruguay.

Petty Officer Richard Wood, injured on HMS *Sheffield*, was one of those who set off on the long voyage back to UK during this time. Here, he recalls his transfer to HMS *Hecla* for the sea voyage north to Montevideo, and thence on to UK by RAF VC10 Casevac flight:

As the end of May approached I learned that, with some other patients who were allocated to the dormitories, we were to be transferred to one of the "Ambulance" Ships for the start of the 8,000 mile journey home. Having visited all the friends I had made on board, including John Strange in the specialised Burns Unit, Captain Clark invited me to visit him on the bridge for a speedy look around before saying his farewell. I suppose as I had been one of the first patients to arrive on board The Hospital Ship he just wanted to wish me well and ask how I had been looked after. He gave me a photograph as a memento, shook my hands, and wished me good luck for my journey homeward.

I collected my possessions, once again in a black plastic bin liner, and soon found myself aboard HMS *Hecla*, one of the Royal Navy Hydrographic Ships which had been converted to Ambulance ships for the duration of the Falklands Campaign. *Hecla*, under the command of Captain Hope RN was to take us to Montevideo in Uruguay, where we would board an RAF VC10 CASEVAC flight for our repatriation to the UK. I was allocated a bunk in the Senior Rates Mess, and found the hospitality most enjoyable for the duration of the journey. I had the pleasure of meeting the Captain during my stay aboard and had a tour of the bridge, during which time Captain Hope signed a copy of a photograph of the ship which I still have to the present day.

There was much concern about our security and safety upon HMS *Hecla's* arrival at Montevideo, as she would also repatriate several Argentine prisoners, who had also received treatment for their injuries in the conflict. Upon arrival we were quickly transferred to a waiting coach and, under armed motorcycle and police escort, taken to Montevideo airport, where an already revved up VC10 was waiting on the tarmac. We were amazed to be advised of the armed guards posted on the top of every high-rise building en route to the airport. The worry of ambush from Argentine sympathisers was so great that every precaution had to be taken to ensure our safety. When the last patient was on board the aircraft it took off and soared quickly to the relief of all concerned. My survival from HMS *Sheffield* must have caused some discussion amongst the aircrew, as The Loadmaster Sergeant came to me shortly after take-off and indicated that the Captain would like me to visit the Flight Deck, where I was invited to sit in the co-pilot's seat for our landing and take-off at Wideawake Airfield, Ascension, for refuelling. The adrenalin rush during those events was amazing; I was absolutely fascinated at how much the pilot had to do. It was a never to be forgotten experience.

* * *

In our operating theatres on board The Hospital Ship we were now usually operating all day and well into the night. Our three teams had united well, and we were all working closely and harmoniously together. This is a very important aspect of Operating Theatre work, whether the Theatres are based on land or at sea. Our work on board The Hospital Ship was extremely arduous, exacting and stressful as will be revealed later in this chapter (see "Working within the Operating Theatres"). The professional demands on us all were very high, and it was essential that we were all totally united as efficient teams in order to maintain our high standards of patient care and safety.

Our training of the QARNNS State Enrolled nurses on the way south had played an important part in this working routine. In normal circumstances, a one-year post-Registration/Enrolment course is undertaken, to train qualified nurses in UK for the Operating Theatre Technique qualification that Senior Nursing Officer Margaret Kerr and myself had gained within The National Health Service some years before 1982. Few of the QARNNS Naval Nurses allocated to work within the operating theatres on board The Hospital Ship had any experience of working within this specialised field, so a crash-course of three weeks as we headed south had to suffice. They all responded admirably in those testing times and we were immensely proud of their achievements.

Our Operating Theatre Team members included:
Superintending Nursing Officer Isa Gauld QARNNS
Senior Nursing Officer Margaret Kerr QARNNS
Senior Nursing Officer Nicci Pugh QARNNS

CPO MA (O) Jim Lacey RN
PO MA (O) Mick Clancy RN
PO MA (O) John Rigby RN
QARRNS Naval Nurse Jo Scade
QARNNS Naval Nurse Denise (Fred) Bassett
QARNNS Naval Nurse June Hendy
QARNNS Naval Nurse Ann Blocke

Jim Lacey, Mick Clancy and John Rigby were Royal Navy Medical Assistants who had an extra qualification in Operating Theatre Technique, denoted by the (O) after their MA rank. The civilian equivalent at that time was an Operating Department Assistant (ODA).

CPO Jim Lacey was another tower of strength for us all in our operating theatres. Jim was an experienced Operating Theatre Manager from The Royal Naval Hospital in Plymouth. The adjacent inset is a brief outline of his background:

In 1982: Chief Petty Officer Jim Lacey RN Operating Theatre "Floor" Supervisor

Photograph: Jim Lacey

I joined the Royal Navy straight from school aged 16. On completion of Medical training I went to The Royal Marines Commando Training Centre (RMCTC at Lympstone in Devon), completed the course and earned my Green Beret. Working in Commando Units took me on extensive travels and I managed to be in at the end when British forces finally pulled out from the Far East. My career took a change of path when I went over to Operating Theatre work. This filled my service time when not serving in Commando Forces.

Prior to joining NP 1830 I was the CPOMA(O) Theatre Manager in RNH Stonehouse, Plymouth having returned to Theatre work the previous year.

Here Jim describes his Operating Theatre role and the implementing of our steam autoclave within the Operating Theatre structure:

My role in the Operating Theatre (OT) on board The Hospital Ship in 1982 was running "the floor" and equipment, and supervising and co-ordinating the Naval Nurses who worked in the OT. Some of these had virtually no previous OT experience prior to embarking. My other task evolved into becoming virtually the sole Operator of our autoclave steriliser, Vesuvius. I never went near the Gasses (Anaesthetic support teams) side, as Mick (Clancy) and John (Rigby) had that covered.

Mick and John could alternate watches if required but I think it was rare. Mostly they would work as long as required, as did most OT staff. I had no one to alternate with. I told Isa (Gauld, the Operating Theatre Superintendent) early on 'if the Theatre is working then so am I'. That's what I said and that's what I did.

Our one and only steam steriliser was an interesting beast. It was an American Armed Forces piece of equipment, measuring approximately five foot high and three foot square. Designed to be robust and portable, it could be used in field conditions (ashore) or at sea as in our case. Ingeniously, it could be operated using either inflammable liquid such as kerosene, or electricity, to heat the water to raise the necessary high pressure steam. A picture is ingrained in my memory of a day early on on the trip south... All the Theatre staff were scurrying around trying to get all the equipment out of the packing cases and see what it was before setting it up. I was sitting in a chair next to a large oblong box-like object with carrying handles on the sides reading the instruction book for a long time. The rest of the staff must have wondered why I was sitting reading while they were beavering away. Finally I had some idea what to do, and had some brawny assistance to lift the thing onto its fold down legs before proceeding further. This wonderful bit of kit could be run on all sorts of different electrical currents. It was far too technical for me, not knowing a single phase current from a 2 phase from a 3 phase. Fortunately for me CPO Norman Carr (Medical and Dental Servicing Section) was there to guide and advise me on what would be best and we settled on using the 3 phase option as being the quickest way to get the Autoclave through its cycle.

When all was connected up the equipment was highly efficient and worked very well. Its only dark side was an occasional tendency to go "over pressure" resulting in an emergency valve literally letting off steam. This was a very noisy and spectacular eruption that frightened the life out of anyone who had not heard or witnessed the event previously. After the first eruption the Steriliser was quickly christened "Vesuvius".

We were fortunate to have Norman Carr with us. The MDSS (Medical and Dental Servicing Section) of the Navy was a specialised branch of Naval CPO Artificers (or electricians), who helped service and maintain specialised hospital, surgical and dental equipment; "Medical Equipment Maintenance Department" would be a more appropriate name. Servicing X-Ray machines, scanners, steam autoclaves and dental drills, etc would be their speciality.

My diary for June 1st reads:

> We have now admitted over 200 patients and are
> pretty busy, so my diary entries are becoming more and
> more disjointed. The 2nd batch of discharges go today to
> Montevideo in HMS Hydra. They are bringing back more
> QARNNS and RN nurses, some much-needed medical
> stores and... we hope... our mail. The staff situation will be
> greatly eased with reinforcements, especially required in the
> specialist Burns Unit where my close friend Chris Asendorf

works, as the ambient temperature and humidity has to be kept so high at 85 degrees F.

We are working watches of four hours on and four hours off, sometimes eight off, but it is pretty wearing for us all, particularly as there are constant pipes and emergency call-outs all day, so it's difficult to sleep. Theatre is going all day and most of the night.

One of our main problems is the making and sterilising of all the dressings for the wards and Burns Unit, as it is very time-consuming on top of our OT commitment. But we are coping well, and have a willing and enthusiastic team. Our Naval Nurses within the OTs are mostly female QARNNS State Enrolled Nurses (SENs) with little or no OT experience, whom we have trained ourselves on the way down.

Our patients now are all types of service personnel, Paras, Gurkhas, Royal Marines, RFA personnel and of course our own first rate RN men. They are all truly wonderful to nurse, whatever field one is working in… always very grateful for everything we do and amazingly resilient to their battle injuries and loss of limbs.

LIMB AMPUTATIONS:

Our Operating Teams worked very hard to save injured limbs where at all possible, often carrying out highly complex and intricate restorative surgical procedures to preserve a damaged limb where viability was considered realistic. Many casualties had both legs or more than one limb compromised, so every effort was made to preserve the second limb in those circumstances. We were all only too aware of the long-term mobility difficulties ahead for single limb amputees, let alone those who had lost more than one limb. In medicine, especially in military surgery, our personnel have to learn to cope with amputation of limbs as routine. Once a limb has been compromised by lack of blood supply, severe bone impact or other complex circumstances, we have to accept that, to save life, we have to learn to face up to limb amputation as a frequent occurrence in a war situation. The Falklands War proved no exception. It doesn't get easier though, as in medicine we always try so hard to save life, sight and limb in that order as a matter of course. We all learnt a great deal about our patients, our colleagues and ourselves during this demanding period, and staff on the wards who were treating and caring for the recovering servicemen faced many a challenge, encouraging and supporting the many amputees through some dark and difficult days.

"HEAL NAVY" became our watchword and motto very early on!

In our working areas two of the main problems that we had to surmount were dealing with clinical requirements within the ship's movement, and maintaining stowage and secure storage of equipment.

The Ship's Movement in The South Atlantic:

Unlike hospitals on land, floating hospital ships move about. In the South Atlantic, the most inhospitable and notoriously windswept ocean on earth, this soon became a very real factor for all on board; patients, nurses, doctors and stretcher bearers in particular. In land-based hospitals, the patients and all mobile equipment are moved around the hospital areas on trolleys with wheels. This concept is unworkable on board a floating hospital operating in extremely rough seas, as the trolleys (none of which were "braked") would obviously career about unrestricted as the ship pitched and rolled. All our equipment, most of which had been supplied for a working Field Hospital ashore, had to be well secured all the time. This was particularly important in our operating theatres where, of necessity, clinical equipment and sterile surgical instruments need to be readily available all the time. We quickly had to re-think this normally "trolley-based" system and adapt as best we could.

Operating Tables:

In all the field units there was an army-pattern stretcher which slotted into a McVicar frame, incorporating an essential tipping device. In our operating theatres the three stretcher bases, which were at a suitable height for anaesthetising and operating, were fixed firmly to the wooden sole (nautical term for floor or inside decking of a ship) of the Operating Theatre. The patient's own stretcher would act as the operating table, and patients were anaesthetised and operated on lying on this stretcher. Sister Margaret Kerr, myself, or one of the OT nurses, would try to remain with our patients as they were carried into this somewhat alarming space until they were anaesthetised.

Our own instrument trolleys were also attached firmly with simple naval lashings to any convenient pillar or bulkhead that was available; fortunately there were three of these in this "veranda" area to which we could lash our trolley bases and storage boxes.

Instead of wheeling the trolleys of sterilised instruments to the operating tables we would carry the trays of instruments to the trolley bases already lashed in place. It worked!

Working within Operating Theatres:

In operating theatres generally the OT Nurses and OT Technicians work in teams of three per patient. In principle, one nurse or technician would "scrub up" (as we call it) and, as the "sterile" person, then handle all the surgical instrumentation and swab usage during that patient's surgery, as well as assisting the surgeon where necessary. Another person acts as "runner", supplying more equipment into the "sterile field" as required. Both those people, the "scrub nurse" and "the runner", maintain a continuous process of checking and counting all the instruments and equipment in use throughout that patient's operation. I will spare the reader too much detail, but surgery, especially trauma surgery, is an extremely messy and hazardous business. The patient's body cavities can be extensive, and this meticulous checking of instruments and equipment as they are used is an essential part of the surgical process, in order to ensure every item that has been used is safely accounted for by completion of surgery and closure of the wound. None of us at the time, of course, had heard the B.B.C. correspondent Brian Hanrahan's iconic expression about the Harrier aircraft – "counting them all out and counting them all in" – but for our Operating Theatre teams on board The Hospital Ship *Uganda*, in the midst of continual life-saving surgery, it was more a case of "counting all our swabs and surgical instruments IN, and then counting them all OUT!"

The third person within this team assists the anaesthetist with the ongoing monitoring, respiratory and other requirements during surgery. As with all closely linked professional teams, all team members rely heavily on each other's skill, efficiency and reliability. In many OT Teams this intricate process can be carried out with hardly a word spoken, as all team members are so well attuned to anticipating other people's needs and requirements; the needs of the patients being always paramount.

Initially Sister Kerr, myself, or our Superintending Nursing Officer Isa Gauld would "scrub up" for operations, but as patient numbers increased we were all soon interchanging roles, with the Nursing Officers working as "runners" and the QARNNS Naval Nurses "scrubbing up" and handling the surgical instruments and essential swab counts that still had to continue vigilantly.

I'm afraid our three-tabled operating theatres on board The Hospital Ship were a far cry from the tranquil havens of peace-time surgery we had left behind. All around us, during surgery, patients were being carried to and from their wards and beds, our steam autoclave "Vesuvius" would be churning through its sterilising process, and other hospital activities continuing apace just yards from where we were working. There were normally two "tables" running at the same time, but from time to time we had to run all three "tables" simultaneously, which was... well... interesting, to say the least!

All the surgical specialties used the operating theatres, so we might well be fixing a broken limb on one table, dealing with skin grafts on another and suturing a patient's wound on "table three". We had to work very fast, and yet efficiently, to maintain patient flow, so that every patient received the necessary surgery as required; it was quite a juggling act to interweave the more severe and urgent cases in with those requiring the routine Delayed Primary Suture (DPS) that is explained in more detail later in this chapter.

In spite of all this frenetic activity continuing around us, our care and safety for all patients remained at the highest professional levels. Our infection rates remained noticeably minimal and, as throughout the rest of the hospital, patient care at all times was of the highest standard.

Surgeon Commander Peter Bull, The Consultant Anaesthetist for The Task Force, enlarges here on some of the technical and practical problems that were now arising from the anaesthetic point of view:

> British Oxygen responded to some of our ventilation dilemma by sending us two Boyle's anaesthetic machines which came in flat packs and required assembling on board – we learned quickly – and also learned how to make do with other less than ideal equipment. We had, for instance, to make plans to recycle some of our disposable equipment such as syringes and, catheters etc., lest we run out and could not be re-supplied. We were, after all, working 8,000 miles from UK, and in somewhat isolated conditions arising from the Geneva Convention restrictions.
>
> Two of our more overwhelming problems however were:
>
> 1. The lack of fresh water. This was solved later by reverse osmosis de-salination plants being transported to us from UK via Ascension Island. These two large machines were assembled on the open deck by the P&O and RN Engineers after they had been transferred by helicopter from HMS *Intrepid*. They were able to draw in seawater and extract the salt, thus producing enough fresh water for drinking, washing etc. – for a modern hospital with easily up to 1,000 persons on board a day. However, the de-salination plants would not work in rough weather, and couldn't be used under three nautical miles from land – so some careful juggling was required as to timing their operation in the mainly wild and windy South Atlantic!
>
> 2. Having to rely on cylinders for our supply of oxygen. We had relatively few cylinders, and needed this valuable gas for other purposes. Oxygen concentrators would have been an enormous help. Oxygen concentrators take in atmospheric air and extract the nitrogen to produce a reduced volume of gas but containing a much higher percentage of oxygen (approx 60-70%) than air (only 21%). The situation was made worse by the "Oxford" mechanical ventilators that we had been sent. They relied on gas pressure unlike the more suitable military–type machine, the East-Radcliffe, which would entrain atmospheric air to function. Two air compressors were provided to drive our Oxford ventilators but only one worked! – so forcing us to use valuable oxygen as the driving gas and/or using hand ventilation via self-inflating bags. *(The technique mentioned in Chapter Seven by Naval Nurse Karen Dawson working on the Intensive Care Unit.)* This vital but laborious task therefore had to be delegated to non-medical personnel in times of extreme need, especially on the

Intensive Care Ward. The Royal Marine bandsmen helped here in rotation and performed admirably – under medical and nursing supervision.

One of our more severely injured patients who arrived on board The Hospital Ship at this time was Sergeant Bill Belcher. Bill was an Air Gunner in three Commando Brigade (3 Cdo Bde Air Sqdn, or BAS) and was injured in action in a Scout helicopter on May 28th.

This is how Bill writes of his war up to that time:

In 1982: Air Gunner Sergeant Bill Belcher RM 3 Commando Brigade Air Squadron (3 Cdo Bde Air Sqn RM)

Photograph: Bill Belcher

In early April 1982, most of 3 Commando Brigade RM (3 Cdo Bde) had just returned from their annual three month deployment to the frozen Northern flank of NATO, Norway, when Argentine marines first settled on South Georgia, swiftly followed by the main amphibious invasion, and occupation, of the Falkland Islands. We hadn't yet unpacked from Norway and the Brigade was put on 72 hours' notice to move to the South Atlantic. I was serving in the Anti-Tank Flight of 3 Cdo Bde Air Sqn, based in Plymouth, as an Air Gunner on Scout helicopters. I was familiar with the structure of Naval Party 8901 in Stanley, as previous service on Landing Craft had brought me into contact with plenty of lads who had served down there. I had already heard of the wild and exposed nature of the Islands.

Within days, the Task Force had embarked, our Squadron had dispersed 15 aircraft across several ships, and on 6th April we were on our way south with the amphibious task force. My half of B Flight (B Flt), were on the LSL *Sir Lancelot* where we stayed for the six week journey south. We trained in all aspects of aviation that were possible; personal fitness, live weapon and missile firings, Argentine force recognition, and general preparation for whatever plans the Brigade staff had in mind for us when we reached the "off". A 6-day stopover at Ascension gave more opportunity for live firing and a chance to modify our aircraft and swap stores around the fleet. We also had contact with other landing elements and a lively banter grew between the various Battalions and Commando Groups who were vying for resources ashore. B Flight were one of the first to commandeer the ex-pats' club in Georgetown – much to the resentment of those still bobbing about at anchor. Someone had to do it.

We left Ascension on the 29th April and, as the journey south developed, we met more and more shipping that was joining the fleet – including amphibious, merchantmen and raw Naval power.

We got our orders for the landing on the 21st May and took an active part in the entry to San Carlos, securing beaches and establishing a hold on the beachhead. The next week was spent supporting the landed elements, moving stores, water and rations up to the hills, reacting to recce and liaison requests from Brigade and dodging enemy air assaults. From leaving UK we always flew as the same crew with myself on the guns / missiles and Lt. Richard Nunn RM as pilot. To the surprise of those elements who were seconded to the Brigade, Royal Marines were trained and skilled in many disciplines: from manning their own light aircraft to driving landing craft, vehicles, forming part of fighting ships' crews and operating complex weapon systems. In our eyes this land campaign was a "Bootie" (bootneck, or Royal Marine) affair and the rest were making up the numbers. Even the 2 star General was a "Royal" (Royal Marine) and my old CO in 42 Cdo.

On the 26th/27th May, 2 Para pushed out of the beachhead and advanced overland on Darwin and Goose Green, with the mission to conduct a "raid" on the enemy garrison at Goose Green. Two Anti-Tank Scouts and 2 Gazelles (Royal Marine Brigade Air Squadron helicopters) were tasked in Direct Support (under 2 Para's control) for the duration of the raid. Lt. Richard Nunn and I crewed one Scout helicopter and Captain Jeff Niblett and Sergeant John Glaze the other. Initially we prepared for an armed sortie, with SS11 missiles, intended for the rumoured HQ Building in Goose Green, but that was cancelled and we spent much of our time lifting ammunition forward and casualties back.

On the 28th May we had been doing much the same from first light when, at approximately 1550 GMT, the call went out that the CO of 2 Para had been wounded. The Battalion HQ called for our assistance to evacuate casualties on stretchers. Shortly after taking off, our pair of aircraft was attacked by two Argentine Pucara aircraft. I was struck in the right leg by cannon fire and the aircraft was damaged and on fire, but Richard Nunn managed to keep it airborne. However, a second Argentine attack killed Richard Nunn, wounded me again in the left leg and caused the Scout to crash. I was evacuated by the other Scout from B Flight to the field hospital at Ajax Bay. Richard Nunn was later buried along with other British fatalities from Goose Green. He was awarded a posthumous Distinguished Flying Cross for his actions that day.

That afternoon, I joined the other casualties from the Raid and underwent life-saving surgery in the hands of the Field Medical Teams, operating under 60 watt light bulbs in the old processing plant at Ajax Bay; not 50 yards from where my Bivvi site had been for the previous week, and with a 500lb Argentine UXB (unexploded bomb) lodged in the roof. After restoring a pulse, blood pressure and vital fluids, my left leg was patched up and stabilised with vein grafts and splints. My right leg was amputated above the ankle and this was pretty much a clean up of what was initially started by a 20mm cannon shell from the Pucara. Lots of morphine, cold legs, hazy memories and a visit from the lads in B Flight whose HLS (helicopter landing site) was next door.

The next day, along with half a dozen others, I was stretchered to a Sea King helicopter and flown out to The Hospital Ship *Uganda* which was now on station in Grantham Sound. I was naked under a pusser's blanket but clutching my trusty pipe that had been rescued from my flying suit the previous night. The deck landing was the most painful I had ever experienced and the WAFU "(Fleet Air Arm speke)" pilot bore the brunt of my anger for slamming it down on deck. So began my three weeks on Sea View Ward. The reception on the ward was both calming and reassuring. Clearly we had entered a clean, bright, organised and well-staffed hospital environment. In contrast to Ajax Bay, we were also out of the combat area and, despite some doubts, under the safety of "Red Cross" Geneva Convention Rules. Not that I was concerned; the agony in both my legs overrode most feelings. The first priority, I guess, was to stabilise my overall condition and then continue efforts to save my left leg. On day four, however, after a change of dressing on my right leg, the medical staff discovered dead and wasted flesh that threatened gangrene. So the decision was taken to amputate above the knee and I was presented with the consent form. The surgeon explained the danger of gangrene and I signed away my right knee and off it came. Another few days of intense pain and then more work on my left leg. I received the mandatory skin graft over the exit wound on the left side of my left leg and the tibia and fibula were roughly aligned and then secured in an open cast so that dressings could be changed. I lost count of the number of times I went into theatre but fortunately I only needed one night in Intensive Care.

Another patient who we all remember very well was Sergeant Major John Phillips. As a Royal Engineers Bomb Disposal Officer who had lost his left arm de-fusing an unexploded bomb on board HMS *Antelope*, John had to make several return trips to our operating theatres as initially he had been severely wounded. He was invariably stoic as he waited in the full glare of a working operating theatre to be anaesthetised. We all admired him very much. 24 years later when we met through our 1982 veterans' association, The South Atlantic Medal Association (SAMA82), John surprised us all by writing a short article about remembering a certain Theatre Sister's kind blue eyes just before he was put to sleep!

This is the start of John's story from when he left UK in April 1982 to when he had made sufficient recovery to be moved from the high dependency "Sea View Ward" to the "dormitory area" on "B Deck":

In 1982: Staff Sergeant Major John Phillips Warrant Officer 2 Explosive Ordnance Disposal Squadron Royal Engineers

Photograph: John Phillips

During Easter leave 1982 I was called by Major Guy Lucas OC 49 EOD Sqn (Officer Commanding 49 Explosive Ordnance Squadron) and informed that after much "table banging" he had secured a place for two Royal Engineer Bomb Disposal Officers on the Task Force. He asked me who I thought they should be. 'Well I'm one and I leave the other nomination to you,' I responded. 'You can't go, you are the Sergeant Major.' 'Sir, I have been waiting 20 years for something like this and I do not want to miss the opportunity.' 'You had better come into the barracks and we can discuss it,' he said. Well, to cut a long story short, I got my way and after considering the experienced members of the squadron, Staff Sergeant Jim Prescott was nominated as the other member of the team.

Not knowing what unexploded ordnance we were likely to be dealing with, I was despatched to the Intelligence Cell at UK Land Forces in Wiltshire, with the brief to find out what weapons the Argentine forces had. This was a complete waste of time. They could not give me the information I needed except for a couple of copies of "Jane's Defence Weekly" which had a few articles they thought might be useful to me. Not a very good start. To add insult to injury they added that 300 body bags had been requested for the Task Force. I did not wish to know that!

Also, as part of 49 EOD preparations I attended the main briefing of participating units at the 3 Brigade Head-Quarters (3 BgdHQ) in Plymouth. It was there that I was informed that we would be sailing on the requisitioned P&O *Canberra* cruise liner from Southampton on 9th April. During my time at 3Bgd HQ I noticed many disgruntled Commanding Officers milling about trying to get their regiments involved with the Task Force. All without success!

After a few days' break, whilst our equipment was packed, Staff Sergeant Jim Prescott and I were taken to Southampton to begin the adventure. That's how we saw it, an adventure. No one actually expected that there would be hostilities. We had just over two tons of equipment. We had taken the full range of EOD equipment which we hoped would enable us to deal with any eventuality relating to unexploded ordnance. Two tons of equipment and just two men!

The time spent during the journey to Ascension Island was filled by fitness training – running around the promenade deck of *Canberra* – and trying to find our equipment which had been lost during loading. It had been loaded from the quayside with Surgeon Commander Rick Jolly's medical equipment and supplies. It took us nearly a week to trace it all. Little did I know then that I would be meeting Surgeon Commander Jolly RN again under very different circumstances. Facilities aboard were fantastic, with Jim and I sharing a twin ensuite outside cabin and eating silver service. At Ascension Island, during the re-organisation which involved a great deal of cross shipping of men and equipment, we were transferred to the LSL (Landing Ship Logistics) *Sir Lancelot* and attached to 59 Commando Squadron Royal Engineers. Back with our own kind! The second half of the trip south was not as comfortable as the first, but was more conducive to going to war.

Again, the time on board *Lancelot* was spent doing fitness training and receiving briefings. However, we always gathered around the ship's Tannoy speakers at midday to listen to the BBC World Service News with its eerie introductory music and varying strength of signal. It was by this method that we learned of the failure in negotiations, the sinking of the *Belgrano* and then the loss of HMS *Sheffield*. The atmosphere on board changed after that.

On Tuesday 18th May we were informed by the OC 59 Cdo Sqn RE that we were now officially on active service. Each man was issued with 200 rounds of ammunition and some additional cold weather equipment.

The surprising thing to me was that none of it had to be signed for. Those things didn't matter anymore. This was for real! Whilst attending a briefing of officers and warrant officers, I was informed by the briefing officer that there was no specific job for me or Jim, and that if the squadron came across any unexploded bombs they would go around them. This lack of understanding of the threat brought it home to me just what a problem Guy Lucas must have had convincing the "powers that be" to put a Royal Engineer Bomb Disposal team in The Task Force. Little did they know!

LSL *Lancelot* arrived in San Carlos on the morning of Friday 21st May with the other ships of the Task Force. As there was little for me and Jim to do I volunteered to man the radio on the bridge and help co-ordinate the offloading of stores. This was a two man job and I worked my shift with a chap named "Smiler", a 59 Cdo. Plant Staff Sergeant. During our conversations he informed me that the first job he had to do on getting ashore was to dig a mass grave at Port San Carlos using the Combat Engineer Tractor. Makes you think, that sort of information.

It was only a couple of hours before the Argentine aircraft arrived. I was on radio watch during the first air raid and saw the aircraft coming in very low. I was under the table at least three times in the first hour but then soon realised how pointless that was if the bridge took a direct hit. The sights and sounds were unreal and all those experiencing it were not yet conditioned to the situation they were in. Many were just watching mesmerised by it all. I recall one young merchant officer on the bridge became quite excited by what he was seeing. It wasn't long before Jim and I got our first task.

HMS *Argonaut* had been hit by two bombs which had failed to explode and they needed assistance. Jim and I were informed that we would be taken to *Argonaut* first thing next morning. The rest of Friday was spent ditching the individual wooden boxes that our equipment was packed in and packing our bergens (military rucksacks) with what equipment we thought we would need. Remember, we did not know what types of bombs were being used against us at that time. I spent a sleepless night going through everything in my head.

On Saturday morning we were transported across to HMS *Argonaut* which was anchored near the entrance to San Carlos Water. After the new experience of climbing a vertical rope ladder, which had been laid down the side of the ship for us, we were met by a Chief Petty Officer who reported that there were two bombs but there was access to only one at the moment. He continued that there were wires sticking out of the nose of one of the bombs and that he had put mattresses each side of it to keep it from moving. Wires, what wires? I was not aware of any bomb that had wires! We were taken to the ship's boiler room where the first bomb was. We immediately recognised it as a 1,000lb British General Purpose (GP) high explosive (HE) bomb. They do not have wires! After a close inspection and to my relief I could explain the wires. When the bomb had entered the ship it had travelled around the boiler room rubbing against the pipes which were lagged. It was the chicken wire in the lagging that was sticking out of the nose cone of the bomb. After carrying out safety procedures (getting the crew on deck and venting the ship) it was then a matter of carrying out a straightforward "render safe" procedure. We were successful. After dealing with this bomb and briefing the CPO that he could now remove the bomb from the ship, we were taken back to LSL *Lancelot*. It was only then did it dawn on us what we had just done. We had passed the "Acid Test".

Next morning (Sunday 23rd May) we were tasked to attend HMS *Antelope* which also had two unexploded bombs on board. This time we had to cadge a lift from a passing Gemini inflatable. As we approached *Antelope* we could see the hole of entry of one of the bombs and, from its diameter, took an informed guess that it would be a similar bomb to that which we had dealt with the day before. We were confident! Once aboard we were shown the location of the two bombs and identified them both as 1,000lb British made GP HE bombs. We decided to deal with the one in the ship's refrigeration unit first as this was most accessible. The crew had sensibly used wooden wedges to stop the bomb rolling around during the ship's manoeuvres.

For reasons I will not go into here, this bomb was a little more unstable than the *Argonaut* one had been. Carrying out the same procedures as the day before, we made three unsuccessful attempts to render the bomb safe.

On the 4th attempt the bomb exploded!

Amongst other things, the blast from the explosion ripped off a closed bulkhead door which hit Jim Prescott, killing him instantly, and at the same time "took" my left arm off at the shoulder. Very shortly after the explosion and still conscious, I was joined by a member of the crew who showed me the way, through the smoke, to an escape hatch. The hatch, when opened, led up to the ship's flight deck, where the majority of the ship's company had gathered. After a long unsuccessful attempt to fight the raging fire Captain Nicholas Tobin ordered the crew to abandon ship. We were all transported to Ajax Bay by the landing craft Foxtrot 4. I was immediately taken to the Field Hospital, the well-known "Red and Green Life Machine" where I again met Surgeon Commander Rick Jolly. Within an hour I was in the operating theatre where my left arm was amputated. I spent the next couple of days in and out of consciousness and remember hearing the noise of the battle of San Carlos Water. I was removed from

Ajax Bay on the morning of Tuesday 25th May and flown by Sea King Helicopter to the Hospital Ship *Uganda*.

The step I took from the stretcher into the helicopter was the one and only time I put my foot on the Falkland Islands.

My first memory after landing on *Uganda* was feeling safe. After many weeks of living in a hostile and wholly male environment it was a fantastic sensation to find ladies working away at sea in a hospital situation, and somehow made things seem OK. It was a great pleasure to smell things other than army kit, bergens and male underwear! I was taken to a ward for observation and stabilisation for some days and, after being issued with "survivors' clothing", down to the dormitories area where we were put into bunk beds. I was given a top bunk initially but negotiated a swap with the occupier of the lower bunk for practical reasons. I couldn't climb into the top bunk having only one arm! During the night the sound of crying could be heard and the occasional groan but no one spoke about the noises the next day. For most of my time on *Uganda* I took my meals in the crew's galley. It was wholesome stuff!

The routine for the duty nurse every night was to ask if everyone had had their medication and were content. On one night a Para soldier who had trench foot asked if he could have some painkillers. The nurse stated that she had already given him his prescribed dosage. He responded by saying that 'those were for my feet I have also got a headache.' The nurse smiled and said something like: 'I bet your mother was relieved when you left home.'. There were also a few minor disciplinary problems in the dormitories which as a Sergeant Major I took it upon myself to sort out.

During my 20 days aboard *Uganda* I underwent a couple of clean up operations. My memories of these are not the operations themselves but the route to the operating theatre from the dormitories. It went past the area used for holding those poor lads who had been burnt during the attacks in Fitzroy Harbour on *Sir Galahad* and *Sir Tristram*. I also recall several bedside visits and chats with a psychiatrist. There were a few times when we were both in tears.

* * *

Our operating theatre work would start each day by 0800 and continue as required, usually well into the night. On the whole, sea conditions were adequately stable to operate while we were at anchor in or around Grantham Sound. But as we headed north of Falkland Sound into the open sea for the hours of darkness we would start to roll; this was not conducive to the careful surgery that was required! The P&O Captains were soon alerted to this problem, and would liaise carefully with us in the operating theatres when they were altering course. With the ship heading into or down wind there would be minimal movement, it was the beam-on seas from port or starboard sides that caused the problems.

This is Theatre Superintendent Isa Gauld's account of her role on board The Hospital Ship:

In 1982: Superintending Nursing Officer Isa Gauld
QARNNS Operating Theatre Superintendent.

QARNNS OT Personnel: Superintending Nursing Officer Isa Gauld with NN June Hendy. April 1982

Photograph: Author's private collection

I was a Superintending Nursing Officer in QARNNS aged thirty-five in 1982, and was in charge of a surgical ward at RNH Haslar when the teams were being selected for duty on board The Hospital Ship. My brother was in the Navy, and I had joined QARNNS in 1969 as a State Registered Nurse with Midwifery as my second qualification.

I joined the Hospital Ship as The Operating Theatre Superintendent – which meant everything which happened in the theatre area was my responsibility – including building it!! I would spend long hours with the OT Teams discussing and figuring out the ways to wash, sterilise and disinfect all the surgical instruments without the usual hospital tools. I spent much time by day and especially at night in rotation with CPO Jim Lacey and the other Theatre Sisters Nicci Pugh and Margaret Kerr watching our only steam steriliser, whom we had called "Vesuvius", chuff away through its cycle to ensure we had sterilised instruments available for the following day's operating; also distributing supplies of sterilised dressings and other requirements around the hospital areas. Night times also included walking around the ship to find where our "customers" for the next day's operating were located in the ship; this was very important as traditionally The Welsh Guards, and also our

Gurkha patients, frequently had the same surname, and the journey to the Operating Theatres from some areas of the hospital had to be carefully worked out in advance.

Overall, though, all our training and hard work paid off. With very few surgical supplies and medicines, and over 500 operations performed, it was largely through good surgical and nursing care that nearly all the young men arriving on The Hospital Ship made sufficient recovery to be transported back towards UK, in the converted survey/ambulance ships HMS *Hydra*, *Hecla* and *Herald*.

* * *

STORAGE OF EQUIPMENT:

In the main we were working with disposable clinical equipment as in military and civilian hospitals ashore. Many lay people and readers will be familiar with the sight of the usual routine intravenous and blood-sampling equipment that was used throughout military and NHS hospitals in UK at that time, even if only from a visit to their GP, or the national television programmes. So it can soon be understood that these mounds of pre-wrapped and sterilised items had to be readily available and sorted efficiently, but at the same time stowed somewhere! Early in the unloading process it was decided to retain the inner cardboard packing that the items were packed in. With careful cutting and adaptation these were soon in use throughout the clinical areas as our "patent storage cupboards", for syringes, needles, etc, all carefully marked for instant use as required. It worked!

Another essential challenge was to fix the patients' intravenous fluid stands, or "drip poles" as we call them, more bits of kit on wheels that had a life of their own on a ship rolling about at sea. Any air inadvertently entering the patients' intravenous systems due to fluid levels swinging with the ship's movements could have fatal consequences. It was a question of extra vigilance, having several pairs of hands available for patient movements and transfers around the hospital areas, and often simply wedging the fluid bottle into an available cardboard storage unit... so they were now serving a dual purpose! On the wards a screw-in pattern was available that could attach to the bed head, but these also developed movement with the ship's motion, as Sister Law describes in Chapter Three.

RECYCLING/SUPPLY FROM UK:

As it became apparent that re-supply of disposable items from UK was not going to be entirely reliable, we devised clever ways of reusing otherwise disposable items in safe ways. One was to allocate a personal sterile syringe to patients who were requiring frequent top-ups and medications; this and other essential sensible usage reductions meant our disposable "stock" was always at a safe working level.

TRANSPORTING PATIENTS AROUND THE HOSPITAL AREAS:

This, again, relates back to the unsuitability of wheeled hospital trolleys on board hospital ships. Because of the shortage of helicopters ashore, many helicopter transports of casualties had to be made to us in military "choppers" not specifically dedicated for casualty transport. It was far from ideal, as our troop carrying choppers were indeed legitimate enemy targets. At one stage military aircraft were only permitted to land on board during darkness. It was another case of "adapt and proceed".

Landing on board had to be literally "touch and go". With the helicopter rotors still turning, a team of six Royal Marine stretcher-bearers would rush forward to unload the casualty from the chopper, transport him in all haste down the steep ramp to the Casualty Reception (or Triage) Area... A hand rail and non-skid tapes had been fitted as the ramp was steeply angled, and very slippery, as it was invariably wet with sea-water. The two outboard Royal Marines would gain traction from the hand rail, the inboard pair steadying the load. One middle-man would carry whatever intravenous fluids were in place, the second middle-man trying to stay in eye contact to reassure the casualty. At the base of the ramp, a chilly but sheltered area invariably soaked with salty south Atlantic sea-water, our casualty/patient labeller or "Tagman" (often our RN Anglican padre, David Barlow) checked the patient's identity (ID). The tagman would check the casualty's own dog tag/service identification disc if he was unconscious, or take verbal name and service number if the casualty was conscious. This ID label was snapped to wrist, ankle or infusion line as appropriate. Speed was of the essence here.

Within the CRA the casualty would be swiftly assessed by an RN Doctor/Consultant who would make a rapid assessment of vital signs and consciousness level. From there the waiting teams of doctors, nurses and P&O off-duty volunteers would take the necessary steps for onward move to either:

1. Operating Theatre for immediate surgery.
2. Intensive Care Unit.
3. Sea View (high dependency ward) for further clinical assessment X-ray, etc.
4. "Dormitory Area" on C Deck for less urgent treatment, or
5. High or low dependency burns units as appropriate.

The RM stretcher-bearers' vital role cannot be overemphasised in this process, which was going on all day, and also through much of the night, as patients were continually moved round the ship's internal hospital areas. They set to in their wartime role in the finest traditions of The Royal Marines. As will be dealt with in the next chapter, many of our patients had to make several return trips to our operating theatres, several from different deck levels, and the manoeuvrings around the ship's bulkheads must have frequently nearly defeated them. Most fighting soldiers would weigh in at well over 12 stone, and their webbing, bergens and kit usually accompanied them.

"Land-based" hospitals in UK, whether civilian or military, have always had the support of vast armies of ancillary staff, whose skills range from "porter-ing" (i.e. transporting patients between the hospital wards and departments), cleaning, cooking and serving meals, as well as administrators and office staff aplenty. We had none of this back-up on board The Hospital Ship, so were thrown very much onto our own resources, in fact coping extremely well in our well-organised teams. But moving the patients and their kit around the clinical areas was indeed a challenge.

Frankly, we would have struggled without the "bandies", as we called them, on board. Furthermore, they remained cheerful under intense pressure, and when it was all over, returned to their delightful musical roles without turning one of the immaculate hairs on their heads. All of us who served on board The Hospital Ship in 1982 remember their tireless work with great respect and affection, and thank them here through the pages of this book.

By early June our troops were advancing steadily towards the Falklands capital of Stanley. With their carefully co-ordinated momentum, two Advance Dressing Stations (ADS) were established ashore, one at Teal Inlet, to the North West of Stanley, and another at Fitzroy settlement, less than 20 nautical miles from Stanley Harbour entrance. We were now receiving casualties from all over the Combat Zone, some being flown directly to The Hospital Ship from battlefield injury for speed or logistical reasons.

Overall, we treated over 150 Argentinian patients. There were no curtains in the ward or high dependency areas and British servicemen often had to be nursed in adjacent beds. It was far from an ideal situation, as former patient Bill Belcher describes in his writing later in the book, but as all the patients in those areas were severely injured it didn't become an issue. Our Naval padre Father Chris Bester spoke fluent Spanish, and was a great help talking with and translating for the Argentinian patients, none of whom spoke English.

Unbelievably, as the troops advanced towards Stanley and the land battles ashore intensified, difficulties were occurring further back in our supply line to and from UK. On May 31st our Medical-Officer-in-Charge (MOIC) Surgeon Captain Andrew Rintoul received a complaint from Montevideo that we were sending too many casualties at a time for onward transfer to UK. This was causing too much administrative work at one time for The British Embassy staff in Montevideo. With our own, and all the Dressing Station levels, at stretching point there was little we could do.

Captain Geoff Hope, the RN Captain of the survey/ambulance flotilla, had also experienced problems on one of his previous trips in HMS *Hecla* in Montevideo. The Uruguayan authorities, who were giving the ambulance ships and The British Embassy every co-operation, suddenly requested an International Committee of the Red Cross (ICRC) certificate that all the 377 boxes of medical stores were indeed destined only for the Hospital Ship and ambulance ships, and not weapons or stores for other warships. In Captain Hope's words, 'The ICRC Representative was reluctant to provide the required certification and something of a deadlock had been reached'. With Uruguay's close proximity to their larger and unstable Argentinian neighbour, they did have to be very careful to preserve their neutrality and to abide strictly by the rules laid down by The Geneva Convention. Fortunately for all concerned, The British Ambassador, Miss Patricia Hutchinson CMG, was a most experienced diplomat and was very much respected by the Uruguayan Government with regard to the casualty transfers and movements. Furthermore, she had spent three years working in Geneva, so was familiar with the workings of the ICRC. She quickly took the initiative and convinced their Head of Mission in Montevideo that there was no alternative but to open and examine all the 377 boxes. Common sense, albeit a labour-intensive outcome, prevailed, and this little known tale can now be added to our "thank-you list" 26 years on. On board, beavering away at full throttle in our floating world of injuries at 52 degrees south, we were, of course, quite oblivious to all these administrative difficulties occurring in countries so far away.

As many will be aware, I have always been known to be much too forthright in expressing my views, and I have to say I learnt much from hearing this tale and realising that warm diplomatic water can also prevail in adverse conditions!

* * *

Back on board The Hospital Ship further south, our routines continued. On June 8th we disembarked another 60 casualties to HMS *Herald*. We were now urgently requiring

"The Fearless Forty". The 40 female Queen Alexandra's Royal Naval Nursing Service Nursing Officers and Naval Nurses on board The Hospital Ship Uganda *as she steams north from The Falkland Islands back home to UK following The Falklands War in 1982.*
Photograph: Author's private collection

reinforcement nursing staff to augment our core teams. To our immense relief HMS *Hecla* brought thirteen additional nursing staff… and joy of joys… seven tons of much-needed pharmaceutical and medical stores. There were also six members of The International Red Cross. The three QARNNS Naval Nurses who arrived in that group augmented our QARNNS Team of nurses from 37 to 40 in number. Thereafter we referred to ourselves as "The Fearless Forty". A photograph of the group can be seen on the previous page. Throughout the entire Falklands Conflict we were the only female military personnel working within the Combat Zone, and our QARNNS Naval Nurses the first female RN Junior Ratings in history to serve at sea.

By early June, with the landing of 5 Brigade (cross-decked to *Canberra* from the *QE2* off Grytviken, South Georgia) on East Falkland, and British troops steadily advancing East towards Stanley, The Hospital Ship was now having to spend longer periods anchored in Grantham Sound to facilitate speedier helicopter casualty evacuations from all three Field Dressing Stations ashore. The need for us to embark casualties and increase patient flow ashore was the priority at this time. We understood that "diplomatic routes" informed Argentina of our movements, but inevitably we felt vulnerable to enemy aircraft attacks. Our MOIC addressed the staff during this period, emphasising our continued protection under ICRC Geneva Convention Rules, adding that the recent arrival of some of their teams, and the presence of Argentinian patients on board should help to strengthen our protection. We had first remained at anchor overnight in Grantham Sound for the night of May 29th, and again on the night of June 6th. On June 7th and 8th we worked out in the new Red Cross Box, just North of Cape Dolphin, embarking our reinforcement personnel, and disembarking patients to HMS *Herald*. This was most fortuitous, as it released bed capacity for what was to arise over the next few days. We returned to Grantham Sound on June 8th, dropping anchor there at 2230.

CHAPTER SIX

"THE SEA-GULLS CRYING"

June 8th – June 14th 1982

As events transpired, it was indeed fortunate that we had disembarked another 60 casualties to HMS *Herald* for onward transfer to UK during Tuesday June 8th, so we had some spare bed capacity. Also, the timely arrival of three QARNNS Naval Nurses and ten RN Medical Assistants to reinforce our now overworked on board teams was very fortunate. That evening, unusually, we had anchored in Grantham Sound overnight for only the third time.

Tuesday June 8th was the fateful day of the Argentinian attacks on the Landing Support Ships *Sir Galahad* and *Sir Tristram* as they were commencing unloading stores and personnel at Fitzroy settlement. Losses were heavy. Our store of spare military beds was immediately brought into use, and hastily assembled in an overflow area called The Music Room that we had earmarked for such an eventuality earlier in hostilities. This hasty conversion of the former Music Room area was, in the main, carried out by Senior Naval Nurse (SNN) Sally Middleton and Senior Naval Nurse (SNN) Marion Stock.

It is worth bearing in mind that five Royal Navy ships had already been attacked and sunk by this stage of the war, and The Hospital Ship *Uganda* had received in the region of a dozen injured or burnt casualties from each of those incidents by early June. So, in reality, although the Fitzroy incident stretched everyone on board The Hospital Ship to the limit, clinically, we were now consolidating a well-rehearsed routine of casualty reception and ongoing treatments.

We started taking casualties at first light on June 9th and on that one day alone we received 159 casualties, the majority of whom were severely burnt, with many other types of injuries arising from the attacks. At one point there were more than four helicopters queuing up to land casualties on the flight deck. One of these was the only surviving Chinook helicopter from the *Atlantic Conveyor* attack, HC1 Bravo November, with 37 casualties on board. This twin rotor helicopter weighs in at 15 tons, so here was a true test for the helicopter-landing pad strengthening pillars, fitted so carefully in Gibraltar in April before our departure! No problem ensued, much to the relief of patients and staff in the now somewhat over-pressed Sea View Ward directly beneath the helo-pad. On the flight deck the enormous chopper perched athwartships, with the rear door hanging, literally, over the open sea. The inevitable joke cracked as the flight deck crew commenced unloading their precious cargo was: 'OK lads – Everybody out… Brits to starboard, Argies to the rear...!' It was a much-needed light moment for those working in such horrendous conditions.

Everyone was at full stretch, especially the Royal Marine stretcher-bearers, maintaining such a crucial ongoing link from flight-deck to CRA. Our Medical-Officer-in Charge, Surgeon Captain Rintoul, made an announcement over the public address system asking for everyone not required on duty in other parts of the ship to report to the Casualty Reception at once. There was a magnificent response; many P&O watch-keepers roused from sleep, and everyone, including the Red Cross Teams just recently arrived, plunged in at the deep end of dealing with mass casualty evacuation. It was testament to co-operation and adaptability in the truest sense of the words.

In our operating theatres all three teams were on watch, and we released one team of three Naval Nurses to SNN Middleton and SNN Stock to help their teams in the newly opened Music Room Ward. Much later that night, when we had departed from Grantham Sound pursued by helicopters with further casualties to embark as we steamed north, I finally closed down the autoclave Vesuvius with CPOMA (O) Jim Lacey. From now on Vesuvius would really come into his own (we never worked out what gender Vesuvius was!) as the workload to supply sterilised dressings required for so many burns patients would now more than double. Vesuvius could only be operated manually, with one of us loading, running, checking and then unloading each 40 minute pressure cycle. Hence this was a time late into the night when the OT Sisters would have finished preparing the next day's supplies of sterilised dressings and instruments that Vesuvius would have sterilised, after our own Operating Theatre schedule.

In effect, the OT staff on board The Hospital Ship had now set up and were running what is called a Central Sterilising Service Department (CSSD) for the whole hospital as, apart from Vesuvius itself, the rest of this usually vital service in normal hospitals ashore seemed to have been omitted from our basic supplies. It was another case of adaptation and innovation. We had adequate supplies to run our own Theatre Sterile Supply Department (TSSU) system, but then had to expand this, to incorporate processing supplies of sterile dressings and instrument packs for all the clinical areas within the hospital. We would deliver the much needed packs of sterilised dressings and instruments round to the wards when our operating theatres were briefly "off watch", usually well after midnight, before turning in ourselves. I would often help my friend, Senior Nursing Officer Chris Asendorf, the burns specialist Sister, with patient care in the High Dependency Burns Unit at these times, which is how I got to know CPO John Strange, Simon Weston, and the other more severely injured patients being nursed in those areas.

Before Chris (Asendorf) joined The Naval Nursing Service (QARNNS) at The

Royal Naval Hospital Haslar in Gosport with me in 1980, she had served a Short Service Commission in The Army Nursing Corps (QARANC). (The full names of all three military Nursing Services can be found in The Introduction.) During this time she had gained much experience working with severely burned military patients at The Army Hospital in Woolwich. This period in her career had also given her a good insight into our soldiers' way of coping with their injuries, and I learnt a great deal from her wisdom and calmness under such difficult conditions on board The Hospital Ship in 1982.

She had spent much time with "two Para" soldiers, and helped me to understand how infantry soldiers in particular felt so bad being away from their battalions, and unable to return to the fighting zone. During The Falklands War this was due to a Geneva Convention ruling that, once a wounded man had been evacuated to The Hospital Ship, he had to remain out of the battle for the rest of the campaign, his only way back to UK being via the route described. For many hardened battle soldiers this was seen by the troops fighting ashore as "a most deplorable fate"… this, in spite of the fact that so many would undoubtedly have perished without us being there. Much kindness, support and encouragement was required at all levels, and talking these issues through with the soldiers in the long hours of darkness was a unique and particular way our traditional nursing skills could come to the fore. By now, groups of casualties who had returned to UK from The Hospital Ship via the routes already described were being discharged from the military hospitals in UK. So we could further encourage those being treated on board The Hospital Ship that the route back home, however lengthy, was working well.

TREATMENT OF BURNS PATIENTS:

Apart from infection, another frequent complication of extensive burns injuries is renal (kidney) function deterioration. So the establishment of daily fluid and electrolyte balance recordings had to be swiftly set up for all burns patients, and they all received intravenous therapy and subsequent monitoring.

Almost all the casualties from the Fitzroy attack treated on board The Hospital Ship were suffering from severe burns, particularly their faces and hands. They were treated with FLAMAZINE cream, a silver sulphadiazine cream renowned for its healing, analgesic and antiseptic properties. The damaged areas, where possible, were enclosed in plastic bags to encourage hand movement within a relatively sterile and enclosed atmosphere. The treatment did look alarming, but longer term results have proved most successful.

Fighting soldiers are used to covering their hands and faces with a dark "camo" or camouflage cream for combat, so a "white camo cream" became the norm in this unit. The less severely injured were able to help those worse than themselves and P&O staff kindly helped out as required when their own watch systems permitted.

The more severely injured were treated in the Specialised Burns Unit run by

Superintending Nursing Officer Marion Hammill, my friend Senior Nursing Officer Chris Asendorf and their teams. This rather enclosed area which incorporated the P&O ship's hospital on B deck had already been prepared for other burns patients much earlier in the conflict; it was up and running most efficiently by the time of the Fitzroy attack. The ambient temperature had to be maintained at 85deg F and had a very high humidity rate; Chris used to say it was "a bit of a sauna" to work in! All the staff that worked there lost at least a stone in body weight by the time we closed that unit.

Simon Weston, a Welsh Guardsman, subsequently known to many as "the face of The Falklands", was among those cared for in the Specialist Burns unit. Simon was a tough cookie, and in spite of his severe burns at over 46% he has done extraordinarily well in the longer term. I was the OT sister who "scrubbed" for his only operation on board The Hospital Ship. We had to skin graft both his eyelids, undoubtedly saving his sight by creating a protective layer for his eyes at that early stage in his treatment. He was another former patient who seemed to recall a certain Theatre Sister's blue eyes just before he was anaesthetised. With the skin grafts in place he was then unable to see for many days.

As soon as patients' conditions were stable enough, our Burns and Plastic specialist, Royal Navy Surgeon Commander Charles Chapman, would seek to commence a programme of skin grafting in Theatres under general anaesthetic. The journey from the Burns Unit to OT was a tortuous one, as they were on different deck levels and we all felt for CPO John Strange, Simon, and the other patients as the RM stretcher-bearers had to manoeuvre them round the bulkheads and ship's passageways. As Doctor Bull confirms later in this chapter, the journey to OT from the Music Room ward area, where the majority of the Welsh Guardsmen were being treated, was less demanding as it was on the same deck level.

Surgeon Commander Chapman had brought with him an innovative "skin graft mesher" which was used to great effect during skin graft surgery. The problem with many of our patients was the availability of skin donor sites, as so much of their bodies were wounded. This device, in effect, reduced the donor area of skin required to be taken for graft by about one third. Again, by commencing this programme of grafts and treatments at such an early stage, future weeks and months of further disruptive surgery were prevented for many patients. It worked!

Surgeon Commander Chapman was subsequently awarded the OBE for his work in this field on board The Hospital Ship *Uganda*.

Types of Injuries:

Penetrating injuries, as in other battles, were the main cause for admission. Mortar, gunshot and shrapnel can all be included in that group. Limb loss or injury from indiscriminately placed anti-personnel mines was high. We treated over 120 burns patients overall, and numerous cold-water-induced foot injuries otherwise classed as "trench foot".

Seventeen patients admitted had sustained penetrating brain injury, skull fractures or concussion. Whenever the inner brain lining or dura had been breached a combination of three immensely powerful antibiotics was administered. This was to prevent infection known as cerebral abscess occurring, before elective neurological surgery could take place as a planned secondary procedure in UK. It worked!

Limb injuries consumed a high proportion of operating theatre time; two of our three operating tables were in use for well over 12 hours daily for several weeks. Chest, abdominal and other categories were all treated as appropriate.

Surgeon Commander Peter Bull enlarges here on some of the issues that were starting to affect us at this stage:

> We were to learn other lessons on how to be adaptable under pressure and in unusual circumstances: for example, that special sterile clothing and prophylactic antibiotics were not essential to maintain our notably low infection rate; and that complicated and expensive laboratory and monitoring equipment, as well as investigations (e.g. blood gas estimation and chest x-rays), could be replaced by good clinical common sense with very little reduction in safety and medical care.
>
> In order to reduce the risks of infection, gangrene and other clinical complications in battle-induced injury, modern surgical technique demands early wound debridement and excision before Delayed Primary Closure many days later (a process often referred to elsewhere in this book as DPC, DPS or Delayed Primary Suture). However, this can necessitate many return visits to theatre and usually numerous general anaesthetics.
>
> This was the fundamental basis of our highly successful line of surgery and treatment on board The Hospital Ship *Uganda* in 1982. Regrettably, this was not always adhered to outside The Hospital Ship and we saw some evidence of this, especially with a young cook from HMS *Glamorgan* after her Exocet attack. One casualty arrived on board The Hospital Ship with synergistic gangrene and an almost unsustainable haemoglobin level of 3.8g *(3.8.grams per 100 millilitres of blood; normal levels in an adult male being between 13g and 18g)*. He was not expected to live.
>
> Anaesthesia (especially the resuscitation and post operative management) played a large part in the success of our campaign, but this could not have been achieved without good surgery and most of all, excellent nursing care – despite the woefully small number – 40 nurses for a potential one thousand bedded hospital! I am most indebted to the work done by my Intensive Care nurses, led by Superintending Nursing Officer Jane Marshall and Senior Nursing Officer Liz Law who had the most strenuous of work patterns. Also to all the Operating Theatre personnel led by Superintending Nursing Officer Isa Gauld with Senior Nursing

Officers Nicci Pugh and Margaret Kerr, and CPOMA (O) Jim Lacey, all of whom greatly exceeded my expectations in their ability to react to the most gruesome of injuries, to say nothing of the long hours.

Ships make for excellent hospital facilities, as so much can be kept on one level avoiding the need to transport very sick patients in lifts to and from theatre or intensive care. In The Hospital Ship *Uganda* we had a series of spaces for the most severely injured along one deck immediately under the flight deck. Admittedly patients did need to be transported down the short but very steep ramp from the Flight Deck helicopters to the casualty area. From there, however, it was an easy progression, either:

1: Aft to the high-dependency Sea View ward (40–45 beds) or 2: Forward to the Operating Theatre (three tables) and Intensive Care Unit (20 beds).

Other areas of the ship were also used because of special features, such as the ship's sick bay, two decks below, because this could be temperature controlled and used as a Specialised Burns Unit (for such as Chief Petty Officer John Strange and Welsh Guardsman Simon Weston). Later in the campaign the forward "Music Room", which had been our recreation space, had to become the Burns Ward, after the influx of 150 patients in three hours from the Fitzroy incident. Also, the old student dormitory accommodation was used for low dependency and recovering patients who could use stairs and showers, or needed non-acute treatment.

I cannot praise my second anaesthetist and colleague, Surgeon Lt. Cdr. David Baker RN, too highly. As a Senior Specialist he could be expected to work alongside me without constant supervision, and also to deputise for me in my absence elsewhere in the ship or during rest periods. Similarly, our anaesthetic technicians, POMA (O) John Rigby and POMA (O) Mick Clancy (both RN Petty Officer Medical Assistants with Operating Theatre specialist qualification), could be trusted to look after anaesthetised patients whilst either of us were attending to more critical matters at the other OT table, or elsewhere within this "acute treatment area" on The Promenade deck.

Back at Ascension (in April), I had come as close as ever to "disobeying a direct order" (an extremely serious Naval transgression) when the Principal Medical Officer of *Canberra* had come aboard to request Doctor Baker, my deputy, to transfer to *Canberra*, as they expected to be overwhelmed with casualties at the time of the Landings. At that stage in the planning, The Hospital Ship *Uganda* was scheduled to be a hundred miles north of hostilities out of harm's way, and to have casualties ferried to us from the shore by ambulance ships. This was soon realised to be impractical as we needed to be within helicopter range in order to have a sporting chance of saving life and limb – also because the ambulance ships only carried general duties' doctors and no Surgical Support Team (SST) personnel or equipment. So, back at Ascension my deputy had helped considerably by agreeing my argument that, with five surgeons on board *Uganda*, having only two anaesthetists was already too few; therefore the request from *Canberra's* Principal Medical Officer was withdrawn; but we did lose one surgeon! If pushed, I believe Doctor Baker would have disobeyed the order to leave.

We already had too small a team for the roles that were subsequently needed to run The Hospital Ship safely and efficiently for a protracted period, especially within these specialised areas:

1. Casualty Reception and Assessment (Triage Area)
2. Resuscitation
3. Operating Theatre
4. Intensive care
5. Pre and post-operative care

I needed help and received this from several sources. A general physician, Surgeon Lt. Cdr. Robin Clark RN, joined The Hospital Ship *Uganda* after the May 21st landings, as his Surgical Support Team in HMS *Hermes* were re-deployed mostly ashore. He helped greatly with the running of the Intensive Care Unit with his senior colleague, Surgeon Commander Mike Beeley RN.

Casualty Reception, Resuscitation and Triage were carried out almost at the same time, and important decisions made on where and how to treat patients had to be made very quickly. Analgesia and intravenous fluid replacement were paramount, and I utilised the help of the most capable to assist here. The Casualty Reception Area (CRA) Senior Nursing Officer Jean Kidd and the Dental (Maxillo-Facial) Officer, Surgeon Cdr (D) Geoff Keeble RN, would carry syringes of diluted Omnopon to be injected liberally, under my strict guidelines, until pain was minimised. We found that even those that required over 20 mg of Omnopon did not suffer respiratory depression, supporting my view that this side effect only becomes apparent if dosing continues after pain is relieved. On occasions there was an excess of 50 mg given within a half hour period.

Notwithstanding the relative shortage of Medical Officers, we had a good balance of specialists and two junior surgical trainees. War is a good place for learning and experience but only if there are enough others to do the training. Nevertheless, these trainees were young, enthusiastic and flexible enough to do what was directed, and overall, at "the sharp end" of the hospital, teams were quickly working harmoniously together within the demands and restrictions I have mentioned.

Overall, we only used two of the Operating Table areas for general anaesthesia, keeping the third for sole use for simple, local anaesthetic procedures, plaster changes, etc. although it could have been utilised for general anaesthetics in the case of need. At busy times we did work at all three tables simultaneously to maintain patient flow. There were less serious injuries too, not requiring anaesthesia but still requiring much work in pain relief and fluid management; for example Trench Foot, which is a non-freezing cold injury. This was mostly a feature of our Argentinian patients. After an initial embargo on helicopter allocation we only took casualties by daylight as, by Geneva Convention, we had to remain floodlit overall and thus, being a beacon for enemy aircraft, would need to sail out of the Falkland Sound each evening. We were indebted to the excellent work done, often at night, at the field surgical stations ashore, especially those at Ajax Bay (Army and Navy), Teal Inlet and Fitzroy (Army).

A section of the Operating Theatre.
Photograph: Jim Lacey

My diary mid-conflict reads:

> *Our line of treatment for the shrapnel and all traumatic*
> *injuries is based on recommendations principally from The*

*Vietnam and Korean Wars; initially to clean, debride and
dress the wound, carrying out Delayed Primary Suture
under general anaesthetic some 5–7 days later. Obviously
every case has to be treated individually, based principally
on the location and severity of the wound(s). This does
necessitate nearly every patient requiring at least two
general anaesthetics and trips to Theatre with all that that
entails, again proving the necessity for an efficient and safe
hospital some short distance from the battlefields.*

By being able to provide these reliable, efficient and highly successful surgical treatments during the Falklands War, the Hospital Ship *Uganda* and her teams were already proving the value of these essential and indeed life-saving procedures. For the majority of injured servicemen treated on board, weeks and months of further follow-up treatments and appointments were avoided.

Sadly, during the second week in June, three of our patients died. All three of them had been fatally wounded before reaching The Hospital Ship. They were all cared for in our Intensive Care Unit, adjacent to the operating theatres. We all felt their loss keenly. One of them, Marine Paul Callan, had been injured in an attack on The Ajax Bay Field Hospital on May 27th, and had put up a brave fight against his overwhelmingly fatal injuries. Paul underwent several operations, received many transfusions, and the finest medical and nursing care we could offer. Our Naval Padre David Barlow was with Paul when he passed away, and subsequently wrote a detailed letter to Paul's parents reassuring them that everything possible had been done to keep Paul comfortable in his last few hours in our care.

Our Royal Marine stretcher-bearer and other available hospital staff, lined the route from the ICU to the Flight Deck when his body was taken ashore for burial with those of his friends who had perished at the same spot at Ajax Bay. Eventually, like many servicemen killed in action during The Falklands War, his body was returned to UK, and he is now buried at The 45 Commando Royal Marine cemetery at Arbroath.

The other two servicemen who died on board were also returned to The Islands for burial ashore with equal respect from all our staff, who cared for them in their last hours.

* * *

BLOOD TRANSFUSIONS:

As with the rest of the clinical requirements, our blood transfusion service was being set up en route to Ascension from Gibraltar, under the direction of our Consultant Pathologist Surgeon Commander John Buchanan RN.

It was operational by the time we left Ascension on May1st. By that time we had several hundred units of cross-matched blood available to last until mid-June, and a working database covering the entire RN and P&O personnel on board. CPO Med. Tech. Bob McGrann and CPO Med. Tech. Mark Trasler were both instrumental in the setting up and delivering of this absolutely vital service. Bob and Mark's little "lab" was just opposite our own "CSSD" packing area. Mark and Bob would be carefully checking, labelling and storing their precious units in the handy cold drinks cabinets on one side of what was a bar area, while our teams on the other (OT) side would be preparing instrument packs for sterilising, folding dressings and rolling bandages, and, of course, chatting away if time permitted. We all became firm friends. I personally remember that part of our work as being almost therapeutic; often following several hours in Theatres dealing with such severe injuries on a daily basis.

In the adjacent inset Mark Trasler tells of his early Naval career within the Medical Branch:

In 1982: Chief Petty Officer Mark Trasler RN Medical Technician 1 (Lab.)

Photograph: Mark Trasler

I joined the Royal Navy as a Junior Medical Assistant in 1971 at the tender age of 16. I spent three years in training to be (in those days) a State Registered Medical Laboratory Technician – now called Biomedical Scientists – reaching the dizzy height of Killick (Leading Hand) when I eventually qualified. In between drafts to Gibraltar I spent over four years at sea, mainly on HMS *Tiger* (Far East, Pacific, Africa and Mediterranean), and in the (previous) HMS *Ark Royal* (USA and West Indies).

1981/82 found me a two-year draft to Royal Naval Hospital Gibraltar, and a chance to enjoy the sunshine, culture, sport, tax-free social life, a smattering of Spanish and some stability. Although a little constrained by being on-call one day in three it was, nevertheless, a somewhat idyllic existence even though the Spanish border was, at that time, closed. In Gib I was promoted to Chief Petty Officer Medical Technician (Lab) (CPO MT1 Lab). The clinical workload was such that "make and mends" (afternoons off) were not uncommon and I took the tax-free opportunity to buy my first ever brand new car – a Honda Civic. Come the end of the draft and time to go home, with a crate of beer in the boot, the proud owner drove the car to the Gibraltar RAF base for a "service indulgence flight" in a C130 Hercules back to RAF Lyneham in UK. That was the last time I saw the car for nine months! This being late March 1982, the car had, very fortunately, caught the final empty flight back to UK before the RAF had far more important logistic work to do! When you undertake this process, you sign a form agreeing to "Exigencies of The Service" which can involve your pride and joy being ditched at sea should flights or sea trips be "diverted".

So I returned to UK in March 1982, only to find myself returning to Gibraltar via RAF Lyneham within a fortnight to join The Hospital Ship *Uganda*, just getting a chance to wave at the new car at RAF Lyneham in passing!

Here Mark describes his work in the Blood Transfusion Service, another crucial link in the casualty evacuation success rate of The Falklands War:

THE PATHOLOGY LABORATORY ON BOARD THE HOSPITAL SHIP *UGANDA*:

The time-honoured matelot advice "head straight for the bar" is never more applicable than when converting a commercial cruise ship into a hospital. A bar has nearly all the attributes needed for a small pathology laboratory. It has worktops, power points, a water supply, shelving, multiple fridges and a telephone – even if all the alcohol has magically disappeared! The L-shaped cocktail bar on The Hospital Ship *Uganda* was no exception, plus it had the enormous advantage of looking out to one side over The Intensive Care Unit in the oak-panelled former Smoking Room, and on the other out over the Operating Tables in the Veranda space – pathology's two biggest customers. The two laboratory technicians, Chief Petty Officers Bob McGrann and myself, had no excuse for not knowing which patients had clinical priority.

Although of necessity somewhat basic, the lab could do all the normal investigations needed for trauma care at the time – medical science has moved on a little since. Full blood counts (to determine scale of blood loss, infection and numerous other factors) used a combination of a small electronic cell counter and a microscope, together with the mark one eyeball. Intravenous fluid replacement was monitored using serum Sodium and Potassium measurements (from patients' blood-sampling,) and recently introduced technology, the Ion-specific Electrode. These vital electrolyte tests had never been previously available at sea, as their measurement traditionally depended on the use of a gas powered flame – far too dangerous a technology for a ship. Vital enzymes and other chemicals that measure liver and kidney function, and tissue death, could be manually determined using special reagent packs and an old-fashioned spectrophotometer to detect colour change. In addition, the bacteria that cause wound infection could be grown and tested against different antibiotics to determine which was likely to be the most effective.

Also on board was a Consultant Pathologist, Surgeon Commander John Buchanan. His main duties included triage, primary resuscitation and clinical photography. Plans to provide a post mortem service proved unworkable due to the lack of private space with good hygiene and lighting. Leading Med Tech (Lab) Paul Wheatley, from the Surgical Support Team aboard HMS *Hermes*, also joined us for a short while and proved particularly useful as casualty numbers mounted from the land battles.

In general, CPO Bob McGrann took charge of the "routine" pathology workload. I had a more roving commission, providing liaison, taking blood samples and generally helping out at Casualty Receiving Stations, sample collection during ward rounds, and, particularly during the slightly quieter periods, undertaking relief nursing duties in the adjacent Intensive Care Unit.

BLOOD TRANSFUSION:

Possibly the most important role of the Medical Laboratory Technicians in war is to provide an efficient Blood Transfusion service — a critical, and lifesaving procedure requiring pinpoint accuracy and organisation to avoid giving the wrong blood type and hastening your patient's demise. A task made doubly difficult by having to take into account numerous critically ill trauma patients all arriving at once, a 10% error rate of the blood group on service dog-tags, the total lack of a timely logistics chain, and Welsh Guardsmen all sharing the same 3 surnames! These days, Field Hospitals in Afghanistan and Iraq rely totally on blood collected in the UK, screened, grouped and processed before being flown out to the Combat Zone. This was not possible in the Falklands War. Units of blood have a shelf life of about 35 days, during which time the therapeutic value slowly reduces, and although 360 units from UK donors were received at Ascension Island, the majority of the blood stock had to be taken from donors within the Task Force and then processed.

The timing of the blood donor sessions is critical. The blood needs to be as fresh as possible for the likely casualties and to last as long as possible. The donors need, at minimum, a couple of days to recover before undertaking arduous duties (e.g. warfare). Once the troops have been landed, donor sessions are almost impossible. The ideal time then is 2-5 days before the amphibious landing. This is fine in theory only, as the date of any intended D-Day is always the top secret! Certainly, no one on a Hospital Ship, let alone those responsible for blood management, would know this vital piece of information.

As it was, 415 blood units were safely collected from on board the *Uganda*, *Canberra*, *Hermes*, *Hydra* and *Hecla*. As always in a potential crisis, the donors were superbly generous and all appreciated the post-donation fluid replacement! Patients aboard The Hospital Ship *Uganda* used 298 of these units (one patient alone receiving more than 50 units). Our colleague ashore with the Surgical Support Team at Ajax Bay, CPO Med Tech (Lab) Stuart McKinlay, used 283 units and HMS *Hermes* used 36. In all, 72% of all the blood stocks was used on patients – a figure hugely in excess of normal UK peacetime rates.

On one particular day just after the landings ashore on May 21st, while transporting blood stocks ashore in *Hecla's* Wasp helicopter (akin to flying in a mini car without any doors), we were just passing the "dippers" (anti-submarine Sea King helicopters) guarding the entrance to Falkland Sound when, with a huge ear splitting roar, two Argentinian Skyhawks flew past at what seemed to be a matter of feet away. Ignoring us sitting ducks, they turned left into San Carlos water to bomb the ships. The anti-aircraft fire certainly made life exciting as we neared Ajax Bay!

BURNS:

Apparently, or so we were taught on the passage down south, modern warfare with over-the-horizon missiles produces many shrapnel wounds but relatively few burns casualties. In fact, burns caused 71% of the injuries amongst those patients admitted from the ships, even if they accounted for only 19% of the UK Task Force admissions overall.

The attack on HMS *Sheffield* produced our first burns patients. One patient, with 46% of his body area badly burnt, proved a real challenge. Taking blood from him for the all-important monitoring of his biochemistry and renal (kidney) function got more difficult by the day, and eventually I resorted to using his big toe! His fortitude under such circumstances was extremely impressive and it was particularly gratifying to meet Chief (CPO) John Strange 26 years later looking so well.

The RFA *Sir Galahad* and *Sir Tristram* bombings, not surprisingly, stretched the whole medical organisation. 159 patients were admitted within three hours – the majority with severe burns. One of the big dangers of burns is fluid loss, and such patients need a rapid and controlled infusion of fluids via an intravenous drip. One way of measuring how much fluid is required is by measuring the concentration of the blood – the higher the concentration of blood cells there are, the less fluid the body has. This is done by a fairly simple test (called Packed Cell Volume or PCV) every four hours at the patient's bedside using a hand-held centrifuge. From the results you can work out, using a formula, how much fluid is needed and how fast it needs to be infused. While CPO Bob McGrann manned the laboratory, dealing with a multitude of other injuries, I looked after the burns patients in the (newly converted) Music Room, Specialised Burns Unit/Ship's Hospital and Dormitories. Blood was taken, the PCV performed, calculations made and, when necessary, IV fluids set up and adjusted. If the hospital notes had not been raised, the results were written on the patient's chest using an indelible marker. This routine was needed for two days before the majority were sufficiently stable. One major shortcoming was that, although the PCV needed doing every four hours, it would take me six hours, working from for'd to aft, to test all the required patients. I then started at the for'd end of the ship again.

Initially, most of the casualties were practically unrecognisable facially, with most having badly burnt faces and hands due to the lack of anti-flash gear. Identifying patients proved particularly difficult with most being called Jones, Davies or Williams. We soon learnt to call them by their "last three" (digits of their service number) e.g. "Jones 684". It took nearly three days to correctly identify all the new casualties, and even longer to work out who hadn't made it to the The Hospital Ship.

One difficult aspect was the number of soldiers with severe nicotine withdrawal who needed a cigarette but, because of their burnt hands, couldn't manage. It was heart-warming to see the P&O staff sitting at their bedsides putting cigarettes in their mouths!

(Note from author: This may sound strange today, but everyone smoked much more in those days, especially service personnel; smoking was part of shipboard and the soldier's way of life. With so much trauma all around us, our on board personnel weren't going to suddenly take this one pleasure away from men who had been through so much by the time they reached us on board The Hospital Ship. Smoking in the clinical areas was always under supervision and adequate ventilation was encouraged.)

Now married to a former QARNNS Nursing Officer, Mark remains in the Service as a Naval Lt. Commander; another Hospital Ship colleague who went on to a most successful RN career after 1982.

CHAPTER SEVEN

"FLUNG SPRAY AND *(THE)* BLOWN SPUME"

June 14th – July 13th 1982

On June 14th, the day of the Argentinian surrender, we had more than 300 patients on board The Hospital Ship. Historically, casualty figures inevitably rise when battle hostilities officially cease and, yet again, The Falklands War proved no exception. We were all very weary and, frankly, at the time, the news made little difference to our working areas. We were so busy that we had asked convalescing patients and P&O staff to help out where they could in B Deck and The Music Room ward. Some help did come across later that day from *Canberra* which was a great support and morale booster.

Surgeon Commander Bull expands:

> After the surrender, the two anaesthetists on board The Hospital Ship, David Baker and myself, were augmented by help from anaesthetists Surgeon Lt. Cdr Ian Geraghty from Ajax Bay and Surg. Cdr Richard Moody from *Canberra*. Also at Ajax Bay were Surgeon Lt. Cdr. Andy Yates and Surg. Lt. Sean Tighe, whilst on other surface ships were: Surgeon Commander Stephen Merrill, also in *Canberra*, Surgeon Lt.Cdr. Steve Squires in HMS *Hermes* and Surgeon Lt. Cdr Chris Stoot in HMS *Invincible*.

The previous few days had seen much fierce fighting ashore, as our advancing troops made for their objectives in a series of carefully planned and co-ordinated assaults on the well dug-in Argentinian defences holding the high ground around the town of Stanley. The battles for Mount Harriet, Two Sisters, Mount Longdon, Tumbledown and Wireless Ridge are well-known, and have been written about at length in the intervening twenty-six years.

For us on board The Hospital Ship, until early June, casualties were being flown to us continuously by day via the routes previously described. But as our fighting troops moved steadily further east, the distance back from "the front line" to the Ajax Bay Main Dressing Station became longer, so more casualties were now coming directly to The Hospital Ship from the battlefields. By this time The Fitzroy Dressing Station was set up and running at full throttle, taking a greater proportion of injured from the Regimental Aid Posts.

One of these was Lance Corporal Denzil Connick, three Para, severely wounded in the Battle for Mount Longdon on June 13th. This is Denzil's complete and unabridged story up to the time of his injury on Mount Longdon and subsequent evacuation to The Hospital Ship *Uganda*:

In 1982: Lance Corporal Denzil Connick 3rd Battalion The Parachute Regiment

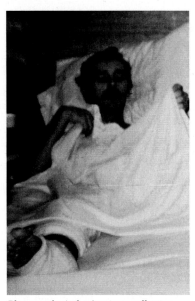

Photograph: Author's private collection

I joined the army in 1972 as a fifteen year old boy soldier in the Junior Parachute Company of The Parachute Regiment. Ten years later I reached the dizzy heights of L/Cpl in the Anti Tank Platoon 3rd Battalion The Parachute Regiment.

For everyone, the invasion of the Falkland Islands by Argentina was a complete surprise. We were geared up and trained as Paratroops for taking on the Russians and counter-insurgency operations and nearly all of this meant that we would probably parachute or air-land into action behind enemy lines. To go to war by sea was never something we imagined we would undertake; a sort of double whammy!

To make matters even worse (as far as we were concerned in the Paras), we were attached to 3 Commando Brigade Royal Marines! The Paras and Royal Marines have always competed with each other in terms of who are the best. Of course we were the best and that's why they needed us to help them; this was our reasoning behind this strange and unexpected development.

The weeks we spent at sea on the huge P&O Liner *Canberra* gave us "some" understanding of the ways of the navy. Learning "Jack Speak"

90

was an education and great fun for us, often to the great irritation of any Royal Navy Officers embarked with us… an example of this was adding to directional signs dotted onboard such as "stern", where we would write underneath "arse end" and so on.

By the 21st May, "D" Day of the landings at Port San Carlos, we were keen to go ashore. The novelty of life at sea had worn off completely and it was time for us to be paratroopers again, win the war and return home to dear old "Blighty".

The respect that the Navy had earned from us on our voyage south was strengthened even more as we watched the regular air raids on our ships anchored in San Carlos. We were also very frustrated at being so helpless in stopping the bombs and cannon fire being inflicted on our friends and comrades. Any childish rivalry had evaporated; we were now bonded together as Brothers-in-Arms; sailors, soldiers and airmen, all for one and one for all… Turtle Power!

The first two weeks ashore we spent marching from the west coast of the island towards Stanley on the east coast… about 70 miles. On the way we relieved a couple of settlements of their unwelcome guests and nursed our sore feet and tired muscles. So far, except for the forced march, horrendous weather and terrain, we had had it reasonably easy. Our brothers in 2 Para had just taken Goose Green and we had lost good mates. Now we were intent on finishing the enemy off and our turn for battle soon came in the guise of Mount Longdon.

Mount Longdon is a high ground feature, along with others, that provides Stanley with an excellent natural defensive ring. The enemy had plenty of time to consolidate their positions on these hills and were ready for us. This was not going to be any pushover; we all knew that we would suffer many casualties and the sacrifice would be high. Longdon is a name that I have recalled every day of my life since the battle, along with the many friends I lost on its bleak craggy slopes.

The battle for Longdon raged for a good twelve hours. The men of 3 Para went in with rifle and bayonet at the cost of some 23 killed in action (KIA) and about 50 wounded; the enemy suffered even greater losses. Amongst those wounded was myself. I was hit by artillery fire on the 13th June that blew away my left leg and shredded my right leg. Two lads with me at the time, Craig Jones and Alex Shaw, died next to me. The shock of witnessing your own injuries as bad as this is a terrifying experience. I knew that without immediate first aid and evacuation I would be dead… very soon. I had already seen the dead bodies of many friends and those of the enemy… was I about to join them? One of our medics at the RAP (Regimental Aid Post) was my long time friend Brian Faulkner. Brian, along with the MO and his team, did a great job of keeping death at bay until my "casevac" (casualty evacuation); they were brilliant.

As luck would have it, even though our RAP was under heavy enemy artillery fire, the medics were able to slide my stretcher along the floor of a little Army Air Corps "Scout" helicopter. They had taken the doors off, so my head was sticking out of one end and my remaining foot out of the other end. Combined with blood loss and the freezing air under the downwash of the rotor blades, I have never felt so cold in my life. I was near death by the time we had arrived at the Field Hospital at Fitzroy Settlement. Had the pilot and observer of that little helicopter not had the courage to land at our "hot" LZ (a landing zone under enemy fire), I would have certainly died.

I learnt some years later that it took about 30 minutes from being wounded to arriving at Fitzroy. I was indeed very lucky, as helicopter casualty evacuation was at a premium. Most of our wounded were taken away overland in the "Volvo BV" snow vehicles.

I remember my arrival in the Field Hospital surprisingly well. The sudden change from freezing temperature to warm paraffin heated tent was so welcome. I also remember thinking that I now had a chance and began to relax. I remember looking up from my stretcher at the medic attending to me and seeing his parachute wings on the shoulder of his shirt. I remember asking if it was okay for me to sleep as the feeling of total exhaustion was so overwhelming but, at the same time, I felt that sleep equalled death and I wanted reassurance that I would not die by closing my eyes and surrendering to blissful sleep and warmth. He said, 'It's okay mate, you're safe now, we will take care of you.' And of course they did take care of me. I awoke the next morning unaware that I had undergone critical life saving surgery during the night. Also unbeknown to me then was that I had required resuscitation (Cardio-vascular resuscitation). My blood pressure was below the recordable scale and my pulse was non-existent. However, by the next day I was awake and feeling like c**p but, somehow, still alive. I was obviously still very dangerously ill and was on the "very serious" list.

Later that morning of 14th June, I was flown aboard the Hospital Ship *Uganda*. I was taken immediately to the Intensive Care Ward and to my surprise and pleasure, put in a bed next to my platoon mate Michael (Mush) Bateman. Mush had been shot through the throat with the bullet exiting through his shoulder. His injuries were also very serious and he breathed through a hole made in his windpipe called a tracheostomy. He had also lost his vocal chords and this meant he could not speak. There we were, both very sick men, barely able to raise our heads from the pillow, weakly acknowledging each other with thumbs up signs, tears rolling down our cheeks and holding hands like frightened children. We were both traumatised by our own injuries, but also coming to terms with the losses of our friends in the previous three days.

I remained on the *Uganda* for the next four weeks. My experiences onboard during that time are amazing; not just from the perspective of my own fight for survival, but from the hundreds of examples of personal bravery and sacrifice from the patients, medics and crew of this wonderful ship, that were instrumental in saving so many lives, both British and Argentinian.

My memories are sad and happy ones with the full range of emotions. The first "happy" ish memory came just hours after coming onboard when the news broke of the surrender of Argentine Forces. I pulled my bed sheet up over my face and just wept, that suppressed sobbing cry of a man who wanted privacy to cry and did not want to show it. I wept for my friends, I wept for myself, but most of all, I wept with relief that further suffering might at last be over.

I remained on the Intensive Care Unit (ICU) ward for some days, during which time I had further surgery and painful salt baths. My wounds were left open and this is done for good reason. Blast injuries involve a lot of muck and debris being blown into your flesh. This muck needed to be flushed away in the salt bath and also air had to be allowed in my wounds to prevent gangrene infection; oxygen is the best prevention of gangrene.

This treatment bath was way below decks from the ICU that was on the upper decks. This bath was also used extensively for treating the many burns' victims of the war, many of which were from the gallant Welsh Guards who suffered so much when their ship the LSL *Sir Galahad* was so mercilessly bombed.

The smell on this deck was rather a strange sort of mixture between antiseptic and cooked pork. I shall never forget that smell or the tormented cries of the men down there that were so terribly burnt. My trips to the salt bath were torture; the journey down the steps on a stretcher was painful, the bath itself was painful, and then the journey back was painful. Before my return journey I was given about an hour to recover and be transfused with about one pint of blood as I would lose about a pint during the bath. I would be given a good dose of morphine and would just float in my drugged state in blissful oblivion.

Morphine is a wonderful drug for pain relief, but it does mess your mind up and can cause you to think and behave very oddly. There I was, lying there after my bath and thinking that my manhood was also ruined along with my legs and that I might not ever "get it up again". This thought came about because I had my leg blown off very high up. It was so close to my privates that it beggars belief… a close call indeed! Anyway, now that you can picture the scene, I am lying there, thinking I'm all alone and decided to test the old boy out. I remember thinking, ah that works and then nothing… I had reached the point of no return and promptly went unconscious. I awoke to a nurse looking at me who said: 'Feeling better now, Corporal?' Talk about embarrassing! I have been reassured that nurses are used to such behaviour and never give it a second thought… really!

Before I was well enough to join the main ward on the ship I asked if I could be moved a few beds away from my neighbour's bed because he was keeping me awake. My neighbour was my long time dear friend Mush as I have already mentioned. My request had nothing at all to do with anything other than the disturbance from Mush every time they cleared his airway that would involve sucking out mucus and blood from his tracheostomy. The sound was a disgusting gurgling noise that would wake me as well as make me want to throw up. It was also distressing to see my friend with panic in his face as he struggled to breathe during this process. Mush was fast asleep when they moved me and was unaware that I had asked to be moved. When he awoke, the first thing he noticed was my empty bed that had been stripped of bedding and my stuff had all gone too. Mush panicked; he thought I had died and began waving his arms about madly and trying to get the attention of a nurse who had no idea what was wrong… don't forget that Mush could not speak. He was trying to ask the nurse what had happened and eventually he managed to get the story that I was only the other end of the room. He looked over at me in disbelief and threw me the "V" sign. He took many years to forgive me; however, we laugh at this little "dit" nowadays.

Eventually, I was moved to the main ward on the ship and was placed in a bed near other mates from my unit. One of these mates was Cpl Ned Kelly. Ned was shot in the stomach, itself a very painful wound that involves delicate surgery usually involving the removal of damaged intestine etc.

Ned is a Glaswegian Scot who was as hard as nails, a great soldier and character. To say that Ned had the constitution of an ox would be an understatement. Within days of some very serious abdominal surgery Ned was as right as rain and drinking more than his fair share of two cans of beer per man per day beer ration. Many of us would not feel like a drink at all and Ned soon caught on to this. He would ask as many people as possible to order their ration of beer even if they didn't want it and give it over to him. Most nights Ned would have at least one slab worth (24 cans) of beer to himself. How he could drink all that after so much stomach surgery is amazing. I did ask him how he did it and he informed me that being "gut shot" did him a favour as he was suffering with an ulcer before he was shot; the bullet shot away his ulcer and the surgery that followed sorted out this problem. He said he had not felt so well in months!

Most evenings we were treated with a film show and a projector and screen were set up in the ward. One such film was the Monty Python film "The Life of Brian". There is a scene at the end of the film where they are being crucified and they are singing the song "Always Look on the Bright Side of Life". We all began singing along and the sight of this was simply amazing for the medics and crew who witnessed this. Imagine all those wounded soldiers and sailors with every kind of injury imaginable, lying in their beds with drips and tubes, swaying to the music and singing this song. I did notice a few tears on their faces.

I think this is a good time to conclude my story. I could tell more; however, I think you have got the idea by now. The Hospital Ship *Uganda* did a fantastic job in saving so many lives. It was not perfect, but nothing ever is unless you're God, but they pulled off their own special miracles. I would love to suggest the Motto for the ship be…

Always Look On The Bright Side Of Life…

…And ever since, I think I have.

Denzil had to make many return trips to our operating theatres while he was in our care. All the teams remember him very well; we all knew what a close call he'd had, and we were as determined as Denzil that he wasn't going to be another statistic on the wrong side for us. The story of how Denzil, his wife Theresa, and I all met up in recent years is continued in Chapter Ten.

* * *

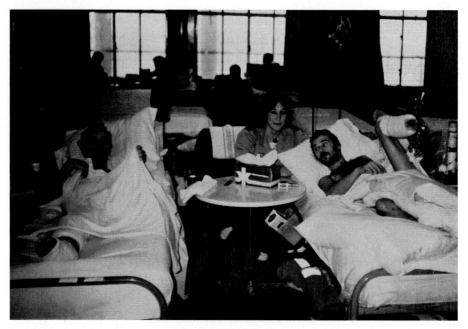

L to R: L/Cpl Denzil Connick, QARNNS SNN Sally Middleton, L/Cpl Roy Bassey in the ICU.
IWM photograph FKD797
Photograph courtesy of the Imperial War Museum, London

By the time Denzil reached us in the middle of June, Sergeant Major John Phillips and Chief Petty Officer John Strange were both well enough for the long return journey by sea and air back to UK. John Strange was transferred to HMS *Hecla* on June 12th, and John Phillips to HMS *Hydra* on June 14th, the day before Denzil and some of the other casualties from the Mount Longdon Battle arrived on board The Hospital Ship.

This is what John Strange and John Phillips wrote about that part of their voyage home:

JOHN STRANGE:

On a ship in the South Atlantic is not the ideal conditions in which to carry out plastic surgery but the operations to graft my hands and arms were carried out with great success by Surgeon Commander Chapman and his competent theatre staff. After five weeks in the capable hands of some wonderful QARNNS Naval Nurses in the burns unit I was soon up and about and fit enough to make the long journey back to UK. This would be by stretcher, back to England via the hospital support ship HMS *Hecla* to Montevideo, and then by RAF transport plane arriving at Brize Norton on the 17th June.

JOHN PHILLIPS:

The next phase of my repatriation was a four day journey to Montevideo aboard the Ambulance Ship HMS *Hydra*. The "passengers" as we were referred to by the crew, were accommodated in their respective messes and were looked after like kings. As I only had one arm, I had a Nelson's Knife made for me by Steve "Robbie" Robinson, the ship's Petty Officer Engineer, which enabled me to cut meat and eat more easily. The crew vacated their cabins and bunks so that we could use them. A great bunch of lads! It was during the journey to Montevideo that we received the news of the Argentinian surrender. We had a little celebration in the mess. On arrival in Montevideo we were transported by coach to the airport where we boarded an RAF VC10 for the journey back to UK. On 17th June I arrived at Woolwich Military Hospital.

Sergeant Bill Belcher, severely injured in action in the BAS Scout helicopter ashore on May 28th, was also now making good progress in Sea View Ward. He describes here how he survived that period and his journey back to UK and The RAF Hospital at Wroughton:

After this early period of trauma, I started taking more notice of events around me and, as well as the constant care of the Naval nursing staff, I noticed the P&O staff helping out with nursing assistance and trying to feed those who were up to it. The Royal Marine Bandsmen were also in constant attendance, as they moved the wounded and helped out with basic nursing care. And then there were the Argentine wounded. I found myself slowly getting surrounded by them after about a week and got particularly peeved with their arrogant, unforgiving and demanding attitudes. 'Agua' became an irritating shout and was often met by some poor orderly having to fetch and carry without thanks or appreciation. I became a little naughty and started reaching for tubes and drips that could be dislodged but failed to reach any of consequence. I had a serious word with the Padre one afternoon and, before I could inflict any long-term damage he had me moved into a British enclave within the ward. After that, just the odd enemy casualty was in proximity and, fortunately, I didn't have to speak much. Throughout though, the Argies got fair treatment from all the medical staff and we often ended up quite close to their hospital ship in the "Red Cross Box" to ship their casualties over.

About ten days after I reached Sea View Ward, there was much commotion and shuffling of patients. Then we heard that one of the LSLs had been hit and burn casualties started appearing by the dozen. Hands wrapped in plastic bags and a lot of burnt Welsh Guards' casualties. Poor sods had been at anchor and had little escape from the burning ship. Many had varying degrees of burns but all were destined for the UK, so The Hospital Ship *Uganda* was under severe pressure due to the numbers. This was a dark day for the Task Force indeed.

By this time, the decision to evacuate me was formally delayed until my left leg was stabilised fully and fit for the long journey home. Then, two weeks after the initial injury, the stitches came out of my right leg and that was it for that side. Further treatment on my left leg followed and then a final "restraining cast" to hold it together was set in place and I was declared "ready to move". I would be on the next survey ship doing the "Ambulance run" to Montevideo. By now, good news of the ceasefire had reached us and The Hospital Ship moved in closer and round to Stanley Harbour. Someone kindly judged me to be fit enough for a bath chair, and one of the nurses pushed me out onto one of the weather decks for my first fresh air for three weeks and direct sight of terra firma.

I felt as though another phase had been reached and the marvellous staff on *Uganda* had pulled me through ready for the next stage. The cast on my left leg was slit to allow for atmospheric pressure and then I was transferred to HMS *Herald*. On board, a central mess deck had been turned into a ward for stretcher cases and we set sail for the River Plate and Uruguay. The crew managed to carry me up to a satellite telephone and I made my first contact with the UK, assuring my fiancée that I was as well as could be expected and 'on my way'. After four days we tied up in "Monte" and the next morning we were moved by stretcher onto the quayside and were greeted by a fleet of Uruguayan ambulances, US sedan style, with one casualty in each vehicle plus driver and medic. We formed a long convoy and drove straight through the city and everything came to a halt as we passed through to the airport. Once there we loaded onto an RAF VC10 fitted for medevac, with a 3-tier stretcher fitting through most of the cabin. Some of the serious casualties were suffering badly by this stage and excellent care from RAF medics was quite timely. I was by no means the worst of the bunch.

* * *

Meanwhile, for us all on board The Hospital Ship there was obviously some feeling of relief that in time, following the surrender, casualty flow would eventually reduce. However, as has been explained in previous chapters, our on-board patients were still going to require much ongoing surgery before we could see any reduction in our daily theatre lists; so basically, we all just continued as before. Later in the day of June 14th someone told us in Theatres that HRH Prince Andrew had landed on our flight deck in a Sea King helicopter with two casualties from HMS *Glamorgan*, asking for one of our apparently highly thought of bacon sarnies; the P&O Chief Purser had promptly obliged!

QARNNS Head Naval Nurse Maggie Freer adds:

> When we heard white flags were flying over Stanley, our ward team toasted the surrender on the 14th June with glasses of orange juice with RN Doctor Jim Warner. The patients were amazing, full of fortitude and bravery, rarely complaining and always trying to help each other out. I have a photo of five patients in their late teens and early twenties in a row in their beds, all with only one lower limb each, all sharing a joke with members of the staff.

In fact, casualties continued to arrive, albeit in lower numbers, for some weeks to come. Many were severe limb injuries from the indiscriminately laid Argentinian anti-personnel mines. Another was a serious facial wound from a "booby-trapped" oil drum. It was obvious to all of us on board The Hospital Ship who treated and cared for all the wounded that they were going to have to face a significant amount of treatment and rehabilitation in the years ahead; many would, of course, live with their injuries for the rest of their days. But somehow, these "aftermath of war" injuries seemed harder for us all to deal with.

QARNNS Naval Nurse Karen Dawson continues to describe her work in the Intensive Care Unit at this time:

> We did shifts or Navy watches of four hours on four hours off around the clock and sometimes if a lot of patients came aboard at the same time we'd stay on duty till it calmed down a bit, especially when the *Sir Galahad* went down.
>
> I can remember we had three patients needing ventilation (external breathing apparatus) and at the beginning we only had one ventilator that worked. We borrowed one from The Hospital ashore in Stanley which was very old, but in fact it was the better one as it balanced itself out when the ship rocked. So we would all work shifts for what we call "hand-bagging"; that's a technique used for breathing for the patients by hand around the clock. Doctor Bull, Doctor Baker and Sister Law trained the nurses how to do this on the way down and we then trained the RM stretcher-bearers in this technique so we could all get some sleep.
>
> I looked after a sailor off the *Coventry* who was found floating in the sea in his lifejacket; he was hypothermic at 28c. He had to be ventilated on the ship's ventilator and the alarm kept going off when the ship rolled.

He was very lucky. Without the ICU facilities we had for keeping people going with their breathing on board The Hospital Ship he could have been classed as dead and unsalvageable. He will always stick in my mind as I had been looking after him for so long, to warm him up and keep him alive; and we had been calling him a particular name which we thought was his. Then, when the wonderful time came when he started to wake up, his first words when he came off the ventilator were: 'Stop calling me Jack, that's not my name!' That still makes me smile, not because we had called him by another name, just the fact he was alive and talking.

I remember another patient with a tracheostomy (an opening into the windpipe to assist external ventilation) which blocked up and he went into respiratory arrest, but we managed to unblock it and bring him round. Then to our shock and delight not long afterwards he decided to bimble off with some other patients and go off to the ship's pictures as if nothing had happened just a few hours before! I can't imagine that happening now.

I nursed an Argentinian who had been shot on his eighteenth birthday. He was quite a mess when he arrived; he'd been shot in the face, and the entry wound went through one cheek and the exit wound through his mouth. I will always remember that look of fear in his eyes when a plane went over us, and also when he regained consciousness and found out where he was. We had a Gurkha soldier who had recovered from his injuries who was waiting to be sent to Montevideo and he had been given a small toy to make and he patiently sat and made it. When he was sent off in the ambulance ship he was told he could take it with him; he was so pleased, nearly to tears. I do remember Denzil Connick from 3 Para; I have a photo of him with some of the other patients when they were getting better on the ward.

The patient I remember the most was Smudge Smith. Smudge was a Royal Navy chef from HMS *Glamorgan* who was very severely wounded when HMS *Glamorgan* was hit by a land-launched Exocet on June 12th. He went through so much; what with losing the arm, the skin grafts, and very severe leg injuries. But he had a good sense of humour considering all that he was going through. The first thing he said to me when he arrived in ICU 8,000 miles from home was that I had a green mini! How could he know this? He had remembered that he'd made my mate's wedding cake the previous year and we had put it in the mini's boot together so I could take it to the wedding… in spite of all his injuries we had a good giggle together and I hope that helped cheer him on his way.

When we all got back to UK I used to bump into him when we were out in Portsmouth. He had his new prosthetic hand then, and it used to hurt when he pinched you, and I won't say where he pinched me! He still had his sense of humour then.

* * *

Our MOIC Surgeon Captain Rintoul was also an ophthalmic surgeon, and carried out several eye operations in Theatre in the next few days. Fortunately, he had brought most of his "eye" instruments with him from RNH Haslar, so it was easy to sterilise these much smaller sets of instruments, as required, in our faithful autoclave "Vesuvius". Vesuvius was continuing to provide sterling service for all our OT equipment and for the much-needed dressing packs, etc now in such demand throughout the hospital. Vesuvius was now an integral family friend, and his (her?) continued reliable running at such high load levels was a tribute to our CPO (O) MA Jim Lacey. The daily temperatures were dropping quickly now as the southern hemisphere (Austral) winter started to bite, and we were glad of the reassuring warmth as we fired Vesuvius up, especially first thing in the cold morning watches.

One of those treated post-surrender was Tim Miller, a Falkland Islander who had been injured some weeks before at his farm on West Falkland. He had gone to the door on hearing a bang, when a second explosion occurred and he felt something enter his right eye with immediate loss of sight and considerable pain. The pain slowly reduced, but the sight didn't return. He realised there was little he could do across on West Falkland with a full-scale battle raging all around him, so carried on with his farming routines until he could be transported to Stanley after the hostilities. He had travelled a considerable distance via San Carlos, HMS *Fearless* and Ajax Bay Field Hospital before finally reaching us on June 13th.

I assisted Captain Rintoul in Tim's surgery. We extracted a sizeable piece of non-ferrous shrapnel from Tim's right eye. He was lucky in some ways; probably due to the heat of the fragment, it was, in fact, sterile when it entered the eye, so no infection ensued. The vision in his left eye was not damaged. The surrender came at a fortunate stage in Tim's treatment on board The Hospital Ship. Another protocol of working under Geneva Convention restrictions is that casualties treated on board Hospital Ships are not permitted to return to the fighting zone; this would also apply to civilians treated on board during a conflict. So, potentially, Tim might have had a much lengthier return journey back to his farm on West Falkland… of about 16,000 miles, via UK! As it was, he spent some time ashore in Stanley with his parents after June 14th, until he returned for his final check-up and discharge from our care later in June.

For our teams in The Hospital Ship operating theatres, the weeks of late June and into July 1982 proceeded with surgical requirements continuing, although daily casualty numbers were now fortunately declining in the weeks following the surrender. Our way ahead seemed uncertain. Casualties continued to arrive, and care and treatment had to be provided.

Another injured soldier who came to us at that time was Robert ("Ossie") Osborn, a Guardsman in the Second Battalion Scots Guards, who had been severely injured in the battle for Mount Tumbledown. By coincidence, Ossie was admitted on the same day as Denzil Connick, whose story is at the beginning of this chapter.

This is the start of Ossie's war, from his voyage down to Grytviken on board the *QE2*, his injury on Mount Tumbledown and his casevac to The Hospital Ship:

In 1982: Guardsman Robert "Ossie" Osborn 2nd Battalion Scots Guards

In 1982 I was a twenty-one year old Guardsman in 13 Platoon Left Flank 2nd Battalion Scots Guards. The Battalion had recently returned to Public Duties in UK from a six-month tour in Northern Ireland (Company Commanders Rover Group in West Belfast). I had joined the Battalion in Germany when they were in a Mechanised Infantry role.

We left Southampton on 12th May 1982 on the *QE2* and sailed to Grytviken via Freetown in Sierra Leone and Ascension Island. Whilst zeroing our night sights off the front of the *QE2* we shot the front rail off! In Grytviken we cross-decked on to the *Canberra* to get us to San Carlos Water.

After a few days in San Carlos we boarded Landing Ship *Intrepid* to sail round to just North of Lively Island, followed by a two-hour trip in Landing Craft into Bluff Cove (well that was the idea). The Navy dropped us well South of Lively Island and we had an eight hour run into Bluff during which our own navy fired at us, but we managed to dodge them.

We arrived in Bluff Cove on 6th June the day before 1st Btn The Welsh Guards came round from San Carlos in the *Galahad*. Although Bluff Cove is within the same inlet of water as Fitzroy, it is about 15 miles to the north by land; there is a small settlement at each inlet.

On 13th June we moved by helicopter to our Forming Up Area (FUA) on Goat Ridge prior to our Attack on Mount Tumbledown. Five minutes after we were supposed to have crossed the Start Line (SL) I was still sitting on it with my back to Tumbledown eating a tin of tuna with hard tack biscuits.

After Left Flank had completed its part of the attack I was detailed to act as a security screen for a stretcher party returning to the Regimental Aid Post (RAP). After a short distance we stopped and swapped places, with the stretcher-bearers becoming the Screen and the Screen becoming Bearers. Five seconds after we restarted we were hit by mortar fire. The person I swapped with, Gdsm David Malcolmson, was killed outright, and my left leg was badly injured.

Another party from Left Flank returning from the RAP were the first to reach us. My first question was where had my glasses gone? They carried those of us who were unable to walk back to the RAP, from where I was helicoptered first to Fitzroy, then to Ajax Bay. From Goat Ridge to Fitzroy my legs were sticking out of the side of the helicopter, with the tarpaulin covering them flapping; it bloody well hurt, and using unprintable language I told the crewman so when we landed!

I was in the field hospital at Ajax Bay when the surrender was announced.

From Ajax Bay I was helicoptered out to "Mother Hen", The Hospital Ship *Uganda*. My first memory was being carried down to "Sea View" Ward and scrounging a packet of ciggies off a young P&O crew member who was nicknamed "Storm". Once on "Sea View", the high dependency ward at the stern of the ship, I met with Staff Nurse (SNN) Diana Aldwinckle, and lost my last piece of clothing (i.e. my underpants).

On the sixth day on board, Surgeon Lieutenant Warner came to see me and explained the full extent of my injuries, and that I was going to lose the leg.

Two days later (five years to the day after I had left school) my left leg was amputated.

I was surprised that the Medical Staff had tried to save my leg, but in the long run for me, anyway, it helped, as it gave me some time to adjust to everything. I remember signing the consent form with Doctor Bull and Theatre Sister Nicci Pugh whilst on the operating table; they were both very kind and seemed to care about every patient individually, which is quite something, considering the job they were doing, and the rate of casualties going through their Operating Theatres at the time.

* * *

Doctor Susie West had joined *Canberra* as Assistant Surgeon on January 1st 1982. She describes the meeting of the two P&O liners north of Falkland Sound on the morning of June 15th:

It is always oddly emotional when two related ships meet at sea. The Hospital Ship *Uganda* was steaming along very close to us. Lots of people came out onto the rails and started waving madly. Little *Uganda* gave a blast on her whistle and *Canberra* gave a huge blast back that echoed round the Sound. *Uganda* replied again with a rather hoarse effort, and once again we responded with a deep full-blooded boom. It brought tears to my tired eyes. I am sure I was not alone.

An extract from Doctor West's report of when she visited The Hospital Ship *Uganda* on June 23rd reads:

> The horrors of war were there for all to see. The ship floats in her own world very far removed from *Canberra's* war-like atmosphere. The Hospital Ship *Uganda* floats in euphoria, surrounded in heartbreak. Only the relief of her patients, that they are alive, keeps the place from falling into tragedy. The patients are very different from ours. *Uganda* took over the job we initially thought we were doing. The maiming I witnessed there is horrible, just horrible, even for me who has a pretty strong stomach. For them the war will never end. Every moment of their lives they will be reminded of it.

* * *

On June 21st we departed Grantham Sound for Port William, where we anchored in the Inner Harbour for the first time at 1500. We remained there until June 29th.

Although we were unaware of it at the time, The Hospital Ship, with more than 40 patients on board, had steamed straight through a live Argentinian minefield! This is how it occurred:

There are two ways to travel by sea from Grantham Sound to Port William (the outer harbour for Port Stanley): the northerly route past Cape Dolphin and The Eddystone Rock, or the southerly route past George, Bleaker and Lively Islands. We chose the latter, which leaves Cape Pembroke to port as you enter the outer harbour of Port William. The day after our arrival in Port William, our Commanding Officer of NP1830, Commander Andy Gough, was speaking with the Queen's Harbour Master (QHM) in Stanley. Commander Gough commented that it was nice to see the minesweeper flotilla at work, exercising off Cape Pembroke under the command of Commander Peter Fish, a Naval colleague and friend of Commander Gough's. The conversation continued along these lines:

QHM: 'Exercising, Andy? They're not exercising! They're clearing the live minefield off Cape Pembroke. Why? Which way did you come in?'

Commander Gough: 'Round Cape Pembroke...'

Both officers leapt to their feet to study the charts and there, in front of them, was the large "cheese" of live mined area, extending at least five nautical miles out to sea to the east from Cape Pembroke. We had steamed straight through the middle of the mined area at 12 knots, and it had not been cleared at that time.

This close shave with disaster arose because The Hospital Ship's status under The Geneva Convention had prevented us exchanging classified or secure information with other ships, and was not the fault of Commander Gough, our P&O Officers or RN Officers. The information about the minefield was indeed classified "Secret", so we weren't given any special instructions about how to approach Port William. Andy has since described his need to "sit down rather quickly" when all this was revealed to him. I suspect a "medicinal tot" might have been called for, as the gentlemen then took steps to ensure that all the many other ships operating in the area were fully aware of the situation.

Once we had arrived in Port William, groups of us were now able to spend a few hours ashore during this time. The first trip I made was with Sister Margaret Kerr, the other Operating Theatre Sister; we needed to exchange some surgical items with our colleagues at The King Edward VII Memorial Hospital in Stanley, so it was very much a work-related trip and we couldn't linger. The other trip ashore was with a group of friends – Sister Jill Lee (Sea View Ward), Sister Jean Kidd (CRA) and Sister Chris Asendorf (Burns Unit). We all wore wellies; Jean's were bright red and caused much mirth to some Paras in their red berets walking in the opposite direction! Even with a watery southern hemisphere winter sun it was still bitterly cold, but for all of us it was just wonderful to feel the earth beneath our feet for a short time. Stanley itself had obviously taken some battering; the few roads were more mud tracks than roads, but there were already many signs of repair going on by troops stationed ashore. We all bought first edition stamp covers from The Post Office; when we got back I had mine framed and treasure them to this day.

Here, QARNNS Naval Nurse Karen Dawson briefly describes her one trip ashore to Stanley on July 13th:

> The one day I went ashore in The Falklands was my twenty-second birthday, July 13th 1982, which was also the day we ceased to be a Hospital Ship. I've got a photo of myself wrapped up as if I was going to the Arctic, as it was thick snow, not what we are used to in the middle of July in the UK. That was the day the group of Welsh Guardsmen were injured while they were clearing snow at the airfield.

…and QARNNS Head Naval Nurse Maggie Freer:

> A week after the hostilities had ceased we sailed from Grantham Sound, and were escorted into Port William by a Hull Trawler which was a familiar sight to me as I come from Grimsby. We then became the hospital for the area and continued to take casualties, including some civilians from Stanley. Our ward and the triage/CRA area were dismantled on 8th July and the Intensive Care Unit then became Stanley Ward. David *(Maggie's husband, who was serving on HMS* Intrepid*)*

came on board several times escorting casualties from the fleet. *Intrepid* sailed for home on the afternoon of 26th June. One of the staff came to tell me and I asked permission to leave the ward to watch them sail. I stayed at the rail watching until the ship disappeared over the horizon before returning to the ward, and it was pretty emotional, I have to say. On board The Hospital Ship we had no idea at that time when we would be going home, and we knew the return voyage would be three weeks, so there was still much worry and uncertainty for us all. Boat trips were organised to Stanley and on the 7th July I had my first taste of dry land since sailing from Gibraltar on the 19th April.

P&O Chief Officer Grahame Burton covers the same period:

On 21st June we sailed into Port William harbour at the entrance to Port Stanley. This was made more eventful, as we found out later, by us having sailed right through a live minefield which was in the process of being cleared. One of the drawbacks of not being in the (communications) loop on matters military! Once at anchor here my workload increased immensely, as many transfers were now by boat, and the ship's boats were often also being used for shore leave. It was all extremely informal for some time after the surrender, and if I wished to go ashore or visit some battle site ashore, it was relatively easy to hitch a ride there and back by helicopter, as there were still a multitude of them criss-crossing the skies over Stanley. Alan Newby, one of the *Uganda* Electrical Officers and also a keen numismatist (coin collector), was with me when we went into the Treasury part of the main government building and asked if they had any interesting items we could obtain. They opened a large safe for us and we purchased several items, including brand new Falkland Island 10 shilling notes which we kept as souvenirs.

Word soon went round the naval ships in Port Stanley that *Uganda* had a large supply of various brands of port in her store rooms, still left on board from her cruising days. There were many requests from RN Wardrooms for transfers, and a healthy bartering system was soon in place around the diminishing fleet still left operating around The Islands. Although we still had patients on board, on Saturday 3rd July we were permitted to proceed on a mini Falkland Island cruise, and on Sunday cruised in Falkland Sound including a brief diversion into Port San Carlos. Monday saw us entering Ship Harbour on New Island off West Falkland, where it had been planned to anchor and allow people ashore. Unfortunately the weather that morning was strong winds with snow showers, and it did not prove possible to anchor. However the scenery looked beautiful, if somewhat bleak, and we could see the few inhabitants who lived there going about their everyday tasks.

Tuesday 6th July found us back at anchor in Port William, and thoughts turning to when we might be released to sail north. It was ironic that we watched videos of *Canberra's* homecoming to Southampton, whilst we were still in the Falklands. On Saturday 10th July we hosted a party on board for the children of Port Stanley. They all seemed to have a wonderful time and several wrote thank you cards to the ship, one of which I kept and used as a bookmark in my diary for many years.

From July 3rd to July 6th we set off on a "Round The Falkland Islands Cruise". Unfortunately poor weather followed us all the way, with snow, sub-zero temperatures and poor visibility. The wind remained resolutely stronger than gale force 8 for the whole three days, and so most of us were glad to return to Port William on July 6th. We still had more than 50 patients on board at the time who were requiring further surgery, treatment and care, so we didn't see very much of the West Falklands coastline.

We did, however, reach our most Westerly point 51.50' S 61.24' West, and our most southerly point, south of Barren Island, 52.30.6'S 59.40'W, which was notable for a ship that had previously not been south of The Equator in The Atlantic Ocean. It also gave us an opportunity to operate the desalinators, which for technical reasons could only be used some three nautical miles from land. We passed Pebble Island, Swan Island, Barren Island and finally Sea Lion Island; although I have to say we didn't see much of them! On arrival back in Port William, *Hydra* came alongside, and we transferred 56 patients for further "on-move" to UK. This was to be HMS *Hydra*'s final return trip, so we said our farewells to this vital link in our onward patient transfer and stores supply route, with much gratitude for their reliable support over the last few months.

On July 7th our RN Padre, Rev David Barlow, and I hosted Canon and Mrs Harry Bagnall on board for a few hours. Canon Bagnall was then Anglican vicar in charge of Christchurch Cathedral and the Falkland Islands Anglican population. As I was one of the few regular Anglican communicants on board this was a great privilege and, unknown to me at the time, the start of a deep and affectionate relationship that I have since built with Christchurch Cathedral Stanley and its incumbent clergy. Sadly, there was no opportunity for us to worship in The Cathedral on this visit... so I quietly made a vow to try to return when I could. It took some 22 years to fulfil, but I eventually made the return trip, more of which can be read in the final chapter of this book.

On July 10th a party of 90 or so Falklands' schoolchildren attended a "P&O Children's Party" on board. We were working in our operating theatres that morning, but could still hear the unusual noise of children's laughter as we worked; it cheered us all up a lot. They were given lunch, a tour of the ship, P&O "goody bags" and some fancy dress and entertainment in the afternoon. These children are now grown-up and some are Stanley residents today.

Leona Roberts remembers the party well:

Leona Roberts (now Manager, Falkland Islands Museum and National Trust in Stanley) (In 1982: Falkland Islander Miss Leona Vidal Age 10)

Photograph: *Author's private collection*

This was the first time we had a chance to really play as kids again, and start to put behind us the fear of the last few months. I was aged ten in 1982, so it was a really big thing at that age being invited on board a ship like *Uganda*, not something any of us would have had the chance to experience. Some of us in The Islands today definitely remember staying on board overnight. That might have been a different trip, but we all remember it well, and it all being a huge adventure, as well as all the excitement of the children's party on board.

Finally, the incoming casualty numbers were reducing, and we could start to de-commission parts of the hospital in a phased way to maintain some operational capability until our role had officially changed. By July 13th we had received our orders to de-register as a Hospital Ship by 1300 on that day. Thereafter, as a troopship, carrying The First Battalion Seventh Gurkha Rifles (1/7th Gurkha Rifles) and 16 Field Ambulance Royal Army Medical Corps (16FA RAMC), we were to proceed to UK with an estimated date of arrival approximately August 8th/9th.

And so it was, during the morning of July 13th 1982, that I was leaning on our last in-use anaesthetic machine in our operating theatres on board The Hospital Ship *Uganda*, the scene of such intense life-saving efforts and tinged with so much sadness for us all, when, once again, the familiar sound of incoming casualty-carrying helicopters reached our ears. It was this course of events I wrote about in some detail in Chapter One, "A Grey Dawn Breaking".

It was a tough day for all the trauma teams on board, but more especially for the unsuspecting injured soldiers who had been cheerfully clearing snow from the runway just some minutes before. Hundreds of injured servicemen had come to our flight deck in the last few months needing our help, care and professional expertise, and so, in that final explosive day, our routines kicked in instantly for them all. Each injured soldier required rapid blood transfusions and fortunately "Mark's Blood Bank", as we now called it, was still operational. There was a genuine moment of near disaster as, unbelievably, two of the soldiers with the same surname – Jones (well, they were Welsh Guardsmen, after all...) also had the same Christian name... but... *different* blood groups. Some hasty re-checking ensued and eventually everyone got the right blood group transfusion! *

    * The Welsh Guardsmen have subsequently told me that's why they all call each other by their surname and the last two (or sometimes three) digits of their service number instead of using Christian names.

In this next section, we read from the memories of one of those soldiers, Lance Sergeant John Jones. He tells us of his early days in the Army as a soldier in The Welsh Guards, his journey from the UK to The Falkland Islands in May 1982, his route from San Carlos to Stanley, and how he and his unit happened to be working at Stanley airfield during the morning of July 13th:

In 1982: Lance Sergeant John Jones "39" First Battalion Welsh Guards

Photograph: Author's private collection

In 1982 I was a Lance Sergeant (LSGT) in The First Battalion Welsh Guards serving as "Alpha" Mortar Fire Controller (MFC) to No 2 Company. The "Bravo" MFC was L/Sgt Dave Edwards known as "65". Being a Jones I was known as "39". This is a tradition in The Welsh Guards that we all call each other by the last two numbers of our Service Numbers, because so many of us have the same surname. I had joined the Welsh Guards in 1974, having given up a not-so-promising career with Nat West bank. I had served in Cyprus, Caterham and Berlin, and it was in Cyprus that I started my life-long attachment to Mortars.

    We joined the requisitioned Cunard Cruise Ship *QE2* with about 5,000 other troops and left Southampton on May 12th (with the rest of 5 Brigade). I didn't think it would actually come to conflict initially, but once we got to Ascension it finally dawned on us that this was for real. When the shooting started rumours reached us thick and fast, including one that we would garrison the place after the Marines and Paras had re-captured it, which was not a prospect that filled us with joy.

We eventually cross-decked to *Canberra* off South Georgia, and arrived in San Carlos Water on June 2nd. We made a dash into San Carlos, landed at the wooden jetty and set off to cross Sussex Mountains, but later retuned to HMS *Fearless* to position ourselves at Bluff Cove, and then move towards Wall Mountain. So it was that 2 Company Battalion, HQ "Recce", and the Machine Gun Platoon landed the day before the *Galahad* and *Tristram* came round to Fitzroy by sea for June 7th. We were about five miles away, inland as the crow flies, when the attack happened. I remember it was a very clear and bright day, with excellent visibility, and we saw the Argentine Skyhawks and Mirages come over very, very low, and later, looking back at the ships, we could all see the great thick black cloud of smoke and a host of helicopter activity. Both Dave "65" and I had many close friends on board at the time, and I had the unenviable task of telling him his brother-in-law was one of those missing. The following day "65" and I were attached to the A1 echelon, and continued moving forward, ending up just short of Stanley when the war ended on June 14th.

Within a few days we were setting up the company's accommodation in Stanley. We were billeted in the court room, and even to this day you can see the nails in the walls where we put up washing lines to get our kit dry. At this time I was the acting company clerk, typing out lists of names of the missing and doing the admin as needed. Fatigue parties were required for various tasks and so, on July 13th, I detailed myself onto one at the airport. I wanted to get some fresh air and escape the claustrophobic atmosphere that hung in the makeshift company office in the Town Hall. I had lost many friends and colleagues back at Fitzroy, some of whom I had known all my army service, and it was taking time to come to terms with it all.

We arrived at the airport on a cold windy morning but it was at least dry. Our task was to clear snow and ice from the runway. By this time the air-bridge was operational and RAF Hercules transport planes would fly to and from Ascension with refuelling en route. We only had our entrenching tools for the job and it seemed a bit of an uphill struggle.

During the morning we were ordered off the runway as a Combat Air Patrol (CAP) of two Harriers was being put up. We shuffled to the edge of the runway and were standing in groups just off the tarmac. I remember watching the Harriers turn onto the runway and begin their take-off. I noticed two very bright white lights appear under the wings of one and thought it looked like it had fired its Sidewinder missiles.

The next thing I knew I was lying on my back and I could hear someone moaning. I thought someone was injured and tried to get up. At this point my left leg came into view and the foot was missing. I thought, 'Christ, I'm hurt, I'd better get some help'…then a wave of pain washed over me. I began to cry out and a group of guys gathered round me. "98" Jones administered first aid but we had no morphine as it had been handed in the previous day. A couple of SAS guys came over and fortunately they still had theirs and I was given two shots. This worked quite well and steadied things a bit. The guy told me 'Remember, you've had two shots… tell them two shots' as he wrote it on my forehead. Helicopters appeared and the evacuation began. I was flown with 3 other guys to the Hospital Ship *Uganda*. Even though they weren't expecting us, and were closing down as a hospital that very day, the staff were magnificent and I was rushed to some place where immediate treatment began. I told everyone who came near me that I'd had two shots; I guess I was a bit like a stuck record. A surgeon asked if I knew what the score was and I said I thought I'd lost both legs below the knees which he confirmed. He said they would need to tidy things up a bit and I asked him to try to keep my right knee as I thought the amputation was very close to the knee. He said he'd do what he could. At this point a nurse approached and asked for my thumb. I asked why and she said they needed to test my blood. I was put out by this as I was "non compos mentis" as they say, and told her my blood group, date of birth and regimental number and showed her my dog tags and anyway wasn't enough pissing out the other end? She apologised but said she had to do it, so I had my thumb pricked and blood tested.

The next thing I remember is moving to the Operating Theatres. There was a pause outside and the morphine must have worn off as it was hurting like hell and all I could think was could they not put me out so I couldn't feel anything any more. The taste of onions and that was it.

From then on all is very much a blur. I remember seeing various people come and visit me on the *Uganda* but I really don't remember who or when and to this day I can't remember the wonderful medical teams that took such care of us. It transpires that 11 of us were injured by the Sidewinder but mercifully there were no fatalities.

As I have described in Chapter One and earlier in the book, our trauma reception routines on board kicked straight back in on that day. During the late morning we patched up all the eight soldiers, and settled them into our last few remaining beds, which by now were conveniently situated in what had been The Intensive Care Unit adjacent to the operating theatres.

By this time, our Royal Army Medical Corps and Queen Alexandra's Royal Army Nursing Corps colleagues ashore were now ready to officially take over from us at the King Edward the Seventh Memorial Hospital in Stanley, known as KEMH. They had, we understood, worked miracles in restoring this formerly delightful hospital to some of its previous working efficiency. The severity of the injuries on that day had precipitated the sensible decision to divide the casualty load between the two military hospital facilities. How very, very fortunate it was that we still had our one last Operating Table and all the essential accompanying equipment still in place for that last fateful day.

Chapter Eight

"THE LONG TRICK'S OVER"

July 14th – August 9th 1982

The next afternoon, July 14th, the eight injured Welsh Guardsmen were all well enough to transfer across to King Edward VIIth Memorial Hospital (KEMH) in Stanley, together with our last on-board patient, another Welsh Guardsman. We knew they would remember little of their time with us, and it was much better that way. Eventually, they would be airlifted back to UK in the recently opened air-bridge route that operated for a few months after The Hospital Ship, now SS Troopship *Uganda*, left The Falkland Islands.

Here, John Jones continues his story from his time in KEMH up to his arrival at The Military Hospital, Woolwich in late July:

> My next recollections are arriving at the old hospital (KEMH) in Stanley; I must have been choppered there but I really don't remember. How long and what happened there I really don't recall; from what I remember there were wooden wall panels painted green... The battalion was now on its way back home with just the few of us left in Stanley, and altogether it was all a bit depressing.
>
> Eventually after about a week in Stanley I was to be flown home by RAF Hercules via Ascension. I remember the ambulances taking us to the Stanley airfield, and just as our stretchers were about to be loaded aboard another Combat Air Patrol of Harrier aircraft was about to go up. This made me very nervous and more than a little anxious. But the nurse was fantastic and steadied my overstrung nerves. I don't know exactly how many of us were being casevacd back to UK. I must have had a big shot of something as the next thing I remember is arriving at Ascension. The tail gate was lowered and the hot humid air flooded into the back of the plane.

We were given an ice-cold drink of orange and the rest of the passengers disembarked and we were left aboard. It got hotter and hotter in the plane and we seemed to be there for ever with our thirst increasing. Eventually we were loaded onto a VC10 for the return leg to Brize Norton. I must have been given another big shot of something as I don't have any real recollection of the flight. At Brize we were transferred onto choppers and flown to an RAF hospital near Marlborough (RAF Hospital Wroughton). There I was greeted by my Mother, Father and my girlfriend, soon to be wife. After what must have been a very difficult reunion for them, things settled down for the night. The following day was another chopper ride, this time to QEMH Woolwich for the final tidying up and then rehab.

* * *

At 1600 on July 14th we weighed anchor, heading initially back to Grantham Sound, where the first Gurkha troops were waiting to be embarked. The next group were embarked from Fox Bay in (another!) gale Force 8.

Here, after 26 years, P&O Chief Officer Grahame Burton reveals the mystery of *Uganda*'s funnel colour change! (Not that any bottles of port might have changed hands, eh, Grahame?) And his thoughts as we finally left The Falkland Islands:

13th July brought news of our forward plans and marked our last day as an officially designated Hospital Ship, and we were then to transport some of the remaining troops back to UK. Instructions were received that the red crosses on the hull and funnel were to be painted over. This was a task for my sailors and it was something that I had been giving some prior thought to.

There was traditionally much rivalry in P&O Cruises between the Officers who had trained with British India (BI) and those of us who were from P&O. Whilst cruising had consolidated under the name of P&O, there were still several senior officers from BI afloat and several ex BI persons in senior positions ashore. The last visible vestige of BI afloat in 1982 was the black funnel of SS *Uganda* with its two white bands, which had been painted white with red crosses prior to the conflict. We P&O officers were always threatening to paint it the P&O buff colour, but of course never did. After it became apparent that our days as a Hospital Ship were numbered, the Bosun and I began securing a supply of suitable coloured paint, however, the only colours, apart from white and black, that we had on board were small supplies of colours for painting the various dormitories. By the time the instruction to "paint out the red crosses" was received, we were ready with enough buff paint, and a break in the weather enabled us to start right away.

All the sailors were set to work painting the funnel a wonderful P&O buff coloured yellow, and by next day I was able to send a message to our management, that the red crosses were now painted over, and that the ship was now resplendent in traditional Troopship yellow. Peter Motion, our Director Fleet, and Frank Kemp, his assistant in the London office, both ex BI personnel, were horrified and wanted to know if the crosses could not just be painted out with white paint, as had been done with the crosses on the hull. Unfortunately it was too late, as bad weather and the fact that we commenced embarking the Gurkha Regiment next day, meant that this really was not possible. As an aside, I had a message from one of the helicopter pilots a day or so later, telling me that one of my sailors had left a rather rude message painted on the top plating of the funnel, where no one would normally be able to see. The Bosun was tasked with having this removed.

Our reverse osmosis plants were now in full operation, thanks to hard work by our Chief Engineer, David King, and 2nd Engineer Peter Johnson, with help from RN Lt. Towers. However, with the increasing numbers of persons on board, it was still necessary to fill up with fresh water whenever possible. On 17th July we berthed alongside the tanker *Fort Toronto*, which had been put into service purely as a water carrier. Just before noon on 18th July we weighed anchor for the last time and sailed on a north easterly course for Ascension Island. I remember standing on the bridge wing taking a last look at the misty outline of the hills of the Falkland Islands and thinking: 'I probably won't be seeing these islands again'…How wrong I was.

We returned to Port William on Saturday July 17th, fuelled and watered from RFA *Fort Toronto* and were ready to depart; but now thick fog delayed our final departure by another day.

At this time there was a very poorly female patient in Stanley called Cheryl Bonner. She was 28 years old, but Cheryl was severely handicapped and needed long-term medical care in UK. At the request of H.E. The Governor Rex Hunt, who had by now returned to The Falkland Islands as Governor, it was agreed we would transport Cheryl up to Ascension, from where she could be flown on to UK for further medical treatment and care. Both Cheryl (and her older sister Shirley who had died aged seven) were born with a debilitating condition that meant Cheryl required 24 hour "specialing", a nursing term that denotes constant specialised nursing care and vigil. Superintending Nursing Officer Christine Poole, who had run the high-capacity "Dormitory Ward Area" so efficiently throughout the War, set up Cheryl's round the clock care with a small team of QARNNS Naval Nurses. SNN Staff Nurse Sally Middleton (now Dr Sally Simmons) worked the night shift, and NN Karen Dawson and HNN Maggie Freer worked within the daytime watch-bill, or rota. Cheryl was transferred to us from KEMH during the morning of Sunday July 18th.

NN Karen Dawson briefly describes Cheryl's little ward area on board:

> On the way back from The Falklands to Ascension I was in the team that helped look after Cheryl Bonner, the young girl we helped get back to UK. It would be nice to find out what has happened to her. She was nursed in the ship's hospital (the same area as the Specialised Burns Unit) which was lower in the ship than the ICU and it was incredibly hot at times, so we were always glad when our shift finished. It seemed strange having just left the snow and ice of The Falklands.

...and HNN Maggie Freer also helped look after Cheryl:

> We sailed for Ascension Islands on the 18th July. I was also in the team who looked after Cheryl Bonner in the ship's hospital until she was transferred off at Ascension to fly to UK. She needed care round the clock, so we set up day and night watches as we steamed up north towards the tropics.

Finally, with smiles of immense relief from all on board, we weighed anchor for the last time from Port William, Falkland Islands on Sunday July 18th 1982. Few seemed aware it was still blowing gale force 8, except the P&O and navigational crew who admitted to having a job turning *Uganda*, now in her troop-carrying role, in the Westerly gale. With the help of a tug all seemed to think *Uganda* made her own determined statement that she was on her way home... and, come hell or high water, she turned in the hazardous anchorage, and we were at last pointing in a northerly direction towards Ascension Island and home. It was a big moment for us all; so many setbacks and false starts seemed to have delayed our departure over the last few days.

Sensibly, we kept some minimal hospital infrastructure operational until the next day, when we were well out of helicopter range from The Islands. Then we finally closed our operating theatres and the adjacent laboratory.

Surgeon Commander Peter Bull, Consultant Anaesthetist for The Task Force, reflects with some post-conflict statistics and thoughts:

> On board The Hospital Ship *Uganda* there were 540 surgical procedures, necessitating 367 general anaesthetics; 47 major sedation techniques and six epidural/spinal blocks were carried out.

Overall there were 652 General Anaesthetics by Army and Navy anaesthetists during the 4-month campaign.

All who served on board The Hospital Ship during The Falklands War were aware that Exocets could not see Red Crosses, so we never felt completely safe, especially after we heard we were even targeted by our own aircraft. The sinking of the *Belgrano* thus removing all enemy ships, was a turning point. Not only did we feel marginally safer but were able to operate closer to The Islands and consequently receive casualties more quickly.

Final packing up of all the remaining stores took some days. But the mood was rapidly lightening as we headed north to warmer weather, resuming our tropical rig by the time we reached Ascension Island. Here, one of our Anaesthetists, Surgeon Lt. Commander David Baker, left *Uganda* and joined the RAF air-bridge, as medical escort for Cheryl Bonner and her onward transfer to UK.

On July 30th we crossed The Equator... now we were officially part of "The North Atlantic Task Force"!

Superintending Nursing Officer Isa Gauld remembers assembling for "Lifeboat Drills" about this time:

> One silly story – from Gibraltar we were all allocated lifeboats if the ship went down. The lifeboat I was allocated would have a surgeon, an anaesthetist and patients as well as myself and one other theatre staff member. We also had room for stretcher-bearers (the Royal Marine bandsmen). We asked each bandsman what instrument he played and chose the most appropriate for our life boat – I envisaged us rowing away across The South Atlantic to strings and harp!!

My diary entry for July 31st reads:

> *Two days out from Ascension. We drip and perspire*
> *through the Tropics, but this time it is all much more bearable*
> *as we know we'll be home in eight days or so. We are now an*
> *"MOD Transport Ship"! We're carrying 1/7th Gurkha Rifles,*
> *16 Field Ambulance RAMC and some RFA cadets. There must*
> *be well over 1,000 military personnel on board at this stage.*
>
> *The entire hospital has now been dismantled, and all*
> *the ward, OT and ICU areas being used as recreation and*
> *exercise areas for the soldiers... and us!*

117

Some mail arrived while we briefly anchored and re-fuelled at Ascension. A new pair of much-needed white plimsolls finally arrived for me posted by a cousin in UK; this was luxury indeed. None of us ever found out why all the nursing staff were not issued with uniform shoes; it was one of those mysteries of life that we accepted with equanimity. There were plenty of "size 7 and over", but of course most of us only wore "size 5 and under"; hence our totally irregular footwear in many of the photographs in this book. The same situation occurred with the orange "once-only suits"; an all-in-one protection garment we had to wear for helicopter flights. These were only available for gents of six foot and over. The majority of the female QARNNS nurses on board The Hospital Ship were short and slightly built at about 5'1" to 5'4". These suits were supposed to stop you drowning should the chopper have to ditch into the sea, but we used to say we'd have drowned in the orange suit first, they were so oversized for us all; we literally swam around inside the suits!

In truth clothing, or "rig", or "kit" as we call it in the Services, was an issue that hadn't really been addressed before our departure. It was probably due to several factors, least of which being that our Naval Nurses were the first female Naval ratings to serve at sea, and also the haste with which the operation was mobilised. We made it up as we went along and tried to accept the situation as best we could. However, no clothing being issued for the patients on board was a different matter. For a variety of reasons many of our casualties, as described in previous chapters, arrived without clothing (burns/ battle injuries, etc), and many from the ships that had been sunk arrived with no possessions; many of them just wrapped in the foil/thermal, or military blankets that were used for warmth. We did not have adequate supplies to clothe patients on board… but P&O, as ever, came to our rescue, and issued what limited supplies they had, although those, too, soon ran out. We did ask for clothing for patients to be supplied via our South American re-supply route, but when it arrived it was some boxes from a charity shop which really upset everyone. This was 26 years ago, and charity shop goods were a far cry from the wide range of reasonable kit you can find in them today. We didn't feel we'd quite reached refugee status just yet, so I'm afraid it went to Davey Jones' locker.

Andy (now Admiral CB) Gough told us all at the April 2008 Reunion he'd given a pair of his underpants to a sailor from HMS *Sheffield*, which we all thought was bit beyond the duty of the then Senior Naval Officer, but it did make the point about the seriousness of the issue!

Eventually some RN shirts and trousers arrived from one of the RFAs, and then more were sent from UK via our re-supply line through Montevideo, which helped enormously. Each casualty did receive a small "comfort bag" on arrival; this contained soap, flannel, a razor, chocolate and a voucher for one pound to spend in the little ship's shop that was in operation all the way through our deployment. There was only one choice of postcard, a picture of *Uganda* in her usual Educational Cruise ship role; most of us seem to have one of those today. These comfort bags were all very welcome… especially the chocolate!

In retrospect, it was all a learning curve; at our de-brief when it was all over we all mentioned the clothing/rig aspect and asked for it to be addressed in future. Compared with the fatalities, the loss of ships, helicopters and equipment early in the conflict, it didn't seem that important. It was more a question of respect and dignity for some very brave and selfless fighting men, many of whom arrived on board with little or no possessions, and who, with so much to address at the time, were also facing a long sea and air voyage to make before reaching UK. Such is the reality of amphibious warfare; with ships being lost at sea, and battles being fought on land, at sea and in the air.

Still, as we headed steadily north we were leaving those dark days behind us. We had no patients on board now, and all were starting to look forward to returning to our homes and families. The "dual-purpose" leaking porthole in my cabin was now coming back into its own, providing a welcome sea breeze as we continued to steam northwards, leaving the Tropics behind by early August.

Our Medical Services Officer, Lt. Cdr Rick Pollard RN set up the "limeys" canteen again that had served us so well on our voyage south; this was the equivalent of a vast tea-urn, that dispensed a bizarre but nonetheless much welcome drink of lime/lemonade flavoured juice to which we could help ourselves as required. It was positioned at the entrance to the main dining area, so all ranks and rates could share a mug together and I have fond memories of many yarns and chats around this traditional Naval "cold drinks dispenser". A forerunner to the filtered water machines to be found round every corner in UK today!

As we continued to steam north we RAS-ed (re-fuelled at sea) as required from the RFAs who were in the adjacent sea areas, and mail seemed to be catching up with us more frequently now.

At midnight on August 5th we were abeam Gibraltar so, in effect, completed our circle on that date. The next day we were overflown by RN Harriers and a Sea King helicopter from HMS *Illustrious*.

The last couple of days as we left The Bay of Biscay, closing to our first sight of land since Ascension, were increasingly exciting and indeed emotional for us all. Although some of the QARNNS nurses on board were married, many of us lived independent professional lives ashore, running our own houses, cars, etc., and were looking forward to finding that freedom and space again. There was also much discussion of the first meals and menus we would all have liked to plan when we first ate ashore. Although the catering on board had been magnificent we were all starting to miss fresh fruit, salads and vegetables. Shopping lists for replacement underwear and other such essential items seemed to feature high in every conversation, as everything we had set off with in April now seemed to be, well, a bit "worn and washed out", as you might say, and a uniform shade of grey or blue. Above all, a longing to see, feel and be near our families and friends again; the excitement was palpable as *Uganda* steamed us all steadily north towards our homes.

Our first sight of land was the Cornish coast. P&O official personnel, VIPs and press were to be flown out from Royal Naval Air Station Culdrose as we closed to Mounts Bay for the helicopter transfer. Many of us, including Rick Pollard, our MS Officer, myself, and my closest friend on board, the Burns Unit Sister Chris Asendorf, came from Cornwall. We were hoping that a rumour that had gone round in the last few days, that personnel who lived in Cornwall might be disembarked to vacate sufficient cabins for the "incomers", might materialise. Hence our smiling faces in a photograph of Chris and I with the coast of Cornwall in the background. Regrettably this hoped-for scenario was not to be, and the Cornish dwellers on board watched their beloved coastline disappear astern with some regret as we steamed away to the north-west from Mounts Bay and the RNAS Culdrose air drop. But we could see, hear and smell England now, and knew it wouldn't be long before we could enjoy a Cornish pasty across The Tamar again.

The accommodation space was indeed very limited in these last two days, and Chris and several others had to move cabins for their last night on board to incorporate the extra passengers, but we all accepted the changes with equanimity. Perhaps I was spared this inconvenience due to the leaking porthole in my own outboard cabin.

Monday August 9th was our last day on board. Most QARNNS Nursing Officers and RN Doctors were allocated press interviews during the morning. The Ministry of Defence had not permitted the press or media aboard The Hospital Ship while we were operational. As medical military professionals these interviews were obviously to follow our strict medical-in-confidence guidelines. My interview was with Laurence Dopson from "The Nursing Times", someone I have spoken with in the last few years; he remembers the day well. A copy on the adjacent page from the August 1982 "Nursing Times" clarifies the situation in print.

Admiral Sir John Fieldhouse, Commander in Chief Fleet; General Sir Frank Kitson, Commander in Chief Land Forces; Surgeon Vice-Admiral Sir John Harrison, Medical Director of The Royal Navy; and Sir John Nott, then Defence Secretary, were among the VIPs who were flown out to us that morning to join the ship as she came to her berth at Southampton.

P&O Chief Officer Grahame Burton continues:

> *Uganda* arrived back in Southampton on Monday 9th August 1982 to a terrific welcome considering it was a weekday. We had been scheduled to arrive on the previous Sunday, but *Uganda* never was a fast ship, and it was just beyond our capabilities. We had, however, embarked the press and several officials in Mounts Bay, Cornwall the previous afternoon, and we had enjoyed recounting our tales to them in the Officers Bar that night. We wanted to display some visible sign that we had also been employed as a Hospital Ship when we approached the dock in Southampton. Fortunately, I remembered that I had removed the large sheet of canvas with a red cross that, when we were a Hospital Ship, had been secured on top of the uppermost wooden games deck to provide aerial identity. I had stowed it away, as a potentially useful piece of kit for later use. Out it came and we hung the large square canvas over the starboard side, to great effect.

The Uganda in action

The Ministry of Defence did not allow either the press or naval photographers aboard HMHS *Uganda* while British and Argentinian wounded were being treated on her.

But last week it released some photographs, taken by amateur photographers, which convey something of the atmosphere of a hospital ship in action

Above: the intensive care unit. Above right: the music room became the burns unit.

Below: Sea View Ward. The pillars provided reinforcement for the helicopter landing pad provided on deck. The noise when the helicopters alighted was deafening in the ward — and at one stage in the campaign helicopters were queueing to land the wounded.

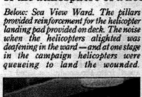

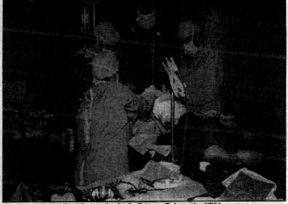

Above: the operating theatre in the ballroom. Below: the ITU.

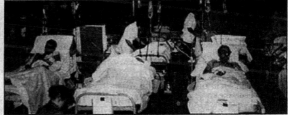

NURSING TIMES AUGUST 25, 1982   1421

This page from August 1982 Nursing Times explains why so few pictures from The Hospital Ship Uganda *exist today.*

Source: Nursing Times

"Please, Sir, may we have some more ships..." Commander Andy Gough RN listens in trepidation as the author speaks with Defence Secretary Sir John Nott; the ship is approaching her berth in Southampton August 9th 1982.
Photograph: Author's private collection

The relief crew was waiting for us on the quayside and we were told to go straight home, without completing a lot of the usual formalities that were required for an official "handover". The P&O Officer who relieved me was none other than Tony Chadwick, who was now released by The MOD from his position at Northwood. The British Government was prepared to pay to restore the ship to her pre-requisition state, and I had been busy preparing a long list of items that had been lost or damaged, and of the structural defects that had occurred due to non-standard operations. I think a few additional jobs might have also slipped into the list from our Superintendents, who knew that the MOD was paying the bill...

Our Flight Deck figures are worth recording:

Total Day landings on the Flight Deck:	1,044
Total Night landings on the Flight Deck:	20
Total Vertrep loads received/sent:	250
Total personnel transported to/from *Uganda* by helicopter:	3,111

Other figures of note:

Days at sea:	113

Total distance travelled:	22,709
(nautical miles)	
Number of casualties admitted as "in patients":	730
(of which 150 Argentinian)	
Number of Surgical operations performed:	504

HNN Maggie Freer wrote of her return and being reunited with her husband, David, and family:

> David and *Intrepid* had arrived back home in the UK to a tremendous welcome at the end of July. He and the family came to meet me when we sailed into Southampton on the 9th August. What an amazing sight to see all the ships and people to welcome us home. I was watching out for them as we came alongside but couldn't see them. Little did I know that David's mother had managed to talk their way onto the press balcony; they could see me and had an excellent view but I had no idea where they were. As we came off the ship and David met me the press wanted to interview us, but I was more interested in getting to see the family and back to my home and a decent bath after only having the timed showers available for our 113 days at sea.

The evening before we had rigged a huge Red Cross banner, which we hung from the starboard side, emphasising *Uganda*'s essential role during that short but vicious campaign, fought so bravely for freedom, so far away. Joined by an increasing number of sailing craft and other small ships, two tugs slowly led *Uganda* past the Cunard Falklands veteran ship *The Queen Elizabeth 2*; funnel blasts were joyously exchanged. A lone Gurkha piper could be heard and seen from his position playing at *Uganda*'s highest mast platform.

Finally, with the same infinite care the nurses had given their patients on board in the last few months, *Uganda* was nursed meticulously into berth 105, just astern of the *Canberra*. You could almost hear *Uganda*'s dignified sigh of relief as her warps secured her to dry land for the first time in four months.

All three of the larger liners requisitioned by the Ministry of Defence in April 1982 were now together.

We were home. It was all over.

Few could have failed to have been deeply moved by the moment. After 22,709 nautical miles *Uganda* had touched land for the first time for four months. We had treated and cared for over 730 patients, and carried out more than 500 surgical operations in our makeshift operating theatres. The QARNNS nursing personnel had acquitted themselves well in what had undoubtedly been difficult, arduous and sometimes dangerous conditions. Our practical and professional skills had shone through, and enabled us to cope with enough trauma and sadness to last us all a lifetime.

Our magnificent Hospital Ship, our professional training, skills and team spirit, had helped see us all through the darkest days. Our motto of "Heal Navy" was as unique as it was appropriate, and had been a constant reminder of the job to be done.

Above all, the bravery, strength and fortitude of the injured servicemen we had treated and cared for would always remain an inspiration for us all.

Surgeon Commander Peter Bull's memory of our approach to the Southampton quayside:

> My overriding memory, however, is our arrival back to UK at Southampton in August 1982, long after most ships had returned and long since we had seen our last patients, the Welsh Guardsmen injured at the Stanley airfield in July. They had been transported back to UK by other routes as we were no longer a hospital, but a troop carrier for the return voyage.
>
> To my pride and amazement we had not been as forgotten as we thought, such was the crowd to greet us – and, right at the front on the jetty in a wheelchair, was the surviving cook from HMS *Glamorgan*, cheering for all he was worth.
>
> It brought tears to my eyes.

(The RN cook from HMS *Glamorgan* was "Smudge Smith", one of the patients NN Karen Dawson mentions in Chapter Seven.)

* * *

So now, with our immense practicality and cheerfulness to the fore, we all rushed to our cabins, grabbed our bags and few possessions, and made our way to the waiting arms of our families. As many seafarers had done for centuries before us, we savoured the moment. With perhaps a slight lift of our chins, a different walk, and a quiet feeling of satisfaction at a "job well done" we made our way down the gangplanks and ashore.

As I picked up my "pusser's grip", the traditional officer's brown canvas Naval hold-all, I glanced back at my little cabin for the last time. I smiled as I thought of the constant battle with the incoming sea-water from the leaking porthole, and moved ahead with the flow of chattering voices to my own family waiting patiently on the quay.

Above: *SS* Uganda *enters No. 2 dry dock in Gibraltar Dockyard, April 16th 1982. She had been requisitioned by The Ministry of Defence in Alexandria on April 10th to serve in The South Atlantic as a Hospital Ship. Photograph: Author's private collection*

Top: *Fitting the stern helicopter landing pad, April 17th 1982. The Students' Common Room, directly underneath the Flight Deck became Sea View Ward, a 44-bed high-dependency ward. The ship's conversion in Gibraltar took 65 hours and involved more than 500 dockyard staff working day and night for 3 days and nights.*

Above: *Vital steel supports being fitted in what was to become Sea View Ward, located directly under the Flight Deck. These pillars became essential anchorage points to lash beds and medical equipment at sea in The South Atlantic Ocean.*

Photographs: Author's private collection

Top Left: *Pre-wrapped mattresses and mountains of stores packed in cardboard boxes pose a challenge for the Intensive Care Unit teams as the ship heads south from Gibraltar. Sister Jill Lee (Sea View Ward) runs to secure some 'FOD' (an aviation term for unsecured debris on airfields and flight-decks!). Photograph: Author's private collection*

Left: *Patients on board in Sea View Ward at stern of ship. Photograph: Grahame Burton*

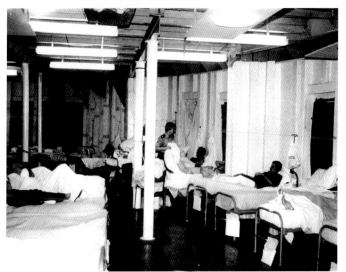

Bottom Left: *Triage/Patient Reception Area under construction at same time. This picture shows how the military stretchers fit neatly onto a pre-constructed hospital bed for initial assessment of casualties on arrival in this area. Photograph: Jim Lacey*

Below: *Order out of chaos: Assembled hospital beds in Sea View Ward were ready for casualties by the time the ship reached Ascension Island. April 28th 1982. Photograph: Jim Lacey*

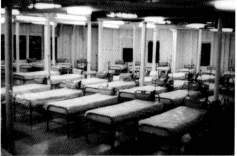

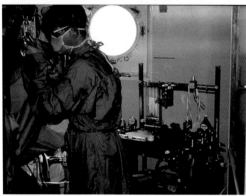

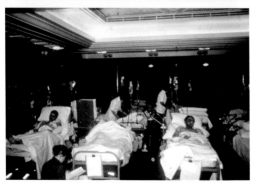

Top: *Starting to assemble The Operating Theatre in what was formerly "The Veranda". Anaesthetic equipment is already being lashed to the pillars to secure items in heavy seas. Our porous-load sterilising autoclave "Vesuvius" in the background is installed and operational.*

Middle Left: *Surgeon Commander Peter Bull (Consultant Anaesthetist for The Task Force) assists during an operation by directing extra portable lighting into a tricky wound during surgery.*

Above: *Teams of RM stretcher-bearers transporting a casualty down the steep ramp from the flight-deck to the Casualty Reception (Triage) Area.*

Left: *The Intensive Care Unit working at full stretch.*

Photographs: Peter Bull

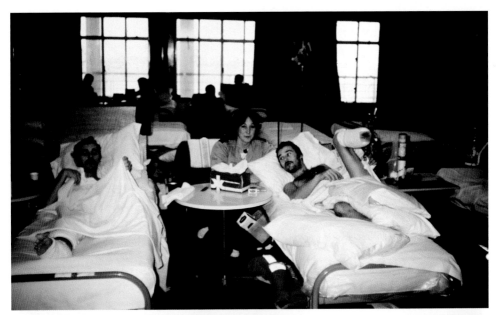

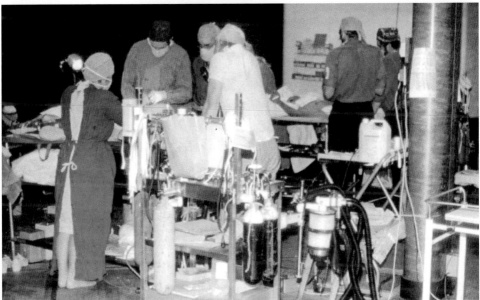

Top: *L/Cpl Denzil Connick (left) and L/Cpl Roy Bassey (both injured on Mount Longdon with 3 Para) with Staff Nurse QARNNS SNN Sally Middleton (centre). Denzil Connick is a founder member and Trustee of The South Atlantic Medal Association. Sally Middleton qualified as a medical doctor in July 2007.The picture was taken by Dr S.J. Townsend, who was serving as a Medical Officer on board the British Telecom ship* Iris, *which was requisitioned by the MOD in April 1982 as a dispatch vessel. It is unlikely Dr Townsend was aware that the Geneva Convention had restricted photography on board The Hospital Ship during The Falklands War. Dr Townsend donated this unique picture with several other photographs to The Imperial War Museum, who are credited with sole copyright of this image. Denzil, Roy and Sally Middleton (now Dr Simmons) have all given their permission to show the picture in this way.*

Photograph courtesy of the Imperial War Museum, London FKD797

Above: *The author (back to camera) working at one of the three operating tables in The Operating Theatre. Equipment lashed to pillars to secure items in heavy seas can clearly be seen. Reason for shoes cast aside – unknown!*

Photograph: Maggie Freer

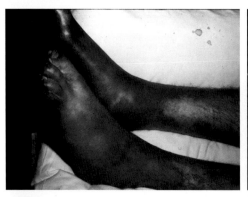

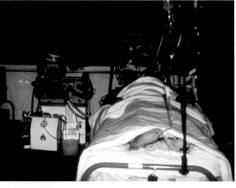

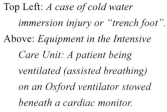

Top Left: *A case of cold water immersion injury or "trench foot".*

Above: *Equipment in the Intensive Care Unit: A patient being ventilated (assisted breathing) on an Oxford ventilator stowed beneath a cardiac monitor.*

Left: *A Tri-Service anaesthetic machine: A simple anaesthetic system for use with or without oxygen supply, and therefore most useful in "the field" or in other difficult/ remote environments. The system draws air (with or without oxygen/other anaesthetic gases) over two volatile anaesthetic agents, Halothane (hypnosis/sleep) and Trilene (analgesia/pain relief). Ventilation can be provided by squeezing the self-inflating bag as shown. An economical, portable and reliable system.*

Bottom Left: *A burns survivor from the Fitzroy attack is treated with the white antiseptic and analgesic cream "Flamazine" in the hastily expanded Burns Unit facility. Photographs: Peter Bull*

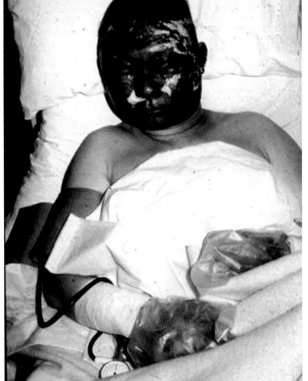

Top Left: *L.to R. QARNNS Senior Nursing Officers Sister Jean Kidd (Casualty Reception), Sister Chris Asendorf (Specialised Burns Unit) and Sister Jill Lee (Sea View Ward) ashore in Stanley, late July 1982. Much mirth was caused by "Jean's red wellies" for some... (see next picture)*

Left: *Red-bereted Paras passing the Argentine Field Hospital also in Stanley.*

Above: *Same trip ashore: A grounded Argentine Puma aircraft in Ross Road West, Stanley, perched between Government House and King Edward VII Memorial Hospital.*
Photographs: Author's private collection

Below: *The Hospital Ship* Uganda *anchored in Grantham Sound early June 1982: A group of recovering patients had just been transferred to HMS* Herald *for onward voyage back to UK via Montevideo (Uruguay) to RAF Brize Norton .*
Photograph: Terry Beddoes from HMS Herald

Above: *Three QARNNS Naval Nurses (NN Denise Bassett and Marion Gay are two) with the author off Ascension Island.*

Left: *"R&R" for QARNNS Nursing Officers as* Uganda *steams north from The Falkland Islands. L. To R: Superintending Nursing Officer Jane Marshall, Senior Nursing Officer Jean Kidd, Superintending Nursing Officer Isa Gauld, Senior Nursing Officers Margaret Kerr, Jill Lee, Nicci Pugh, Liz Day, Superintending Nursing Officer Christine Poole, Senior Nursing Officer Liz Law.*

Bottom Left: *Superintending Nursing Officer Isa Gauld and my colleague Theatre Sister Margaret Kerr share a joke on deck as* Uganda *steams north as a troopship. The beige-painted funnel can clearly be seen behind Isa Gauld.*

Photographs: Author's private collection

Above: *The Hospital Ship* Uganda *anchored in Port William after the Argentinian surrender. A snow-covered Mount Low can be seen in the background.*
Photograph: Author's private collection

Left: *Conversion to troopship for the voyage back to UK. The Geneva Convention red crosses are being painted out and re-painted with traditional trooping buff colour. July 13th 1982.*
Photograph: Zak Coombs

Below: *Personnel of Naval Party 1830. The Hospital Staff on board Her Majesty's Ship* Uganda *as she steams northwards from The Falkland Islands to UK. August 1982.*
Photograph: Author's private collection

Top: *"The Fearless Forty": The forty Queen Alexandra's Royal Naval Nursing Service Nursing Officers and Naval Nurses on board The Hospital Ship* Uganda *as she steams north to UK . During The Falklands War we were the only military female personnel working within the Combat Zone. The QARNNS Naval Nurses were the first female RN junior ratings in history to serve at sea.*

Above: *Fire hydrants from Southampton's tugs as they escort The Hospital Ship (now officially a troopship) into Southampton Water. August 9th 1982.*

Photographs: Author's private collection

Top: *Finally, on August 9th 1982 after 113 days at sea,* Uganda *approaches berth 105 in Southampton Docks. Although officially a troopship, we had hung a huge Red Cross banner from the starboard side of the ship as we entered Southampton Water.*

Photograph: Maggie Freer

Above: *Crowds of families and friends wait to welcome us ashore as The Hospital Ship berths in Southampton Docks just astern of the Canberra. August 9th 1982.*

Photograph: Author's private collection

Top: *Following her re-fit in the River Tyne after The Falklands War,* Uganda *soon returned to The South Atlantic to serve as troop carrier between The Falkland Islands and Ascension Island from 1983 to 1985. Here, she heads north from Port William for the last time on April 4th 1985. She is flying a traditional paying-off pennant from the signal mast.*

Above: Uganda *then spent a year moored in a deep water anchorage in The River Fal in Cornwall. Eventually, in April 1986, she was sold by P&O to a Taiwan shipyard for scrap. In this poignant picture she leaves UK waters for the last time on May 20th 1986. Escorted by four tugs from Falmouth Harbour Commissioners,* Uganda *heads south from The River Fal towards The Suez Canal and her final anchorage in The South China Sea. The National Trust property Trelissick can be seen on a hill behind the ships.*

Photographs: SS Uganda *Society*

THE PASK CERTIFICATE OF HONOUR

AWARDED BY THE COUNCIL OF THE
ASSOCIATION OF ANÆSTHETISTS
OF GREAT BRITAIN AND IRELAND

To The Defence Medical Services of the United Kingdom
in recognition of the services of anaesthetists
in the Falkland Islands Campaign 1982.

Royal Navy

Surgeon Commanders P.T.Bull, S.B.Merrill and R.A.Moody:
Surgeon Lieutenant-Commanders D.J.Baker, A.J.Yates and J.F.Geraghty M.B.E.:
Surgeon Lieutenants S.Q.M.Tighe, S.J.Squires and C.J.Stoot.

Army

Lieutenant-Colonels J.Anderson and R.J.Knight:
Majors M.D.Jowitt and A.K.Banerjee: Captain R.C.D.Wagon.

M. D. Vickers.

dated the **23rd** day of **September 1983**   PRESIDENT

Above: PASK Certificate of Honour: The Association of Anaesthetists of Great Britain and Ireland awarded all the fourteen Service Anaesthetists involved in Operation Corporate with the PASK Certificate of Honour in recognition of the outstanding success of their mission in 1982. A copy of this unique Award is on permanent display in The Falkland Islands Museum in Stanley.

Photograph: Author's private collection

Far Left: *Queen Alexandra's Royal Naval Nursing Service: This QARNNS officer's uniform epaulette shows the crossed "A"s of Queen Alexandra's monogram entwined with a naval anchor above the Geneva Red Cross. The small red stripe denotes the rank of Senior Nursing Officer.*

Left: *The Military Cross: The purple and white ribbon carries an engraved silver cross. The Military Cross is a gallantry award that can be granted to any rank of The British Armed Forces on active land-based service. In November 2009 Able Seaman Kate Nesbitt RN became the first woman in The Royal Navy to receive this award. (See Appendix One – Military Females in Combat Today.)*

Bottom: *The Order of The Royal Red Cross: The dark blue ribbon with crimson edges carries the red-enamelled golden cross. The Royal Red Cross is a military decoration for exceptional services in British military nursing. (See Appendix One – Military Females in Combat Today.)*

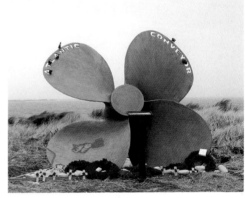

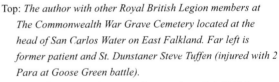

Top: *The author with other Royal British Legion members at The Commonwealth War Grave Cemetery located at the head of San Carlos Water on East Falkland. Far left is former patient and St. Dunstaner Steve Tuffen (injured with 2 Para at Goose Green battle).*

Middle Left: *Memorial cairn at the site where Col. "H" Jones VC Commanding Officer 2 Para fell during the battle for Goose Green, May 28th 1982.*

Above: *Memorial to The* Atlantic Conveyor *at Cape Pembroke on East Falkland. This is the original ship's propeller.*

Left: *Looking East to The Welsh Guards Memorial at Fitzroy. The ship in the background is MV* Tamar *delivering stores to outlying settlements on The Falkland Islands.*
Photographs: Trevor Johnson

Bottom Left: *Falkland Islanders Tim & Jan Miller, Shirley Hirtle and the late Terry Peck MBE with former Welsh Guardsmen Wayne Trigg and Charlie Bale at The Liberation Monument in Stanley, November 2003. Both Tim Miller and Wayne Trigg were treated on board The Hospital Ship* Uganda *in 1982.*
Photograph: Author's private collection

Top: *BLESMA members gather at The Inaugural Hospital Ship* Uganda *Reunion held on board P&O Cruises*
Aurora, *April 18th 2008. L to R: BLESMA Assistant Secretary Ernie Stables; former patients Bill Belcher MBE,*
John Phillips DSC,"Ossie" Osborn, Terry Bullingham and John "JJ" Jones. Bill, John, "Ossie", Terry and
"JJ" have all contributed to White Ship – Red Crosses.
Photograph: Author's private collection

Middle Left: *Former P&O Master at Arms Stan Selwood (centre) with former P&O Electrical Officer Alex Jamison*
(left) and former P&O Engineering Officer Chris Freeman at the Inaugural (2008) Hospital Ship Reunion.
Photograph: Derek Houghton

Bottom Left: *Consultant Anaesthetist Dr. Peter Bull cuts the ceremonial cake with St. Dunstaner Terry Bullingham*
and serving QARNNS Naval Nurses at the 2009 Hospital Ship Uganda *Reunion.*
Photograph: St. Dunstan's Simon Rogers

Above: *Falkland Islander Sea Cadet Tansi Bonner with SAMA82 returning veterans John Callaghan (HMS*
Glamorgan, *right) and Steve Kay (HMS* Exeter, *left, with Standard) at Stanley Liberation Monument, June 2006.*
Tansi is a great-niece of the late Doreen Bonner and cousin of Cheryl Bonner (see Chapter Eight).
Photograph: John Callaghan

Top Left: *QARNNS Senior Nursing Officer Sister Nicci Pugh outside The Sister's Mess, Royal Naval Hospital Haslar, Gosport, Hampshire. October 1980.*

Top Right: *The author (front row, second from right) after completing the Short Introductory Course at Britannia Royal Naval College, Dartmouth, February 1981. The Burns Unit Sister QARNNS Senior Nursing Officer Christine Asendorf is second row, third from right.*

Above: *The author aged three with her mother in one of the family's boats.*

Right: *Post-Falklands War: The author in the Operating Theatres, Royal Naval Hospital Gibraltar, November 1983. The small South Atlantic Medal ribbon with rosette denotes time spent within the Combat Zone.*

Photographs: Author's private collection

CHAPTER NINE

"THE LONELY SEA AND THE SKY"

Uganda's Final Chapter
August 1982 – August 1986

N one of us could have known in August 1982 how soon *Uganda* would be returning to The Falkland Islands and The South Atlantic Ocean. After a 3-week re-fit at Smith's repair yard in The Tyne she left Newcastle on September 18th 1982 to restart her educational cruising programme from Southampton. In honour of the men lost on board HMS *Coventry* during the Falklands War, 470 schoolchildren from the City of Coventry, with their teachers and the Mayor of Coventry, sailed on this mini-cruise from Newcastle to Southampton. Also invited were senior figures from P&O, Naval Party 1830 and senior Army and Royal Naval Medical Services officers and other dignitaries.

All traces of her heroic role during The Falklands War had been removed. Gone were the helicopter landing pad, the de-salinators, the hospital and clinical involvement and the satcom systems. Her rust-streaked hull had been grit-blasted off and meticulously repainted in the dry dock, and overall she was a delight to the eye as she berthed once again in Southampton on September 20th. On September 25th *Uganda* left Southampton with 300 cabin passengers and 870 students for the Mediterranean. There followed rough Channel and Biscay passages, so things were definitely "getting back to normal".

It was all too short-lived. On November 23rd 1982, P&O announced that *Uganda* would be chartered to The Government as a troopship again, sailing between Ascension and Port Stanley. There was now a requirement for a regular sea "shuttle" between The Falklands and Ascension Island linking to the RAF VC10 (latterly Tri-Star) onward flights to UK from Ascension. The runway at Stanley airfield could only accommodate Hercules C130 transport planes; with their limited range the cost of at least two in flight refuellings was becoming prohibitively expensive. So an alternative sea-bridge was considered more appropriate for the intervening years until the new Falklands military airbase and runway at Mount Pleasant were completed in 1985.

A north sea ferry, *St Edmund*, managed by Blue Star Line and renamed SS *Keren*, was similarly requisitioned, and the two ships were swiftly re-fitted for this ongoing service in The South Atlantic.

Uganda and *Keren* both served in this troop-carrying and military support role until April 1985. It was a very demanding time for both the ships, and their ship's companies. *Uganda* herself was too large a vessel to enter and anchor in Stanley's shallower inner harbour. Only the smaller *Keren* could enter "The Narrows" and berth alongside in Stanley Harbour. So both ships, in effect, spent the next two years at sea or at anchor, with no shore-based maintenance or support facility available during that time. One ship would be loading in Port Stanley, the other in Ascension and vice-versa. As in 1982, all loading of stores, troops and personnel to and from *Uganda* was done by helicopter or small boat transports. The Falkland Islanders, however, regarded both ships as their vital link to UK, and a great affection built between the ships, their crew, and The Falkland Islanders at that time.

The late Terry Peck MBE was the founder, and former Chairman of the Falkland Islands branch of The South Atlantic Medal Association (SAMAFI). Terry was a loyal Falkland Islander, former head of the Falkland Island Police Force, and had been a member of the Legislative Council in the past. He had done many brave and daring things during the Invasion in 1982 and worked closely with 3 Para as a local guide and scout during the advance on Stanley. The first thing Terry said to me when I returned to The Islands in 2003 as a returning SAMA82 veteran was: 'We can't tell you how much The Hospital Ship *Uganda* meant to us all in '82, Nicci.' He went on to explain: 'The wounded soldiers could see The Hospital Ship with her red crosses in all her anchorages around the battlefields, and see the helicopters ferrying the injured out to her at all hours of the day and night. They knew if they could make it there they'd be OK.'

He said it was a great pleasure and privilege to welcome the first nurse, and the first person who served on board *Uganda* as a Hospital Ship, back to The Falklands.

'What you may not realise is how dear we all still hold *Uganda* today, as she was our only link to UK from 1983 to 1985, until they opened the new air base at Mount Pleasant. All Falkland Islanders hold *Uganda* in a very special regard.'

Finally, in April 1985 the Mount Pleasant military airfield in The Falkland Islands was opened by HRH Prince Andrew, air links re-established with UK, and both ships could be released from their arduous roles. The *Keren* became the *Sirocco* in 1986, and returned to The Channel Islands, where she traded for some years as the *Rozel*.

Terry Peck, his dear wife Eli and I remained in close touch until Terry's death in 2007. Terry also told me that he and Eli met on board one of *Uganda*'s successors, the requisitioned former cruise liner *Cunard Princess*, on one of the south going routes after the Mount Pleasant Airport had been opened in 1985.

And who was the Commander and Executive Officer-in-Charge of *Uganda*, as she ploughed her way between Ascension and The Falkland Islands for those two vital years, as The Falkland Islanders' only link to UK? None other than our one and only Grahame Burton, P&O Chief Officer on board The Hospital Ship *Uganda* for all her Southern Atlantic sojourn in 1982. (And, many suspect, the procurer of all that beige funnel paint while we were at anchor in Port William!)

Grahame Burton recalls how the Appointment arose… and tells us of an interesting custom he observed at Dakar airport during his crew-changes, travelling to and from Brize Norton to join the ship:

In August 1982, *Uganda* was sent to Smith's Ship Repairers on the River Tyne, and I went off on a nice long holiday with my family to Western France. *Uganda* was refitted for her Educational Cruising and was scheduled to resume her itinerary with her 25th September sailing from Southampton. It was the wish of P&O that those of us P&O personnel who had served on board *Uganda* during The Falklands War should re-join *Uganda* in North Shields, participate in a promotional cruise down to Southampton, and then sail on the first few cruises, to provide some continuity. I rejoined on 17th September and remember having Dr Hope, who at the time was in charge of the Seafarers Education Service, seated with me for dinner. He was a man whom I had often heard about, and whose organisation provided the libraries carried on board ship, and it was a pleasure to meet him. I stayed with *Uganda* for three more cruises until 4th November, when I flew home to take my remaining leave.

Sadly whilst on leave I was advised that the revenue from Educational Cruising was declining, and that P&O had received a lucrative offer from the Ministry of Defence to charter *Uganda* for two years as a sea-borne transport ship, running between Ascension Island and Port Stanley, whilst the new airfield was being built at Mount Pleasant. I was obviously a prime candidate for service with this new venture, especially with my RNR background. So on 9th January 1983 I rejoined *Uganda* in Southampton where the ship was in dry dock, and a much improved helicopter deck was fitted, along with some other military equipment, including a secure communications room. Whilst still employed by P&O, my new title on board was to be Executive Officer. The Troop Officer, an Army Major Royal Corps of Transport, and I, were jointly responsible for the efficient running of the passenger side of the operation. Our passengers included Falkland Islanders and all the different personnel who at the time were living or working in the Falklands, including reliefs for the military personnel ashore, afloat and in the air.

The schedule was approximately ten days at sea each way between Ascension and Port Stanley, with five days spent in the Falklands and three at Ascension. My tours of duty were two round trips on and then one trip off. Flights were from Brize Norton to and from Ascension on RAF VC 10s, with a refuelling stop at Dakar. We were not allowed to remain on the plane in Dakar, but not allowed into the terminal either, so we were usually told to stand under the wing whilst the refuelling took place. I never did understand that one. The accommodation provided at Brize Norton prior to the flight was to be in a shared room for all Merchant Navy personnel, but fortunately I found I was able to use my Lt.Cdr's RNR ID card to secure a room of my own. I remained with this duty until early 1984, when P&O promoted me to Deputy Captain and I joined *Sea Princess* for Mediterranean cruising.

Uganda returned to UK, entering Falmouth Harbour, Cornwall on April 25th 1985 to lay-up while her future was decided. In spite of no major maintenance having been carried out for 18 months she had steamed home at an incredible average speed of 16 knots.

On May 4th *Uganda* was moved up river to a deep-water mooring off Coombe Creek in The River Fal. By another strange coincidence, a former Chairman of The South Atlantic Medal Association, P&O Captain Martin Reed, was the P&O Captain who relieved Captain Scott-Masson on April 26th 1985, and took *Uganda* up the River Fal from Falmouth to her laying up deep-water mooring.

Uganda proceeded up the narrow and twisty river with tugs ahead and astern, and the engines just ticking over at "dead slow". She was to remain in this peaceful Cornish deep-water anchorage near "The King Harry Ferry" until May 20th 1986.

During her last year afloat on this south-west river backwater, a small team of caretaker engineers and watch-keepers remained on board. Just ashore at Tolverne was the well-known "Smugglers Restaurant", a delightful thatched cottage run as a tea room and boat hire business by Peter and Elizabeth Newman. Roger Marshall, a P&O engineer, was one of the officers assigned to remain on board during this time and, with The Newmans, started to create what is now affectionately known as *The Uganda Room* within this ancient seafarers' haunt ashore. Much *Uganda* memorabilia, artefacts and items of interest can be found today at this unusual and delightful spot, nestling at Tolverne on the shores of the River Fal in Cornwall.

By now I had returned to work in Cornwall, and was continuing my nursing career as a civilian Operating Theatre Sister at The Royal Cornwall Hospital nearby. I had my own little cruising boat and often used to sail friends up the River Fal to look at *Uganda*'s now rusting hulk on the deep-water moorings. And, yes, the same porthole on the port side of the ship could still be spotted even from the water... apparently, it would seem, remaining neither open nor closed, some four years after The Falklands War!

In spite of the unstinting efforts of the SS *Uganda* Society to find her some sort of preserved role as possibly a museum or hotel during this time, eventually all efforts came to nought, and *Uganda* was sold by P&O for scrap to a breakers' yard in Taiwan.

On May 20th 1986, *Uganda*, her name now changed to *Triton*, left Falmouth, Cornwall on her final voyage towards Taiwan and the South China Sea. Crowds had gathered on the

Falmouth viewpoints near Pendennis Castle and The Peninsular Drive to see her off. She was joined on the water by many small craft, and a Sea King helicopter from the Royal Naval Air Station at Culdrose made a poignant "kiss" landing on the remnants of the helicopter landing pad astern.

* * *

Fifty-six days out from Falmouth, they arrived off Kaohsiung Harbour in The South China Sea on July 15th 1986. The voyage south under the command of Captain J.D.Coxe to Taiwan through the Mediterranean and the Suez Canal was not without incident, and more detail can be read of Captain Coxe's account in:

"UGANDA The Story Of A Very Special Ship" published by the SS *Uganda* Trust.

Uganda was anchored with eight shackles of cable, handed over to the Taiwan shipyard, and left with a new red ensign flying from her mast.

A month later, while still at anchor, she was struck by typhoon Wayne, and driven ashore just south of the entrance to Kaohsiung Harbour. There, within a few weeks, the wind, waves and weather overcame her and she essentially began her own breaking up process herself. Perhaps she felt, as an ancient and dignified old lady with so much history inside her keels, that she just wanted nature to return her to the elements she had so loyally served for so many decades.

145

Chapter Ten

"A LAUGHING FELLOW-ROVER"

1982 – 2008

So, where did it all end? And what happened to all those mentioned in these pages? After we left the ship in August 1982, the QARNNS Nursing personnel were given two weeks' leave, and then returned to our posts at the various Royal Naval Hospitals and Establishments which we had left in April. I suspect Marks and Spencer's sales of both ladies' and gentlemen's underwear took a rapid boost in late August 1982! I spent much of my leave sailing round the coast of Cornwall in my little boat, reminding myself that sea passages could be enjoyed, away from gales, minefields and enemy aircraft. I particularly remember the enjoyment of sailing in the peaceful and closely wooded rivers and creeks of the South Cornwall coast, so far removed from the windswept and barren Falklands coastline.

Naval appointments and postings, held back since the war had started, were now being implemented.

Royal Navy Commander Andy Gough had already been appointed as Executive Officer (XO, or 2IC) to HMS *Glamorgan* way back in March 1982. However, this was before his temporary appointment to The Hospital Ship as Commanding Officer of Naval Party 1830 and Senior Naval Officer of SS *Uganda*. He finally joined *Glamorgan* as her Commander in September 1982. Following commands at sea of HMS *Broadsword*, HMS *Beaver* and HMS *Brave* he was appointed Rear Admiral in 1997 and awarded CB, Companion of the (Order of the) Bath, in the Millennium Honours List 1999/2000.

Many of the QARNNS Nursing personnel were soon dispersed around the globe; Christine Poole went to Hong Kong (HMS *Tamar*), and I went to relieve a colleague at The Royal Naval Hospital, Gibraltar. My close friend Chris Asendorf from Cornwall, who had already served a short-service Commission in Queen Alexandra's Royal Army Nursing Corps prior to joining the QARNNS at the same time as I did in 1980, returned to civilian nursing and soon married and started a family. Margaret Kerr continued her medium-term Commission: after a year as Senior Nursing Officer at The Royal Marines Commando

Training Centre at Lympstone in Devon she then ran the Operating Theatres at The Royal Naval Hospital Stonehouse, Plymouth.

Jim Lacey returned to his job as Operating Theatre Manager at Royal Naval Hospital Stonehouse, before returning to Commando Forces again. He spent the remainder of his time there, finally leaving the services in 1992 after nearly 26 years.

Jim summarises his life "in Civvie Street" after he left the Services:

> On leaving the RN I completed the necessary courses to work for the Offshore Oil Industry as a "Rig Medic". I worked in the North Sea for a year, relishing working for just two weeks at a time, to have two weeks off. Coupled with a 2-berth cabin to myself, hotel standard food and excellent working and recreational facilities, I was a very happy boy.
>
> My next job took me to Baku, Azerbaijan working for the Oil industry, on-shore in a clinic on my own before the clinic expanded to include a Doctor and later several doctors and support staff.
>
> My Grand Finale took me to the Sahara Desert in Libya working for a German Oil Company. It was a super job – the climate, food, accommodation and facilities were superb. Having spent six years doing the job I decided to call it a day and now enjoy life in early retirement.

Mark Trasler, who worked in the Blood Bank and Laboratory, concludes the story of his career:

Lt.Cdr. Mark Trasler RN on active service in Kosovo 1984.

Photograph: Mark Trasler

After 37 years, I am still serving in the Royal Navy Medical Branch, one of the good number (but rapidly reducing) who can still wear uniform and the South Atlantic Medal with pride. After 18 years as a Junior, then Senior Rating, a Commission followed in 1989. Soon afterwards, I found myself serving in a Hospital Ship again, on board the RFA *Argus* during the first Gulf War.

Thereafter, wider responsibilities resulted in land-based deployments to Bosnia, Kosovo, and all around the Gulf region. I am currently the Royal Navy lead Officer for a project to introduce a readily available electronic healthcare record to the military medical, dental centres and hospitals, ashore, afloat and deployed.

In 2007, as Lieutenant Commander Mark Trasler RN, I was awarded the MBE for services to Defence Healthcare, and was honoured to be able to wear The Award with The South Atlantic Medal for the first time at The Falklands 25th Anniversary Commemoration Ceremony on Horse Guards Parade on June 17th 2007. It was a pleasure and privilege to meet some representation from The Hospital Ship *Uganda* on that memorable day, attend the Ceremony and march down the Mall to Buckingham Palace with Isa Gauld, Christine Poole, Nicci Pugh, Jo Scade, Marion Stock, Geoff Keeble, Derek Houghton and Carl Keeble, all of whom are referred to in this book in some way.

Many of our colleagues reassessed our own lives and values following The Falklands War. In 1983 I married Paddy Hargraves, a QARNNS Nursing Sister and midwife, (and colleague of Nicci Pugh), whom I met on the Maternity Ward at RNH Gibraltar. We celebrated our Silver Wedding in 2008.

Maggie and David Freer's return to "Life on Land":

On our return to UK we were both granted two weeks' leave and took a short holiday. David was drafted back to RNH Haslar and I returned to the Out Patients Department at RNH Haslar for a period, before I handed over to another Staff Nurse. I was "discharged shore" on pregnancy leave in 1983 and became a full time mother, having a second child two years later. It was difficult to integrate back into work after that, as the QARNNS was all I had ever known. I eventually found my way into practice nursing and now work as a Specialist Practitioner with an interest in respiratory medicine and combine this with being a Practice Nurse Trainer and Regional Respiratory Trainer for Education and Health. I am currently studying for an MSc in First Contact Care on a distance learning contract with Sheffield Hallam University, due to graduate in May 2009.

I still miss the QARNNS but keep contact with former colleagues as a committee member for the QARNNS Association, and am now helping Nicci (Pugh), Alison Harris (P&O) and Christine Poole with the Hospital Ship *Uganda* Reunions, which we hope to continue until the thirtieth Anniversary of The Falklands War in 2012.

Initially David was able to develop his career in medical computing within the Navy, but was made redundant as a Charge Chief Medical Technician (CCMT) under options for change in 1996. He has continued to work in medical computing, first in the NHS and now within BT Health as a programme manager.

Naval Nurse Karen Dawson returned to RNH Haslar for some months. She was unable to secure the draft to RNH Gibraltar she had hoped for, so instead arranged a "swap draft", as we called them, with someone from RNH Stonehouse in Plymouth.

This is her own story of her subsequent nursing career as it continued in QARNNS until 1988, and thereafter as a civilian nurse:

> After a few weeks' leave when we got home, I went back to my old job of working on E3 ward at RNH Haslar, but I couldn't settle, so I did a "swap draft" (a location exchange with another service person with similar qualifications) for a year with someone from RNH Stonehouse (Plymouth). Back at Haslar in 1983 I then got a draft to HMS *Sultan* sick bay for two and a half years which was great. By June 1985 the QARNNS rating of Senior Naval Nurse (SNN) had changed to Leading Naval Nurse (LNN) which I gained that year, the same year I married my husband who was a submariner in the Navy. We didn't go on honeymoon straight away, as on the Monday afterwards I had to be in a Guard of Honour for the Duke of Edinburgh at Hampton Court!
>
> When I left QARNNS from RNH Haslar in 1987 I continued in nursing until my children were born in 1990 and 1991. In 1999 my husband's 22 years in the Navy were up and we didn't know if he had a job. So I undertook a Return to Nursing Course and he helped more at home and with the children… a bit of role reversal which neither of us minded at all.
>
> In 2001 I passed my conversion course to Staff Nurse (now called Registered General Nurse or RGN) and then changed jobs completely and went to work as a Recovery Nurse back at RNH Haslar in the Operating Theatres… bearing mind I had never worked in theatres in my life even through my training! Nicci and the OT Teams on The Hospital Ship would have been proud of me!
>
> I have been there ever since; it's a super job. I am now a Senior Theatre Practitioner, I've completed my Mentorship Course at level 3, and I'm now doing my Diabetic Course. I am still working at RNH Haslar (it's just called The Royal Hospital Haslar, now) but only until 2009 when RNH Haslar is sadly due to finally close.
>
> I always said I would stay till the end and even tie myself to the front gates in protest at the closure, and now it seems that day is nearly upon us.

Superintending Nursing Officer Isa Gauld RRC, who had been the Operating Theatre Superintendent, recounts:

> On return home I moved into Occupational Health and worked in most of the Royal Naval Establishments in the South of England. I rose to the rank of Royal Naval Commander and the Matron of Post Registration Training and Development at RNH Haslar before leaving the service in 1999. I was awarded the Order of the Royal Red Cross by The Queen for my services to nursing in QARNNS. I am currently continuing in the Occupational Health field in industry. I enjoy the countryside and walking my dogs, and still feel the relief and wonder of being alive.

Surgeon Commander Peter Bull:

> After the campaign, I returned to RNH Haslar to continue my duties as a Consultant Anaesthetist. I resigned my commission in 1983 having served over 18 years. I wished to fulfil my desire to practise as an Obstetric Anaesthetist, and the Navy had by then been denied a Maternity Unit in which I could have specialised.
>
> 1984-present: Consultant Anaesthetist at Kings Mill Hospital, Nottinghamshire – now part of Sherwood Forest Hospitals NHS Trust. I also volunteered to the RNR for three years to help at HMS *Sherwood* in Nottingham when they were short of medical support.
>
> In 1997 I was one of very few Hospital Ship *Uganda* representatives at the 15th Anniversary Reunion of the Falklands Campaign in Gosport, and was the only Medical Officer from The Ship to take part in the March Past in the presence of Lady Margaret Thatcher, who, of course, had been Prime Minister at the outbreak of the Falklands War. (There was also one Dental Officer, Surgeon Commander ((D)) Steve Taylor who had served on board HMS *Hermes* during The Falklands War.)
>
> Some personnel from The Hospital Ship *Uganda* were finally acknowledged in the 1983 New Year's Honours List, and they are listed further on in this Chapter.
>
> However, The Association of Anaesthetists of Great Britain and Ireland, under the President, Dr Mike Vickers, chose to award all the 14 Service Anaesthetists involved in Operation Corporate with The PASK Certificate of Honour in recognition of the outstanding success of our mission. A framed copy of this unique and prestigious Award is on permanent display in The Falkland Islands Museum in Stanley, and can be seen within the pictures in this book. It is a medal awarded to anaesthetists "For Acts of Great Courage

or Valour". No Service Anaesthetists were awarded post-conflict Honours; it was ever thus. There were 9 RN and 5 Army Anaesthetists within the War Zone but many others were subsequently motivated by our action, and they too volunteered for specialist anaesthetic training within the Services, which led to further meritorious achievements in subsequent wars, eg The Gulf, Iraq, Afghanistan.

In September 1982 Superintending Nursing Officer Jane Marshall and I attended a de-briefing session with Surgeon Captain John Drinkwater at the Naval Medical Directorate in London. Realistically, all we could do was leave a "shopping list" of items that we hoped might be included should Hospital Ships be requisitioned in the future. There wasn't that long to wait.

In 1990/1991 RFA *Argus* was brought into service for the same purpose in The Persian Gulf to stand by in the event of British casualties during the first Gulf War. In order to alleviate some of the communications and other difficulties we had encountered in 1982 on board The Hospital Ship *Uganda* because of Geneva Convention restrictions, *Argus'* role then and now remains as a Casualty Receiving Hospital. RFA *Argus* is unusual in having two roles: as well as her primary CRH purpose, she also has a role in aviation training and equipment carrying; she does not therefore qualify for ICRC insignia or protection.

RFA *Argus* is now the home of The Royal Navy's Afloat Primary Casualty Receiving Facility and has recently been re-fitted in Falmouth dockyard for this purpose. The re-fit includes a purpose built Triage facility on the Flight Deck, the availability of a new computerised tomography (CT) scanner, and ongoing improvements to the lift systems for transporting casualties around the clinical areas on board the ship.

Today, in 2009, all the Military Hospitals that were running so efficiently in 1982 have now been closed, the last being The Royal Naval Hospital, Haslar, Gosport in Hampshire. This had become The Royal Hospital Haslar in 1996 when it became Tri-Service. The Ministry of Defence withdrew from the site in 2006, and final closure was in 2009.

On arrival back in UK today all injured servicemen are now treated in one Military-Managed ward of The Selly Oak Hospital in Birmingham, using a Tri-Service partnership arrangement with the National Health Service. If appropriate, ongoing treatments and rehabilitation for injured servicemen and women then proceed at The Defence Medical Rehabilitation Centre, Headley Court, Epsom Surrey. This long-established medical unit is now run under the administrative umbrella of The Royal Air Force, although Command structure rotates between The Army and Royal Air Force. Some 200 + personnel, which include specialist medical and rehabilitation teams of all remedial and therapeutic specialities, work to continue to maintain the world-class reputation of this centre of excellence, which Headley Court Centre has now become.

Military and QARNNS Naval Nurses are now trained within a Tri-Service degree course at the Royal College of Defence Medicine in Birmingham.

* * *

Back in the late summer and autumn of 1982 various engagements and weddings took place as the year drew to a close. Sister Liz Law, who had helped run the Intensive Care Unit, quickly promoted her boyfriend Howard Ormerod, (who had survived the sinking of *Atlantic Conveyor*) to fiancé, and they were married later that year. Sister Jean Kidd, who had run the Casualty Reception Area, married Surgeon Lt. Cdr Ross Adley, a registrar anaesthetist who had worked ashore at the Ajax Bay Field Hospital, and another QARNNS Naval Nurse married her Royal Marine boyfriend who had served ashore in 42 Commando.

This is the final part of Liz Law's (now Mrs Howard Ormerod!) story as she recalled in 2008:

> Following our return home on board *Uganda* (now as a troop-carrying ship) on 9th August 1982, wedding plans were in full swing. Howard had taken part in a BBC Documentary as a survivor of a sunken ship. During the filming of this he had revealed that I was still down south working as a Nursing Officer on board The Hospital Ship *Uganda*. As a result the local press were camped on our doorstep both in Plymouth, and on my parents' doorstep in Doncaster, awaiting our return. They subsequently filmed a part of the wedding on 2nd October and used it in the documentary.
>
> I remained in the service as a QARNNS Senior Nursing Officer until August 1985 when, at the end of my commission, I decided to explore other clinical areas. I then worked as a Community Macmillan Clinical Nurse Specialist in Cornwall until 1989 when we moved to Oxfordshire. I still work as a Macmillan Clinical Nurse Specialist.

There were a number of married ladies amongst our QARNNS teams on board; most of the husbands had been serving within The Task Force at sea or ashore; by some extraordinary coincidence a number of babies were born some ten months after we all came ashore.

On November 19th 1982 Sister Jill Lee and I were privileged to attend The Grand Task Force Reunion Ball sponsored by "The Daily Express", and held within the hangar area on board HMS *Hermes* in Portsmouth Naval Dockyard. This magnificent function was organised by an old friend and colleague of ours, Surgeon Lieutenant Commander (D) Steve Taylor, a Royal Naval dentist who had served on HMS *Hermes* during her time in the South Atlantic. Sister Jill Lee had worked on Sea View Ward on board The Hospital Ship and we had worked together on C5, a busy surgical ward at Haslar, before The Falklands War. We both wore our QARNNS "Mess Dresses" with the little shoulder tippets (part of the evening uniform that covered one's shoulders, not unlike the top part of a cape or cloak) and it was fairly obvious no one had a clue who we were, but it was certainly an evening to remember!

A Service of Commemoration and Thanksgiving was held at St. Bride's Church, Fleet Street in London on Saturday December 4th 1982 for members of Queen Alexandra's Royal Naval Nursing Service on their return from The South Atlantic. It was a charming service conducted by The Staff Chaplain at The Ministry of Defence. Nearly all the QARNNS personnel who had served on board The Hospital Ship attended. As a group we had heard of The Victory Parade in London on October 12th, but we were not aware of any personnel from The Hospital Ship *Uganda* who had been included or attended. It was a delight to hear recently, from his contribution to this book, that former patient Sergeant Major John Phillips DSC had participated; also QARNNS Superintending Nursing Officer Christine Poole ARRC with Naval Nurse Sue Offen.

In the New Year's Honours List 1983 Surgeon Commander Charles Chapman was awarded the OBE, Senior Nursing Officer Jean Kidd the MBE, and Senior Naval Nurse Marion Stock the BEM.

People often ask how we all coped with such a rapid transition back to "normality". In many ways it was probably the best thing to get back to a work routine and try to put the whole thing behind you. Like other veterans, everyone had to come to terms with their experience in different ways. Personally, I didn't want to talk about it very much; even if one had wanted to, no one seemed very interested, and there was that recurring theme in the Services of "those who went" being somehow different from "those who stayed behind". It was probably better to pretend it had never happened. I have to say I couldn't quite understand this attitude, as those who had served on board The Hospital Ship were only too aware that for the majority of our former patients, their lives would have changed so dramatically. You couldn't help but wonder where they were and how they were coping. Everybody certainly thought about each other more than we had realised, and many have now expressed a wish that we could have met up over the years, as have other Task Force veterans. There is, and always will be, a strong bond between men and women who have shared dangerous and difficult things together. For us, in 1982, this was undoubtedly enhanced by that extraordinarily unique relationship formed between the military patients, doctors, nurses and other support teams who were, literally "all in the same boat". Frankly, it was not quite the same as other experiences that can tie people in the ordinary walk of civilian life.

In 1985 at the end of my Short Service Commission, I returned to work at The Royal Cornwall Hospital in Truro. In 1984 I had applied for a Nursing Sister's position in The Falkland Islands at the civilian hospital, King Edward VII Memorial Hospital in Stanley, but, unfortunately, my application was lost in a tragic hospital fire they experienced the same year. It seemed I might not be going to make the return journey south so soon.

It was during this time that *Uganda* made her final return from The South Atlantic, and was laid up in The River Fal, just a few miles from my cottage in Cornwall; this was when I used to sail round her rusting hull in my little sailing boat, inspecting that familiar non-closing porthole... this time from sea level and the outside of the cabin!

The twentieth Anniversary seemed to pass us by as a group; we were probably all too busy trying to pay our mortgages and cope with the demands of ever-escalating careers in the National Health Service and private sectors.

Nearly all the RN Medical and QARNNS Nursing personnel who had served on board The Hospital Ship *Uganda* went on to continue outstanding careers within the medical profession. All the Naval doctors eventually held Consultant posts, and the majority of the nursing staff steadily upgraded and improved their qualifications over the years. Likewise, the RM stretcher-bearer/bandsmen, and indeed the P&O personnel, who had helped us all so willingly and cheerfully through our darkest days.

P&O Captain Grahame Burton tells here of his last years with P&O:

> I subsequently served in several P&O ships (and ships of their subsidiary, Princess Cruises) until, in 1992, I was appointed to the command of *Pacific Princess*, cruising out of Vancouver, Canada, to Alaska. For those familiar with the US television series "The Love Boat", this was the ship that was featured, and I have subsequently often recounted how my first command was as "Captain of the Love Boat". In 1995 after a spell in command of *Royal Princess*, I was assigned to the building of the new P&O liner *Oriana* in Germany. This was shortly before I was asked to transfer to a shore position, as Vice President of Marine Operations for Princess Cruises, in Los Angeles, California. I remained in that position until 2001, just before the takeover by Carnival Cruises, when I left and formed my own Marine Consultancy Company.

Cheryl Bonner, whom we had nursed on board *Uganda* on the way back up to Ascension, was cared for for many years in The Ockenden Venture Home in Camberley, Surrey. Her mother, Doreen Bonner, who had cared for Cheryl at home in Stanley until 1982, had been tragically killed during the hostilities, and her father Harry died later that year. Funding for her long-term care was obtained through The Falkland Islands Appeal.

Her uncle, Don Bonner, now aged 80, who had been Sir Rex Hunt's chauffeur and butler at the time of the Argentine invasion, told me:

> Regrettably, Cheryl's condition never really improved. She lived in various homes in UK where there were trained staff to care for her all the time. Cheryl sadly passed away last year (2007) at the age of 51. Her ashes came back to The Falkland Islands and have been buried with those of her parents and older sister Shirley in The Stanley Cemetery.

The Bonner family remain very well-known in The Falkland Islands. They are now well into their fifth generation of Falkland Islanders. Jack Bonner, known as "JB", used to own all the land surrounding San Carlos Water before the larger Falkland Island settlements were divided up during the 1960s and 70s. Bonner's Bay remains a good safe small craft anchorage within San Carlos Water on the east arm of the inlet, just over one nautical mile from the carefully tended and much-visited British Cemetery at the head of San Carlos Water. Don (Cheryl's uncle) continued working at Government House for several subsequent Governors of The Falkland Islands and now lives in retirement in "Chauffeur's Cottage", just behind the main Government House buildings on Ross Road.

Tim Miller, one of the civilian Falkland Islanders we had treated on board The Hospital Ship, now lives on the outskirts of Stanley. I have since met Tim many times in The Falkland Islands, and in UK, through our work with The South Atlantic Medal Association (SAMA82), and have become good friends with him and his wife Jan. They now run the thriving Stanley Garden Centre, and associated Stanley Growers, and supply much of the fresh produce and flowers for all The Falkland Islands. Tim retired from The Falklands Legislative Council (Leg Co) in 1986, and can often be relied on for an outspoken line in the weekly Falklands newspaper "The Penguin News". Every year since the formation of SAMA82 during the 15th Anniversary Year in 1997, Tim and Jan have opened their house to SAMA82 returning veterans, mainly Welsh Guardsmen. The maintenance, and indeed recent additions, of seat, flagpole and daffodil plantings at the beautifully maintained Fitzroy Memorials are all due to their continuing help and support for returning veterans to The Falklands over the years. Another thank you, to Tim and Jan through these pages!

* * *

And what about our other former patients, you ask; the very reason The Hospital Ship *Uganda* was requisitioned in the first place?

The first thing we should mention at this point is that not all war injuries are entirely physical. Although, of its nature, this book tends to focus on the physical trauma of battle-induced injury, there is today a collection of traumatically induced conditions that we now link together as a post-traumatic stress condition, known within the medical profession as Post Traumatic Stress Disorder, or PTSD. Sufferers from this condition can be helped through a charity linked to SAMA82, called Combat Stress www.combatstress.org.uk

Within the limitations of this book, however, we are focussing on those injured with physical, as opposed to psychological disorders, being mindful how closely the two are linked.

Many of the veterans who have contributed to this book are writing down their thoughts and experiences for the first time. Following are the latter parts of their stories.

Chief Petty Officer John Strange RN was one of the first casualties from HMS *Sheffield* to arrive on board The Hospital Ship *Uganda* on May 12th 1982:

> Once back in UK, after one night at RAF Hospital Wroughton I was transferred to the Royal Naval Hospital Haslar in Gosport, Hampshire; close to my wife and family and under the watchful eye of Surgeon Commander Dewar and his staff. After some more minor skin grafting, I soon recovered sufficiently to be discharged from hospital and return

His Royal Highness Prince Charles visits CPO John Strange and other injured RN personnel from The Falklands War at RNH Haslar. August 1982.
Photograph: John Strange

home. However, it was to be June 1983 before I was declared fully fit for service again. Whilst having treatment in Haslar I was referred to Odstock hospital where I was fitted for surgical gloves and vests to reduce the keloid scarring to my hands and body. During my time in hospital I received many letters and cards from well-wishers from all over the world. One letter in particular came from a man in Southampton who became a very good friend and introduced me to the Rooksdown Club which was named after a hospital that treated burns casualties from The Second World War. He was Mr Geordie Reay, Chairman of the Rooksdown Club, who had received horrific burns during World War Two.

In August 1983 I was drafted to HMS *Tamar* in Hong Kong for two years to work with the Royal Navy Clearance Diving Team as the diving equipment maintainer. This was a married accompanied post which meant that I could take my wife and children with me. On return and after some leave I left the Royal Navy in March 1986 after 22 years' service. After three years as a Technical Author I joined the Civil Service and spent the next 17 years, firstly as an Instructional Officer for 11 years, and then as a Health and Safety Officer for six years, before retiring in 2006.

I still remember the events of the 4th May 1982 clearly and at our annual remembrance church service still feel a great sadness for those who lost their lives, some of whom were personal friends of mine. I also remember the care and treatment, without which I would not have survived, that I received during my long road to recovery from doctors and nurses alike on the various ships and hospitals where I was treated and would like to thank them all for their dedication and professionalism.

John Strange
Ex CPOMEA HMS *Sheffield*

Petty Officer Richard Wood, injured and temporarily blinded during the same attack on HMS *Sheffield*, writes:

Our arrival at RAF Brize Norton was greeted by our families and well-wishers as well as the nursing staff (PMRAFNS) from RAF Hospital Wroughton where we were accommodated overnight. We were taken by coach to the RAF Hospital and, en route, we were flagged down by a very excited landlord from a nearby public house, who donated a very welcome bottle of light ale for every returning serviceman on the coach.

The following day we were transported by coach to RNH Haslar near Portsmouth and after further Medical Examinations were sent home on sick leave. I had suffered shrapnel damage to my eyes and face, and burns to my ankles and face. The shock and trauma from the scenes I had witnessed just prior to my sight being lost (thankfully not for ever), the loss of my friends and colleagues, and witnessing some of the severe injuries sustained by fellow servicemen, did set me back emotionally for some years. Care and treatment for my eyes, and psychiatric care continued at RNH Haslar and at RNH Gibraltar where I was posted from 1982 to 1985. I was medically discharged from the Royal Navy by the Medical Board at the Institute of Naval Medicine, Alverstoke in February 1987.

I had arrived home on 1st June 1982 after a momentous journey, and much wonderful and loving care by the Medical and QARNNS Nursing Staff to whom I will be forever grateful.

Despite all this I will never regret joining the Royal Navy. Remembering the words of my late father as I left home in 1966, 'It will either break you or make you' I feel certain I didn't disappoint him, as, in spite of all the setbacks and injuries, in some ways it did "make me".

Chief Petty Officer Terry Bullingham RN, who was blinded in the Argentinian Dagger aircraft attack on HMS *Antrim* on May 21st 1982:

After a week on board The Hospital Ship, HMS *Herald's* Wasp helicopter transferred a party of us to the ambulance ship for the 6-day passage to Montevideo and the subsequent 15-hour RAF VC-10 flight to Brize Norton eventually arriving in a ward in RAF Hospital Wroughton on Victory Day (14th June).

After an overnight stay, the Naval casualties journeyed to Royal Naval Hospital Haslar by road. I was informed by Professor Bob Cooling at Moorfields Hospital that what was left of the retina on my right eye was not worth putting back – at least I knew my bottom line. Surgeon Commander Bob Telfer removed some shrapnel from my left knee that was causing a problem and I was discharged from the medical system.

Autumn 1982 and winter 1983 were spent undergoing basic rehabilitation at St Dunstan's, Ovingdean, near Brighton. The training was intensive and thorough, comprising: learning to type, read and write braille, in addition to mobility using the long-cane technique. Following this, I became an information officer at the Fleet Air Arm Museum, RNAS Yeovilton, where I was reunited with "Humphrey", HMS *Antrim's* much-loved venerable Wessex helicopter, by now part of the current Falklands exhibition. Strange to say, feeling "his" familiar components was quite reassuring. The Museum environment was extremely useful as it allowed me to get used to dealing with the public in my new role, within the social life and support of shipmates I had known for years. During winter 1983, I decided it was time to move on and I left the RN in February 1984.

Further training at St. Dunstan's followed and I subsequently enrolled as a student Technical Officer for the Blind in Leeds during Winter 1984 and Spring 1985, subsequently taking a post with Grampian Society for the Blind, in Aberdeen. After a year's experience as a field-worker, I did a 2-year Social Work course in the City, returning to field-work on completion.

Autumn 1990 saw me as a social-work lecturer at an RNIB college in Birmingham. In summer 1993, I took up my final position as a public speaker for St Dunstan's, finally retiring in 2005.

During the 1980s and 1990s I used to race walk (a St. Dunstan's tradition) and I have completed the "Action Heart" London-Brighton run on my tandem. My main hobby is model engineering using "Meccano" and I am pleased to be a member of several guilds. I am the proud possessor of a Myford "Super-7" lathe that I have adapted for my use. I assist my wife, Maria, on our allotment, by digging using a 6' X 4' wooden frame. High-fidelity audio and tape-recording, using open-reel machines, is another interest that I have maintained since my teenage years. I don't really miss television since the pictures on the radio are so much better. The choice of radio programmes has increased dramatically over the last 26 years and I find I can follow most sports relatively easily, although this has been an acquired skill.

I look back to my time on the hospital ships with nostalgia, since it surrounded life-changing events and exemplified the very best of the comradeship and mutual support that is so much part of Naval life. I have deliberately avoided mentioning the wonderful Queen Alexandra's Royal Naval Nurses and members of the various ships' companies individually, as the things they did for me are simply too numerous to mention. I would just like to take this opportunity to thank them all.

Terry Bullingham
19 July 2008

Sergeant Bill Belcher RM lost his right leg, and very nearly his left, during the battle for Goose Green on May 28th. He describes here his progress from his arrival at Brize Norton onwards:

Arrival at Brize Norton came after an overnight flight and stopover in Dakar. There the journey reached a low point. We were moved onto rickety old mini buses, with whitewash on the windows, about nine to a vehicle, and driven to the hospital at RAF Wroughton. I was in excruciating agony after being rattled across country roads for 45 minutes. I was not alone in suffering and I understand the need to avoid the public gaze but that was no way to treat so many suffering souls. Even Uruguay could do better.

At Wroughton, the three services were queuing up to "claim" their respective personnel and, rather than being sent onwards to RNH Haslar, I realised that Wroughton was much closer to my fiancée than anywhere. So I asked the Air Force if they could cope with me and then pleaded with the RN to let me stay there. It took a while to get the OK but then common sense prevailed and I was left at Wroughton. Much constructive surgery later, bone grafts, external fixation, nerve reconstruction and soft tissue repairs, and my left leg was rebuilt by the RAF Orthopaedic surgeons. I had truly been through the medical hands of all three Services and their combined efforts had saved what remained of my lower limbs and gave me the hope of walking again.

My gratitude is forever extended to each and every person who contributed to my survival and recovery; from my colleagues in the Gazelle helicopter who applied initial first aid, to the Remedial Gymnast at Headley Court who made me run again.

After seven months at RAF Wroughton, and many visits to the local limb centre, I was ready for rehabilitation at RAF Headley Court. About six months there, on and off, and I returned, walking, to the Air Squadron who had now moved to Yeovilton. During this period I was married to Lynn and upheld the promise that we would "tie the knot" when I could walk reasonably. Soon after, the Admiralty Board sent for me and offered me a desk job until the end of my current engagement, or medical discharge. I took the latter to avoid the financial penalties of "finishing my time" as normal.

A short period of resettlement followed and then I was sent on Terminal Leave and the hunt for an alternative career began in earnest. Mention of the Civil Service had been made during resettlement and I stumbled across an advert for clerical staff with the MoD in a local paper. I applied, went for test / interview and started in Oct 84. The post was office based, within five miles of our home in Oxfordshire, and well within my capabilities. I have stuck with the Civil Service to this day and have, hopefully, continued to contribute to Defence from the logistic end of the spectrum. All three Services have continued to be engaged since our particular "Combined Op" and they have relied on maximum support from the UK Base.

John Jones, a former Welsh Guards Lance Sergeant who lost both legs in the Stanley Airfield incident in July 1982, completes his story describing his treatment at Woolwich Military Hospital, his rehabilitation, return to civilian life, and his subsequent most successful civilian career:

Woolwich is another chapter, and all I really want to say is that it was a very interesting and courageous time with the wards full of recovering casualties from The Falklands War. I made some lifelong friends there whose courage and determination were an inspiration. The manner in which they bore their pain and suffering and dealt with the trauma and nightmares should never be under-estimated, nor the care and support from the nursing teams. I personally was not a good patient as I had a bad attitude to authority and rules. However each of us has to deal with things in their own way and perhaps that is how I coped. I trust that should any of the team that I may have made life difficult for read this, they will accept my apology for my behaviour at this time. Smoking when I shouldn't have been, sneaking out to the pub, complaining about cold tea being just some of the manifestations of my reaction to the loss of both legs.

During this period I was in a wheelchair and learnt to hate it. It appears that when you are in a wheelchair people can think you've lost your brain as well as your legs. They don't look you in the eye and they talk down at you and talk to anyone who is with you about you. It's really frustrating and very annoying. Since leaving Woolwich I have only been back in a chair once and that was during an extended period of six weeks when I couldn't wear my legs.

On 27th November 1982, four and half months after the incident, I walked, rather unsteadily admittedly, down the aisle of the Guards Depot church as I married my girlfriend Teresa. Unfortunately this union did not survive past 13 years. This achievement of being able to walk again was down to the professional care and support I received from all the medical teams I encountered; be they on The Hospital Ship *Uganda*, the hospital ashore in Stanley, the casevac teams who brought us all back to UK, the staff at Woolwich and the staff at the limb fitting centre at Roehampton.

I left the Army in August 1983 but had been working in London since the April having moved to Basingstoke. I found the commuting a real drag and after 18 months got a job with the AA at Basingstoke in their accounts department. I eventually ended up managing the department until I was made redundant in May this year (2008) after 23 years' service.

Simon Weston OBE was another Welsh Guardsman and patient in 1982, and, over the

The author with former patient Simon Weston OBE at her home in February 2007 (see overleaf).
Photograph: David Fitzgerald

years, he has become one of our most well-known former patients treated on board The Hospital Ship *Uganda*. Simon's further treatments and the reconstructive surgery of his face continued in UK for many years, and several television documentaries and programmes have been made about his experiences. He has written about various aspects of his life since 1982 in numerous books, most of which are still published and widely available today. Some of the titles are: "Walking Tall" (October 1989), and "Going Back" (April 1992), both published by Bloomsbury Publishing plc., and "Moving On" (September 2003) published by Piatcus books. Simon was awarded an OBE in The Queen's Birthday Honours in 1992 for his wide-reaching charitable work. During the 25th Anniversary year of The Falklands War Simon made a television documentary focussing on his medical care and casevacs in 1982. The picture on the previous page was taken at the author's home in February 2007 during the filming for that documentary "Saving Simon".

* * *

This is the final part of Ossie Osborn's contribution. As a Guardsman in the 2nd Battalion Scots Guards, Ossie was injured by mortar fire during the battle for Mount Tumbledown on June 13th 1982. Ossie has described how he subsequently had to have his left leg amputated on board The Hospital Ship in Chapter Seven. He continues his story from that time onwards:

> Some days later the journey back to the UK started by my being transferred on to the Survey (Ambulance) Ship *Hydra*, up to Montevideo. I was one of very few who managed to sneak crutches off the *Uganda*, and I still have them. From the port in Montevideo we were transported individually to the International Airport to fly back to the UK on a VC10 via Ascension.
>
> There was a mad moment on the road from the port to the Airport. Whilst waiting to be loaded on to the VC10, 2 of the ambulance crew spotted an Argentinian civil aircraft taxiing in and asked if I fancied having a shot at it? Jokingly I said, 'Yes, why not?' so they called over one of the Uruguayan soldiers to ask if I could borrow his gun, his answer: 'Borrow, yes, but it would not be any good, as he didn't have any ammunition…'
>
> The VC10 landed at Brize Norton from where we were transferred to RAF Hospital Wroughton for post flight Medicals.
>
> It was here that I met my parents, my first comment to my Dad being: 'I put my big foot in it this time, Dad'. From RAF Wroughton we were helicoptered to Queen Elizabeth Military Hospital (QEMH) at Woolwich.
>
> For my first Sick Leave I arrived home to a big welcome from the village. It was a total surprise; I told my Dad I would get him back for not telling me about it… it took me nine years, but I got him back on his 70th!
>
> I was offered Rehabilitation at Chessington or Headley Court but

refused it. With instructions from Roehampton and help from a Paralympic Disabled Lady in the next village to my parents, I decided I could get on better myself. By the time they offered it I was already competing in Disabled Sports, had just been to my first Regionals and was about to go to my first National Championships.

Before I lost my leg I would walk or run everywhere and had only driven Military vehicles off-road. I got my first car via South Atlantic Fund / Regiment / Local Dealer, then given a 4 ½ day, 1,000 mile driving course, followed by passing my test. I stayed in the Army completing just short of 24 yrs, first as a Swimming Instructor (I couldn't swim before I lost my leg), then a spell in the Training Office, before running the Gym and Swimming pool complex at Chelsea Barracks. I finished working for the London District Physical and Adventurous Training Office and was in the Field 99% of the time.

After finishing in the Army in 2001, I spent the first six months acting as a full time carer to my Dad who had just been diagnosed with Parkinson's disease. After his condition stabilised I then worked as a guide at a stately home, before being offered the job I now hold as Assistant Curator in the Queen's Royal Lancers Regimental Museum. I was also appointed as The Cannon Master to His Grace the Duke of Rutland. This is an honorary position, of which I am extremely proud. The cannons

BLESMA member and former Scots Guardsman Robert 'Ossie' Osborn fires one of the eighteenth-century cannons at Belvoir Castle for Falklands Liberation Day, June 14th 2007.
Photograph: 'Ossie' Osborn

are original eighteenth century cannons, and I fire them at Belvoir Castle at The Duke's request for Events, Anniversaries, etc. On June 14th 2008 we had a special seven-cannon firing for the Liberation of The Falkland Islands 26th Anniversary and we are all hoping very much His Grace will allow this to continue up to the 30th Anniversary.

In 1988 I was awarded a Douglas Bader Flying Scholarship from which I obtained my Pilot's Licence; during the same year I gained my Speedboat Driver's Licence.

My first Sports competition for East Midland Regional Superstars was 141 days after my leg was amputated; my first International was the 1986 World Championships in Hungary.

In 1991 at the Inaugural Disabled ex-service Championships I won three gold, two silver and a bronze; the same year I got into the Army Shooting Squad. In 2001 I got into the Able-Bodied National Squad.

I have competed in 226 County, 76 Regional, 126 National and 58 International Championships in the following events:-

Athletics, Swimming, Air Weapons, Road Racing, Volleyball, Table Tennis, Small and Full Bore Pistol, Dragon Boat Racing, Cross-Bow, Water Polo, Gallery Rifle, Bowls, Weight Lifting, Slalom, Power Lifting, Archery, Small-bore, Target, Full Bore, Classic and Light weight Sports Rifle.

Gaining: 927 County (507 Gold), 211 Regional (87 Gold), 444 National (185 Gold), 202 International Medals (94 Gold).

3690 Medals Overall. (1076 Gold)... So you can see I'm quite a competitive bloke.

I mention all this because, in some ways, once I knew the leg had to go, I had to face up to a new and different way of life. I've just carried on working hard and enjoying all these sports and the new friends I've made. Some of the things I might never have got to do if it hadn't been for the injury, which is a funny way of looking at it, but it's true.

* * *

This is the final part of the contribution from Sergeant Major John Phillips DSC. As a Royal Engineers Bomb Disposal Officer, with Staff Sergeant Jim Prescott CGM, John successfully de-fused an unexploded bomb on HMS *Argonaut*. John was then seriously injured, losing his left arm, de-fusing another unexploded bomb on HMS *Antelope* on May 23rd. John was a Trustee of The British Limbless Ex-Service Men's Association (BLESMA) until 2009; his final paragraph is of particular interest:

It was during my stay at Woolwich that I made up my mind to get fit

BLESMA Member and Trustee John Phillips DSC wears his new prosthetic arm. October 1983.

Photograph: John Phillips

and return to duty. What had happened had happened and I would just have to get on with it. What sparked this determination was a visit from a stranger who introduced himself to me as the new Sgt Major of 49EOD Squadron. They had replaced me! I immediately responded by saying 'No! I am the Sgt Major of 49 Sqn.' That was it! A few days later I had agreement from the doctors to discharge myself into the care of my wife who was a registered nurse. After all, the only treatment I was getting at this stage was regular new dressings and she could do that. So armed with a box of dressings, lotions and pills I went home!

I returned to duty as Sgt Major immediately after the August Bank Holiday 1982. I was determined to prove that little had changed – although it had – and that I was able to carry out my duties. After a final medical assessment it was agreed that I could stay in the Army and, after a chat with the boss, I was also permitted to go back onto the duty roster as an operational bomb disposal operator. Although it was stated on the Orders for the Victory Parade through London in October, that "no wounded would be on parade" I was there. I could march but could not swing my left arm, so what?! A great day.

A day or two before the Victory Parade I had been called to the Commanding Officer's office to be told that I had been awarded the Distinguished Service Cross (DSC) for gallantry during the Falklands Conflict. I was also informed that Jim Prescott had been awarded a posthumous Conspicuous Gallantry Medal (Navy) (CGM), the only one awarded for the conflict. Both these awards are unique to Army personnel and the Corps of Royal Engineers is very proud of them. The CGM is a very rare award. Since its introduction in 1885 there have been fewer awarded than Victoria Crosses. In 1993 this medal was replaced by the Conspicuous Gallantry Cross. Both Groups of medals are now on display in the Royal Engineers Museum in Chatham.

Writing this has reminded me of when I was preparing to go to

Buckingham Palace to receive my medal. It looked as if my prosthesis (artificial arm) would not be ready in time for the investiture. As I wanted to look "normal", and being a true Royal Engineer having been taught to improvise, I asked my wife to find something to fill the sleeve of my uniform to which I could attach the prosthetic hand, which was ready. We came up with the idea of filling one of her tights with wool to which we attached the hand. When this was done we attached it to my shirt and put the jacket on to view the outcome. It looked very good and it was comfortable. However, as I was looking in the mirror admiring the workmanship, I began to notice that my artificial arm was getting longer! After about a minute it was touching the floor. The tights had stretched under the weight of the prosthetic hand. This was the first time we had laughed since my return home. The arm did, eventually, arrive in time for my investiture.

In May 1983 I was promoted to Regimental Sergeant Major. After two years I received a Regular Quartermaster Commission and was promoted to Captain (QM). My last position in the Army was as the Training Officer (Army) at the Defence Explosive Ordnance Disposal School (Bomb Disposal School). The fact that I had only one arm raised the level of attentiveness of the students I had the pleasure to teach. I chose to leave the Army prematurely in 1989 and had a very successful career as a Senior Technical Officer (Explosives) with the Health and Safety Executive in London. I took early retirement from the Civil Service on my 58th birthday and have never looked back. I spend my time as a volunteer with SSAFA Forces Help and as a Trustee of BLESMA and SAMA82, all of which keep me very busy indeed!

My family and I will always be grateful to all those in Ajax Bay, on The Hospital Ship *Uganda*, on HMS *Hydra*, RAF Transport and those at Woolwich Military Hospital who patched me up and got me back safely.

BLESMA (British Limbless Ex-service Men's Association) are unfortunately seeing more and more young men coming home from active service having lost limbs. In the past 5 years there have been more than 140 such cases. That's 140 more people who have to have the determination - together with the support of their families - to readjust and get on with their lives.

(BLESMA membership categories include servicemen and women amputees, loss of sight, loss of eyes and loss of use of limbs.)

John Phillips DSC WO2 (SSM) 49 (EOD) Sqn RE in 1982. Trustee, British Limbless Ex-Service Men's Association. February 2009.

I feel it is fitting to end this chapter with these thoughtful words from Senior Nursing Officer Liz Law, who helped so many seriously wounded servicemen on the road to recovery from her position as Senior Nursing Officer in The Intensive Care Unit:

> When we finally transferred the last of our patients on 14th July we were de-registered as a Hospital Ship. We were then able to bring home other troops. It was not long before the decks echoed to the footsteps of some 600 1/7th Gurkhas and the personnel of 16 Field Ambulance. We had, by now, dismantled all the beds and re-stored the medical equipment. Apart from a few marks on the carpets, all that remained were our memories:
>
> - The memories of the three men whose lives we could not save.
>
> - The bravery of those whose lives would be forever changed either because of physical or mental trauma.
>
> - The remarkable recoveries witnessed, against all odds.
>
> Elizabeth Ormerod (nee Law)
> July 2008
>
> THE END
>
> Although, of course, this is not the end for all those involved...

The Final Chapter

THE SOUTH ATLANTIC MEDAL ASSOCIATION (SAMA82) AND THE INAUGURAL HOSPITAL SHIP *UGANDA* REUNION

April 2008

So, this isn't "The End" of our story. This is really just the beginning of another chapter…

… In 2002 I joined The South Atlantic Medal Association (SAMA82) after hearing Michael Nicholson's programme on Radio 4 – "Falkland Islands Families". By now I had left the National Health Service, and with a little bit of spare time available, wanted to help 1982 veterans and the injured servicemen who had passed through our care, should the opportunity arise. I had not heard of this veterans' association until then and, apart from contact with Sister Margaret Kerr, the other Operating Theatre Sister, and Sister Chris Asendorf, I had little contact with any other personnel who had served on board The Hospital Ship.

Very few, if any, Hospital Ship personnel were SAMA82 members at that time. The Secretary of The Association was then Denzil Connick who, as a Lance Corporal in 3 Para, had lost his left leg and most of his right on Mount Longdon in June 1982. Denzil's contribution to this book has been told in full in Chapter Seven. We all remember him very well from 1982, and Denzil and I quickly re-established a mutual friendship and respect which has strengthened through our work with SAMA82. I have a deep regard for what he has achieved since his life-threatening attack in The Falklands, and have become friends with both Denzil and Theresa, his wife, over the years.

The South Atlantic Medal Association, Registered Charity number 1118842 www.sama82.org.uk was formed in 1997 during the 15th Anniversary year of the

Falklands War. There are various membership categories that include all veterans of the 1982 South Atlantic Campaign. Through a network of Branches throughout the UK and our Falkland Islands Branch (SAMAFI) we aim to promote a sense of pride and comradeship amongst veterans, their relatives, and the Falkland Islanders. We work closely with other veterans' associations in matters of Welfare and other related issues. We also aim to maintain and strengthen our links with The Falkland Islands. As an Association we are deeply committed to helping sufferers from Post Traumatic Stress Disorder (PTSD). Each year our Committee works with our branch in The Falkland Islands (SAMAFI) and The Falkland Islands Government, helping veterans from 1982 make return pilgrimages to The Islands, as part of a healing programme for all involved. As this final chapter will reveal, it was my great privilege and pleasure to help SAMA82 with this complex process from 2003 to 2008.

In 2002 at the 20th Anniversary year, and again in 2007 at the 25th Anniversary, SAMA82 arranged for groups of some 200 1982 veterans to make return trips to The Falkland Islands. Veterans genuinely want to make this trip, to pay their respects to their fallen comrades, to come to terms with their sites of trauma, and also to see how much the events of 1982 mean to The Falkland Islanders. The enormity of this undertaking should not be underestimated. The Falkland Islands are 8,000 miles from our shores, and remain almost as difficult to get to now as they were all those years ago! The flights to and from Brize Norton via Ascension, in two legs of about 7-9 hours each, are often the first time veterans have flown "long-haul". Many of those selected continue to suffer today from PTSD symptoms and need much help and support to undertake such a long and indeed utterly exhausting journey, in both practical and emotional terms. But veterans really do want to make this trip very much indeed, and every group is well over-subscribed.

As well as the larger "milestone years", SAMA82 works closely with our Branch in The Falkland Islands, SAMAFI, to arrange smaller trips at least twice a year. These are usually timed to coincide with November Remembrance Day Services and June 14th Liberation Day, both of which are supported widely by all The Falkland Islanders.

In November 2003 I was selected within the SAMA82 system, to make my first return trip to the Islands with a small group of veterans, two of whom had been former patients on The Hospital Ship. At that time, SAMA82 membership, and indeed incoming finances, had fallen off; we were not yet a Registered Charity, and for a number of reasons things were difficult within The Association. At the same time a new Rector had just arrived at Christchurch Cathedral in Stanley, and also a new Governor had been installed at Government House. Terry Peck MBE, the founder and then Chairman of SAMAFI, and a key member in The Islands in the return pilgrimage process, was not in the best of health, and the overall co-ordination of the system was much in need of improvement.

The trip was, simply, a life-changing experience for me, as it was for all in the group. We all stayed with host families in Stanley, and Falkland Islanders drove us in their own vehicles, giving their own time, to the various memorials and battle sites as we required. Every site of military significance from The Falkland War is marked by a carefully maintained Memorial, which The Falkland Islanders themselves help to care for with assistance from The Commonwealth War Graves Commission. This alone is a source of great comfort to the families and friends of those who gave their lives so far from home.

There are several other aspects to this unique "return pilgrimage" process that veterans describe in their own ways later in this chapter. But for us all, to have the opportunity to walk in peace and without danger on land and battlefields that have been ravaged by conflict and war is not only a privilege, but also an immensely healing and calming experience. This, combined with the warmth and generosity of The Falkland Islanders themselves, the unpolluted atmosphere, the vast skies, ever-changing seas and unique wildlife, all combine to ensure that everyone who makes the effort to undertake the long journey south returns home refreshed and renewed by the experience.

My own host in Stanley was Shirley Hirtle, a fourth generation Falkland Islander, who could not have been kinder, more thoughtful and supportive, as at times the emotions obviously ran high. Mind you, I was a disappointment to her in some ways… Shirley was then a working "bachelor lady", and she told me jokingly that when she'd put her name down with Terry Peck to host veterans she was rather hoping to meet a couple of handsome Paras or Royal Marines! So being allocated a boring white-haired old nursing lady was not quite what she had in mind!! Shirley and I have remained firm friends and I'm sure will remain in close touch for the foreseeable future.

On return to UK I teamed up with Andy (Curly) Jones, another SAMA stalwart, then Secretary of SAMA Wales. At the request of then SAMA82 Chairman Captain Martin Reed, Curly, myself and the new SAMAFI Chairman, Gary Clement, initiated a new SAMA Pilgrimage Support Team within the SAMA Association framework. Sadly, Terry Peck died in 2006. During that period of difficulty and changeover at all levels within The Association, Curly, SAMAFI and I arranged numerous veterans' return trips to The Falklands, and eventually, between us, helped several dozen veterans, and the widow of a soldier killed in action, to make the restorative journey in the smaller groups. At that time, each return trip to The Islands was costing well over £1,000 in flight fares alone; this had to be obtained from Veterans Associations, other related charities, or indeed the Falkland Island Government themselves. All in all, it was a time-consuming, complex and expensive process, but nevertheless it was a privilege and pleasure to help veterans in this practical way. I hope I was able to help our team to gradually improve the system during the years I was involved. In that time I made numerous return trips to The Islands, some at my own expense, did much bridge-building behind the scenes, and made many lasting and meaningful friendships in The Falkland Islands that I know are cherished by us all.

Fortunately for everybody, since the 25th Anniversary Pilgrimage, all Falklands War veterans are now entitled to apply for "military indulgence" or subsidised flights to and from The Falkland Islands which will greatly ease the financial burden on all concerned. I, and many others, had campaigned very hard for this concession over many years; it is a sensible move forward which we know will help a great many people in the years to come.

Currently, and since 1982, veterans have been "hosted" in Falkland Islands homes for their visits. This is a truly unique and very special arrangement that works extremely well for everyone concerned. The Falkland Islanders, including the next generation since 1982, remain eternally grateful to members of The Task Force for all their sacrifices on their behalf, liberating them from their unwanted and uninvited rulers. The people of The Falkland Islands are the kindest, most thoughtful and generous of hosts and many of them open their homes to returning veterans on a regular basis. However, as the years advance, and in the available years that this process can continue, more veterans will want and indeed need to return to The Islands accompanied by family members or carers. So, with this in mind, a "Veterans' House" has recently been built and opened in Stanley, and this will enable groups to make the return trip within a more flexible accommodation system. The house has been named "Liberty Lodge" and was opened in February 2009 by The Commander of The British Forces and South Atlantic Islands, Air Commodore Gordon Moulds, himself a veteran of The 1982 Falklands War.

In 2007, at The 25th Anniversary of The Falklands War, a number of National Events to commemorate and remember The Falklands War and the Liberation of The Islands were organised. I was fortunate to attend a number of these including: The Service of Remembrance and Thanksgiving at The Falkland Islands Memorial Chapel, Pangbourne; a Service at Trinity House; a Reunion with 1/7th Gurkha Rifles, and the principal function in Horse Guards Parade on Sunday June 17th 2007. With over 8,000 other Task Force veterans, a contingent of 6 QARNNS Nurses from The Hospital Ship *Uganda* assembled for the Service of Commemoration, and then marched down The Mall to Buckingham Palace. It was a unique and memorable week during which countless friendships were renewed and much camaraderie restored.

The Hospital Ship *Uganda* was also included in The Imperial War Museum's Falklands 25th Anniversary Exhibition in London. For some reason still unclear to me I was selected to participate in this meaningful Exhibition, which linked to an ingenious interactive website where memories, spoken recollections, memorabilia and superb photographic exhibits could all be viewed from the comfort of one's armchair at home. Several Falkland Islanders were included in The Exhibition, including Tim Miller, at whose eye operation I had assisted all those years ago.

Another participant was Bill Belcher MBE, a severely injured Royal Marine aviator, who had been thrown from the back of a Brigade Air Squadron Scout helicopter. It had come under attack en route to collect casualties from 2 Para, including the mortally wounded body of Colonel H Jones from the battle at Goose Green. Bill lost one leg and nearly the second in this attack, in which the RM pilot Lt. Richard Nunn was killed.

Bill had made many trips to our operating theatres on The Hospital Ship, but of course we hadn't met or been in contact since he left The Hospital Ship to return to UK in 1982, so it was quite an emotional reunion after all that time. Bill, his wife Lynn and I remain in close touch as the years advance. Bill concludes his thoughts later in this chapter.

A surge of renewed interest in our former Hospital Ship, from personnel who served on board and from the injured servicemen we had treated and cared for, was emerging. As the only person from the Hospital Ship involved with 1982 veterans through SAMA82 I was unsure how to harness all this interest. Initially, I couldn't quite understand why it was happening. In time I realised that personnel from nearly all other ships and units from The Task Force had, of course, been meeting on a regular basis for the intervening 25 years. Not so with The Hospital Ship *Uganda* personnel, most of whom seemed to have disappeared into thin air! An opportunity came our way when I met with Derek Houghton at the 25th Anniversary London Falklands Event in Horse Guards Parade on June 17th 2007. Derek had been our P&O Accommodation Officer on board The Hospital Ship in 1982. Although we had lost touch in the intervening years, we recognised each other straight away and established contact soon after the momentous events of that memorable week.

THE INAUGURAL HOSPITAL SHIP
UGANDA REUNION – APRIL 2008

And so the idea of a Hospital Ship Reunion was born, and The Inaugural Hospital Ship *Uganda* Reunion was held on board the P&O cruise ship *Aurora* in April 2008. The planned Event was initially started as "a pie and a pint in a pub", but P&O Captain Grahame Burton and Derek Houghton's contacts within P&O were able to accommodate us as a group during the cruise ship's changeover during an April weekend. By complete coincidence, it was the same date, April 19th/20th, 26 years before, that *Uganda*, as Her Majesty's Hospital Ship *Uganda*, had left Gibraltar Dockyard for the uncertainties of The South Atlantic.

The Event was an overwhelming success. We had come full circle. Nearly 200 former personnel attended, which included the widows of P&O Captains Brian Biddick and Jeff Clark, 20 or so of our most severely injured former patients, RN Medical Doctors, QARNNS Nurses, Royal Marine stretcher-bearers and P&O personnel, many accompanied by their partners or wives. Few of us had met in the intervening years. Lady Thatcher sent us a Letter of Support, and Andy Gough (now Admiral, CB), and I presented St. Dunstaner, and former patient, Terry Bullingham with a Braille copy of all the documents relating to the Function.

The Falklands War, fought far away and long ago, will always be part of the lives of those who participated. Hopefully, with the support and strength of some of our veterans' charities, St. Dunstan's, The British Limbless Ex-Servicemen's Association and The South Atlantic Medal Association, we will now, as a group of professionals reunited after 26 years, have the motivation to support and encourage each other by remaining in touch as the years advance.

Colleagues, former patients and others who attended The Function on board *Aurora* express their feelings about the whole experience:

P&O Captain Grahame A. Burton RD FRSA FNI:
(In 1982: P&O Chief Officer Grahame Burton RNR)

Photograph: Author's private collection

Several of us were recently thrilled to be able to arrange a special Hospital Ship *Uganda* Reunion on board the P&O Cruises superliner *Aurora* in Southampton in April 2008. The idea for this came during the week of National Commemorations for the 25th Anniversary of The Falklands War. A group of us met at the wreath laying at the Merchant Navy Falklands memorial in Trinity Gardens, Tower Hill, London, and the main Event in Horse Guards Parade on Sunday June 17th. So many old and new friendships were rekindled, and it occurred to a group of us that personnel from The Hospital Ship had not had the opportunity to meet since 1982, unlike most of the other ships and units involved in Operation Corporate.

It was all a bit of a leap into the unknown, as we had few contact details from so many different personnel now widely dispersed all over the world. But our hard work and diligence paid off, and the Event was an overwhelming success. Nearly 200 of us based ourselves at an adjacent hotel for the weekend and gathered on board *Aurora* on Sunday April 20th, the exact weekend date *Uganda* had sailed from Gibraltar in her new Hospital Ship livery 26 years before. Another Falklands veteran, the Cunard *QE2,* was moored directly astern of *Aurora*, most uncanny for the 1/7th Gurkhas who had joined us, as they had voyaged south to The Falklands on board her in 1982.

We had very much wanted to include our former patients in this unique occasion. The Event Organiser and former QARNNS Theatre Sister, Nicci Pugh, who seemed to know many of the 1982 veterans through her work with The South Atlantic Medal Association, worked ceaselessly with Derek Houghton, our former Accommodation Officer on board *Uganda*, tracking everybody down. It was a memorable day, described by the now Admiral Andy Gough CB as "simply, a triumph". Now, we all hope to continue to keep in touch, certainly up to the 30th Anniversary in 2012.

Quite a group of P&O personnel who had been *Uganda* crew members during the conflict attended, and we discovered that there is now a website devoted to pictures and notes about current and ex P&O Officers of our generation. So, as the Latin motto on the P&O crest states:

"Quis Nos Separabit"
"So – Who Will Separate Us?"

Captain Grahame A. Burton.
August 2008

* * *

Dr Peter T. Bull MBCh.B, FRCA: Consultant Anaesthetist:
(In 1982: Surgeon Commander Peter Bull RN. Consultant Anaesthetist to The Task Force)

Photograph: Dr Peter Bull

Our First Hospital Ship *Uganda* Reunion was held in April 2008 in Southampton, when nearly 200 of us met at a local hotel to relive our memories and then attend a lunch celebration aboard the P&O Cruises superliner SS *Aurora* – kindly provided for us for the afternoon during her changeover, by P&O. It was unique in that we particularly wanted to include as many of our former patients as possible, and SAMA82 member Nicci Pugh was able to harness her Association work to contact some of them. It was an emotional experience after so long, but made us realise how incredibly well most of our former patients have fared in the intervening years, and also how grateful many of them were to have been under our care. Of necessity, they had left us as soon as they were fit to travel back to UK, and most of us had never seen or heard of them since.

One of our more well-known patients (though not our most severely injured), Simon Weston OBE, was unable to join us but hopes to be able to as future events unfold. I was able to talk with many others, whose survival and rehabilitation were a pleasure to behold. The Event was widely covered by the National and local press, television and BFBS.

Many of the amputees belong to BLESMA, The British Limbless Ex-Servicemen's Association, and several Falklands veterans are also St. Dunstaners, the Charity for blind ex-Servicemen and women. So, with South Atlantic Medal Association members aplenty there are now several Charities and Service Associations that help link all this aspect of war together.

The publication of this little book arose following the success of our 2008 Reunion. Many attendees approached the Organiser, former QARNNS Operating Theatre Sister Nicci Pugh, asking how we could collate all this information before it all fades with our memories as the years advance. Nicci valiantly took on the task, and this meaningful publication has arisen entirely from her diligence and hard work in gathering all the necessary information. Our thanks must also go to Falklands veteran David Connett, who helped Nicci in the early stages of the publishing process, and subsequently Melrose Books near Cambridge, who have seen the project through to completion. Our special thanks also go to Major-General Julian Thompson for agreeing to write the Foreword for us.

Dr Peter T. Bull MBCh.B, FRCA
August 2008

* * *

Commander Isa Gauld RRC:
(In 1982: Superintending Nursing Officer Isa Gauld QARNNS)

My involvement with SAMA 82 was not until very recently – I eventually got my membership just after our Inaugural Hospital Ship Reunion in April 2008. I hope to be able to get more involved in the future.

Unlike Nicci, who has been closely involved with The Association, 1982 veterans and many of our former patients for some years, I had mixed feelings about the planned Reunion. I had visited some of the Welsh Guardsmen when they were in The Military Hospital Woolwich later in 1982, and very few of them seemed to remember their time on board The Hospital Ship, which was probably a good thing. So I was wondering what the reactions would be.

Photograph: Sandra Rowse

However, I was very surprised at the memories of both staff and patients; for many the recollections were crystal clear, and the former patients were really pleased to have been included in such a unique event, and to have the opportunity to meet and speak with the nurses, doctors and other teams who had helped them all those years ago.

And, of course no one seemed a day older!!

It was very necessary to meet again, and a real tonic for all. Many said they wished it had happened earlier, so now we're all in touch as a group, I'd be confident we'll continue in a lower-key way for some years to come.

* * *

Lt. Commander Mark Trasler, whose Laboratory skills with the vital "Hospital Ship Blood Transfusion Service" we have read about in such detail earlier in the book (in Chapter Six), concludes his thoughts on how he, and the personnel on board The Hospital Ship, coped in 1982:

Lieutenant Commander Mark Trasler MBE RN:
(In 1982: Chief Petty Officer Mark Trasler RN Medical Technician MT1 (Lab))

The Falklands War was probably the most influential event of my service career. A unique experience in that, on board The Hospital Ship, it ultimately relied on old fashioned technology and, more importantly, old fashioned values. The challenge was enormous and was met with adaptability, innovation and pure hard work. The harsh reality of war, with the inevitable human loss and misery, was all too evident and I felt we came close to being overwhelmed. But news of the surrender came, not only just in time, but with a huge sense of relief that the death, injury and suffering would sometime cease. That said, the job satisfaction as a health care professional was enormous, and I am proud of (the albeit

Photograph: Mark Trasler

modest) part I was privileged to play. The bravery and heroism of our patients, and potential patients, was probably the most remarkable factor and I am honoured to remain in touch with them and, where possible, support them, through The South Atlantic Medal Association. The Inaugural Hospital Ship Reunion that Nicci Pugh and Derek Houghton organised on board the P&O Cruise Ship *Aurora* in April 2008 pulled all these feelings together in a unique and memorable way.

* * *

State Registered Nurses Maggie and David Freer:
(In 1982: QARNNS Head Naval Nurse Maggie Freer and husband
Chief Petty Officer David Freer RN Medical Assistant Medical Technician MT1)

QARNNS SNN Marion Stock BEM with HNN Maggie Freer at The Inaugural Hospital Ship Reunion. April 2008 .
Photograph: Author's private collection

The First Hospital Ship Reunion in April 2008 brought all these forgotten thoughts and memories back into focus and it was a real privilege to meet former patients, especially those David and I had both treated on separate ships in The Task Force. Also, (to meet) many of our colleagues whom we hadn't seen in the intervening years. We had been considering joining SAMA82 for some time and have now both done so, and I've volunteered to help Nicci and her teams with the administration of future Reunions. Many said they wished it had happened before, so now we've all finally made contact again, I'm sure some of us will now keep in touch, certainly up to the 30th Anniversary of The Falklands War in 2012. Although our memories may fade as the years advance, our former patients live with their injuries from 1982 on a daily basis, so we can support and encourage them in this way by letting them know they are far from forgotten, even after all this time.

* * *

Karen Dawson (now Harwood):
(In 1982: QARNNS Naval Nurse Karen Dawson)

I heard about the reunion in 2008 from one of the Bandies (RM stretcher-bearers on board The Hospital Ship in 1982) and then my neighbour told me I was in the "Navy News" and I should read it as there was a Hospital Ship Reunion coming up. It was the first time most of us had met for 26 years, apart from Nicci who belongs to The South Atlantic Medal Association and seems to be in touch with everyone, especially lots of the former patients.

During the few days before The April Reunion I did start to get nervous about meeting people I hadn't seen for 26 years, when we were all younger and slimmer! I'm good at remembering faces, but not names, and was worried I might not recognise people after all this time. I went with my husband and arranged to meet Les Aldridge who'd been an RN Medical Assistant on board; Les and I were classmates in training, and we've stayed in touch.

The Event on board *Aurora* was on Sunday April 20th 2008. Some of us based ourselves at a Premier Inn near to Southampton Docks for the weekend, so people started to arrive on the Saturday afternoon; it was very strange it was the exact date The Hospital Ship left Gibraltar 26 years ago; they said it was a coincidence, but you can't help but wonder.

Nicci and Derek were there to greet everyone. They had a brilliant information pack and name badges which really helped. As soon as we all saw each other we started to recognise faces, and that was it. It was just fabulous to see all the old faces that I had lost contact with and have always wondered what they were up to. Most of us had brought photo albums; it was amazing seeing us all in colour pictures 26 years ago. I hadn't taken that many pictures in 1982 as we weren't allowed to take photographs around the clinical areas.

Uganda had a beauty all of her own and I will always remember her with both sad and happy memories. It was a time in my life I will never forget however old I get.

AURORA IS JUST "WOW".

What else can you say! She is just amazing!

We arrived at the Southampton Docks early and went to the arrival area on the quayside. Nicci was already there and needed to get things on board early to set up for the day, so we went through the strict security together. As we queued to get on board, all the wheelchair passengers from the last P&O cruise were disembarking; were there more than in 1982, we wondered? We had been allocated the Crow's Nest on the top deck and ironically next to it was a small room called the *Uganda* Room with a small model of the SS *Uganda*. Nicci had not known of this so how spooky was that? Of all the ships in the P&O fleet they chose the *Aurora* or did the ship choose us because of the day? That just made the day a bit more special.

As we were early we had a chance to go round all 13 decks of the ship, and what luxury, so very different from the *Uganda*. As more people started to arrive they were not so lucky as us and had to wait a long time to get on board. Teas and coffee were served (and home-made biscuits!) whilst everyone was meeting up and photos being taken. There were lots and lots of hugs and smiles and especially fond memories coming flooding back, even though some of them were sad.

We were then all escorted to the dining room for a sit-down silver service lunch. The food was excellent and the speeches were very emotional. Commander Gough (now Admiral) had us all in stitches, as well as making us all realise how difficult things were for them at the time.

The patients were the stars of the day and it must have taken a lot of courage to bring back all the bad memories of the pain they went through.

I was really looking forward to meeting Smudge Smith whom I nursed on ICU, but at the last minute he was genuinely unwell; we all hope he'll make the next event.

I was also hoping to speak with John Strange who was one of the first patients I looked after on The Hospital Ship, but we missed each other as he was so busy; there were nearly 200 of us altogether, so it was quite a crowd.

After the lunch and speeches we went back up to the Crow's Nest with the fabulous views right over Southampton Water... and the sun shone for us all! Now we all want to keep in touch and not leave it so long. Our time slot on the *Aurora* was up and we had to disembark to allow the next group of passengers on board so they could sail to the Mediterranean. What lucky people – I know a few of us would have liked to have stowed away somewhere! Time went too quickly, so many things

BLESMA member and former Welsh Guardsman John Jones shares a joke with the author as they walk the decks of P&O cruise liner Aurora *for The Inaugural Hospital Ship* Uganda *Reunion. April 2007.*
Photograph: Author's private collection

to find out now, but hopefully we will all keep in contact now we've had this amazing experience.

Thanks need to go to Nicci and Derek for making this all happen, and now they deserve some rest.

* * *

John Jones was a Lance-Sergeant in the Welsh Guards and was injured in the Stanley Airfield Incident on July 13th 1982. He was treated on board *Uganda* but had to have both legs amputated below the knee. He attended the Function with his wife Jane and I spent quite a bit of time with them both over the weekend. John was interviewed by the BBC at the Function on board *Aurora*, and said:

> I just wanted to shake the surgeon by the hand and
> thank the whole team for their dedication, sheer courage and
> care which meant that so many of us did come back alive.

After the event John wrote:

John Jones:
(In 1982: Lance-Sergeant John Jones First Battalion Welsh Guards)

> Thanks to the work done by the SAMA82 Pilgrimage Committees I, along with many hundreds of 1982 veterans, have been fortunate enough to return to the Falkland Islands in groups spread over many years. Nicci has explained in this book how this process works, and how deeply important it is for us all.
>
> I found the experience very emotional, particularly the first time, but at the same time it provided some sort of "closure" for me… whatever that means. The whole place seems so much smaller, and the jetty where we first landed is still there, but it does seem very small now. During my first trip I found my old trench near Wall Mountain from where I saw the ships hit in Fitzroy on the 8th June. The little cove where the Welsh Guards landed, immortalised thanks to the wonders of TV, looks very peaceful and has no visible sign of the tragedy that occurred there except for the memorial crosses on either side. It all seems so long ago and yet so fresh.

* * *

Bill Belcher MBE also attended the Function with his wife Lynn. Here Bill concludes his thoughts, as well as describing a poignant gesture that he and Lynn achieved during his recent trip to The Falkland Islands over the 25ᵗʰ Anniversary in November 2007:

Bill Belcher MBE:
(In 1982: Air Gunner Sergeant Bill Belcher RM)

Bill Belcher MBE RM following the Falklands War Twenty-Fifth Anniversary Comemorative Service and march. June 2007 .
Photograph: Bill Belcher

Over the years, I have been extremely fortunate to be able to return to the Falkland Islands, both alone and with close family, and have met many generous, honest and caring people. I have been impressed at the way the Islands have been developed, grown and settled by more ex-pats. The exodus from the islands to the UK has mainly been stemmed and the increased opportunities have raised the retention of young people and quality of life befitting the 21ˢᵗ century. Long may that continue.

2007 marked the 25ᵗʰ anniversary of the conflict and we could not let it pass without appropriate commemoration and remembrance of the events that changed so many lives. I was invited to assist the Imperial War Museum with their display in London, and worked on the snapshot of our action on the 28ᵗʰ May, and assisted with the Opening Ceremony. Here, for the first time for 25 years, I reunited with Nicci Pugh, one of the QARNNS OT Sisters on board The Hospital Ship *Uganda* in 1982, and both admitted to a tad of emotion at that moment. Little did any of us realise that inside the nurse was this author struggling to get out!

On 17ᵗʰ June I took part in the Parade on Horse Guards and surprised myself by yomping all the way down the Mall in the company of so many proud and distinguished old warriors.

I also participated in a special display at the Waddington Air Show where one of our restored Gazelles from 1982 became the centre of an aviation themed commemoration of Operation Corporate. Finally, and to round off the year, my wife and I travelled down to Stanley for the Remembrance Day parades and to join in the latest pilgrimage by SAMA82. Once again, a chance to witness amazing hospitality, generosity and friendliness from our hosts and everyone we met.

On our last day, I managed to plant a young fir tree where our aircraft came to rest all those years ago. It stands alongside a cairn that now marks the spot where we finished that last sortie, and ended the struggle to evade a determined adversary.

His gravestone is still neat and tidy, in the Argentine cemetery further inland from Goose Green. But that is another story.

To top off the commemorations, the medical staff and crew of the Hospital Ship *Uganda* held their own first reunion in April this year (2008). Their many former patients were included in this unique event and we were honoured to meet on board the P&O cruise ship *Aurora* in Southampton. We were wined and dined, met fellow patients, and most importantly, the nurses, surgeons, anaesthetists and Bandies who had formed up in Gibraltar

The author with former patient and BLESMA member Bill Belcher MBE at the opening of The Imperial War Museum's Twenty-Fifth Anniversary Falklands War Exhibition. Bill's former Commanding Officer Lt.Col. Peter Cameron MC RM behind them.
Photograph: Imperial War Museum

as we headed South in the Amphibious Task Group. Such a pleasure to see those folks who had had helped save my life so long ago.

Bill Belcher MBE

August 2008.

Bill and Lynn Belcher at the commemorative cairn near Camilla Creek House on East Falkland, where Bill and Lt Richard Nunn DFC RM crashed in 1982. November 2007.
Photograph: Bill Belcher

Ossie Osborn tells us about his return trips to The Falklands, and his time at our Reunion in April 2008:

Robert ("Ossie") Osborn:
(In 1982: Guardsman Robert Osborn 2nd Battalion Scots Guards)

I'm a BLESMA member, and was on the first South Atlantic Medal Association (SAMA82) return Pilgrimage to The Falkland Islands in 2002. In 2007 I made my own way back for the 25th Anniversary Pilgrimage, staying with Bill and Clara McKay on both occasions. Bill and Clara and their family have become very good friends. They open their house and their hearts to me; it is wonderful how kind everyone is in The Islands to returning veterans. I hope to get back to the Falklands again in the near future.

After the big Commemorations of the 25th Anniversary of the Falklands War in and around London, I heard through BLESMA of the first Hospital Ship *Uganda* Reunion which was being held on board a cruise ship in Southampton in April 2008. This was the first time anyone from the Hospital Ship had met, and all the former patients were included. Amazing! I signed up straight away. I wanted to meet up with all the Navy medical teams who had helped me after my injuries. It was a brilliant weekend.

People had travelled from all over UK and abroad; we all based ourselves at a nearby Premier Inn, and were on board *Aurora* by 1000 on the Sunday morning. There were nearly 200 of us altogether. I specially wanted to meet and talk with Diana Aldwinckle, who was the QARNNS Staff Nurse on Sea View ward who had been so good to me, and Sister Nicci Pugh who I knew by then had assisted at my operation when the leg was amputated. I sat with Sister Margaret Kerr, the other Theatre Sister on board *Uganda*, and Chief Jim Lacey, for lunch. I also spent time with Doc Beeley and Doc Bull; they were all very kind and professional, and didn't mind talking about my treatment at all. I'm going to keep in touch with all the group now, as I think they did a fantastic job for us all down there, and no one ever seems to mention them.

I like their new name which is HUGS 2009; the letters stand for Hospital Ship *Uganda*. Anyway, that's what nurses do a lot of, and they're a great crowd of lasses (and some gents, of course!).

During the whole time I was on the Hospital Ship in 1982, I got the best treatment and, more importantly, care from the Navy Medical team that was possible, especially members of QARNNS – "The Fearless Forty".

A Big Thank You To All "<u>HUGS</u>".
You'll always be Special to me
When the Army's Hurt, QARNNS Heal!

Ossie Osborn
July 2008

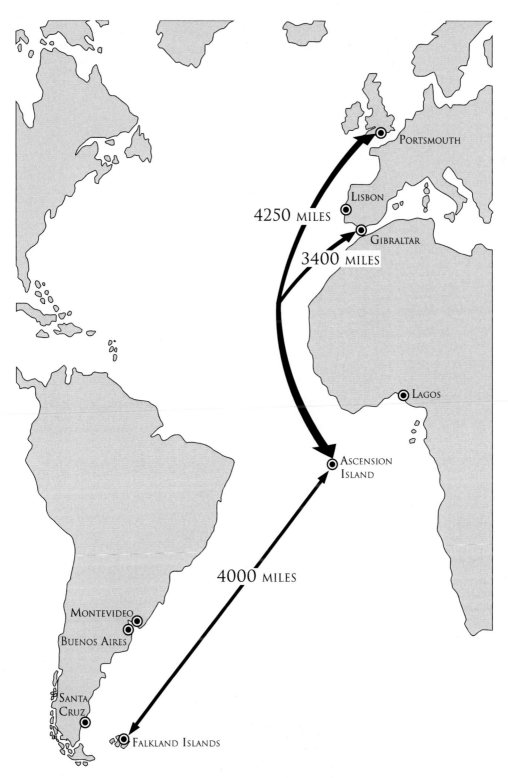

PORTSMOUTH

LISBON

4250 MILES

GIBRALTAR

3400 MILES

LAGOS

ASCENSION
ISLAND

4000 MILES

MONTEVIDEO

BUENOS AIRES

SANTA
CRUZ

FALKLAND ISLANDS

Distances between UK, Ascension Island and The Falkland Islands.

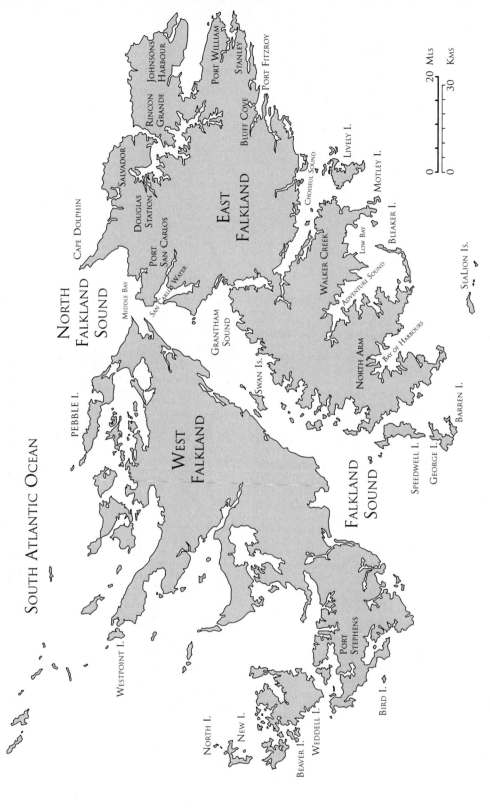

Outlines of East and West Falkland Islands, showing some of the anchorages used by *The Hospital Ship Uganda in 1982 (e.g. Grantham Sound, Middle Bay and Port William.)*

Locations of the three Military Field Dressing Stations ashore during the 1982 Falklands War (positions are approximate).

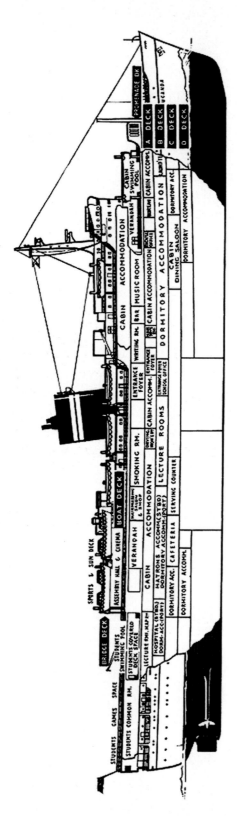

Profile of SS Uganda following her conversion to Educational Cruising in 1968. The majority of hospital facilities were located on the Promenade Deck during her requisition to serve as Her Majesty's Hospital Ship Uganda throughout the Falklands War in 1982.

Source: SS Uganda Trust

Margaret Thatcher

19th April 2008

Twenty six years ago the Hospital Ship Uganda departed Gibraltar for the uncertainties of the South Atlantic. Only a few days before the ship had been host to hundreds of schoolchildren cruising in the Mediterranean. She was now sailing to war.

For the doctors, nurses and support staff on board, the following months would be the ultimate test of their professionalism and dedication. In the most difficult of conditions the ship became a refuge for the men who had given their all and now lay badly injured, in desperate need of life-saving treatment. Sadly, some did not make it through but what is remarkable given the circumstances is that so many of the patients did.

As you gather to mark those months, now over a quarter of a century past, the vivid memories of the skills, the courage and the comradeship of staff and patients alike will be uppermost in your minds. For some of you, the bonds forged aboard Uganda will have survived well after your return. But for all of you, those moments will remain a life-long testament to all that was achieved.

Last year, at numerous events across the country, we saw that the people of Britain have not forgotten all that you did for us in that conflict. Today, again, we honour and salute you.

Margaret Thatcher

THE RT. HON. THE BARONESS THATCHER. L.G., O.M., F.R.S.
HOUSE OF LORDS. LONDON SW1A 0PW

A copy of The Letter of Support from Lady Margaret Thatcher for The Inaugural Hospital Ship Uganda *Reunion in April 2008.*

APPENDIX ONE

MILITARY FEMALES IN COMBAT TODAY

Today, since the implementation of the Equal Opportunities Act in the early eighties, women serve in nearly all specialities in the British Armed Forces, except those where the primary duty is "to close with and kill the enemy".

There are currently around 18,000 women serving in the British Services, and approximately one in five of the 8,000 troops serving in southern Afghanistan are female. Women serve in a number of units on the front line, which include piloting combat jets, other fixed-wing and rotary aircraft (helicopters) and serving as medics, interpreters, in transport and bomb disposal.

Women have also served within Britain's Special Forces for more than 20 years.

Since 2003 seven female members of The British Armed Forces have died on operations – five of whom were killed in enemy action. Many more have been wounded. In November 2008 Captain Kate Philp had to have a leg amputated below the knee after the Warrior mini-tank she was commanding ran over a 50kg bomb in Afghanistan. Captain Philp is believed to be the first woman combat amputee in British military history.

The most recent to be killed was Corporal Sarah Bryant of The Intelligence Corps who was killed on June 19th 2008, along with four members of the Territorial SAS, when their "SNATCH" Land Rover was destroyed by a roadside bomb in Afghanistan.

British servicewomen have also recently been the recipients of some of the highest British awards for gallantry. The first woman to be awarded the Military Cross was Private Michelle Norris of the Royal Army Medical Corps while attached to the Princess of Wales's Royal Regiment in Iraq. Under sniper fire Private Norris saved the life of a critically injured colleague during a fierce battle in Southern Iraq in 2006. In March 2008 Flight Lieutenant Michelle Goodman, a Royal Air Force helicopter pilot, was awarded The Distinguished Flying Cross after rescuing a severely wounded soldier from the centre of Basra at night. Under heavy fire, she managed to land the helicopter close to the injured soldier, who had been given only fifteen minutes to live, enabling him to reach safety and successful surgery in time.

In 2009 Able Seaman Class One Kate Nesbitt became the first woman in the Royal Navy to be awarded the Military Cross. Able Seaman Nesbitt spent thirty minutes administering medical care while under Taliban fire to a soldier who had been shot in the neck. The

Ministry of Defence said: 'Able Seaman Nesbitt's actions throughout a series of offensive operations were exemplary. Under fire and under pressure her commitment and courage were inspirational, and made the difference between life and death. She performed in the highest tradition of her service'.

Following the same tour of duty in 2008/2009 Lieutenant Commander Alison Hofman, the QARNNS Commanding Officer of the Medical Treatment Facility at Camp Bastion located in The Helmand Territory of Southern Afghanistan, was awarded the Order of the Royal Red Cross (RRC) for her 'consistently high standards of nursing and military achievement at The Camp Bastion Hospital'.

Speaking recently on the subject of females working within combat zones, a spokesman for the Ministry of Defence said: 'Women continue to serve bravely on the frontline in many ground support roles. Currently, females within the British military framework do not serve in roles where they may be required to engage the enemy deliberately in face to face combat, often at the point of a bayonet.'

Of all nationalities of troops serving in Iraq in 2008, approximately 11,000 women served alongside 127,000 men. American female military roles are similar to those of British female military personnel; they are deployed as members of some ground combat units, as aircraft pilots, and at checkpoint duties searching Iraqi women. This latter role led to a tragic incident in Fallujah in 2005 when four American female servicewomen were killed in an ambush. US Commanders believe the females were specifically targeted in that incident, as Iraqi women are searched at checkpoints by US female military personnel to avoid upsetting Islamic cultural sensitivities.

Canada now has full gender integration within its Armed Forces. The Canadian Armed Forces opened all military occupations, including combat roles, to women in 1989; only their conventionally powered submarines were excluded, and by year 2000, women submariners were also accepted. Today, women make up some 15% of the Canadian military. Approximately 225 women are part of their Regular Combat Force with 925 in Combat Reserves. In May 2006 Canada experienced their first loss of an active combat female soldier. Captain Nichola Goddard died on the front lines during a battle against The Taliban in southern Afghanistan.

There is no doubt that overall, modern warfare is changing. What was once a clearly defined and symmetrical "front line" is now very hazy indeed. All those who currently serve in these overseas forward units have to work and travel in dangerous areas on a daily basis. The risk of suicide bombings and roadside attacks doesn't exclude servicewomen; and civilians, women and local children are all equally at risk.

Other countries seem much in line with our own British military statistics on this issue: Women represent 19% of all French military personnel; they serve in all posts including infantry, but not in submarines or in riot control. Germany has no restrictions for females in the different military branches. Women make up 13% of Australian forces, with some restrictions; New Zealand has no restrictions within its defence force. Pakistan has recently started to recruit women for combat roles. Israel reduces their normally three year conscription to two years for females who serve in non-combatant positions.

Appendix Two

WOMEN WITHIN THE SERVICES AND THE ROYAL NAVY TODAY

I n 1993 the WRNS (Women's Royal Naval Service), which had been created in 1917, was disbanded and, from then onwards, women joined the Royal Navy on an equal footing with men. Women now serve on at least one third of all the Royal Navy ships; the only specialities they are excluded from are diving and submarines. This is for physiological reasons and remains under review.

Likewise, The Women's Royal Army Corps was disbanded in 1992, and now 70% of the Force is fully gender-mixed.

Women in all three Services now receive equality in pay, opportunities and working conditions with the men who work at sea and ashore.

In all three British Services, The Royal Navy, Army and The Royal Air Force, the number of servicewomen in senior appointments has continued to increase since 2005; in 2006 there were two female Army Brigadiers, and 20 female Colonels; and at least 20 female Group Captains in The Royal Air Force.

In 2004 Commodore Carolyn Stait CBE RN was the first Royal Navy female to reach the rank of Royal Naval Commodore in direct competition with her male counterparts; Commodore Stait is delighted to make the following entry for this book:

> Like Nicci and her QARNNS contemporaries in the eighties and nineties, all other female Royal Naval officers and ratings had to adapt to the changes happening around us. The WRNS as an entirely separate service effectively came to an end when we became subject to the Naval Discipline Act in 1977, but it took another 15 years before we had adopted the same insignia and rank/rate titles as our male colleagues. Gradually, professional training was delivered in mixed classes, and thus the separate professions for WRNS ratings and officers disappeared. The biggest change, of course, was the decision to send Na-

val women to serve in front-line units at sea. In the late eighties, the then Captain Alan West (former Captain of HMS *Ardent* in 1982, now Lord West of Spithead) led the work that resulted in female RN officers and ratings serving at sea in major warships from 1990. Amongst the first female RN personnel at sea were the complement of HMS *Brilliant* as she sailed for front-line service in the first Gulf War that year. Naturally, there were some teething problems and some of the die-hard traditionalists were never going to accept such a change without a lot of chuntering into their hammocks. But the quality and capability of seagoing women eventually convinced all but the most intransigent and bigoted of sceptics, and it is now simply inconceivable to imagine an RN surface ship doing its job without female crew members as an integral and essential part of the ship's operational performance. Women still don't serve in our nuclear submarines, and no western power has yet sent women to sea in nuclear-powered submarines. None of the British Armed Forces accept women in front-line fighting units that may have to engage in hand-to-hand combat; so, for example, there are no female combatant Royal Marines.

I had entered the Women's Royal Naval Service in 1975 as a Cadet Wren Weapon Analyst, wearing blue insignia and with aspirations that could realistically look no further than eventual attainment of the two-and-a-half blue stripes that signified a First Officer WRNS (equivalent of a Lieutenant Commander). I left the Royal Navy at the end of 2007, wearing the broad gold stripe of a Naval Commodore (the equivalent of an Army Brigadier).

In my final appointment in the Service, I was the Naval Base Commander, Clyde, and held that Command appointment for three-and-a-half years. In very broad terms, I had responsibility for some 6,500 military and civilian personnel who worked in the Base (including the crews of the base-ported submarines and ships); I managed an annual operating budget of £190m; I was responsible for the safe operation of several mobile nuclear reactors at any one time (whenever a nuclear sub – UK or foreign – was alongside); and was responsible for the custody, maintenance and fitting of the bulk of the nation's strategic weapon stockpile.

Not in my wildest dreams as an 18-year old in 1975 could I, or anyone else in the Royal Navy or the Women's Royal Naval Service, have dreamed of such an outcome.

I first met Nicci in 1983 when the Task Force had returned from The South Atlantic and we both held appointments in Gibraltar. She was already an experienced offshore sailor with a recent Transatlantic sailing passage under her belt, and I knew how much she believed in encouraging females to serve at sea as well as on land, even in those early days.

She and her colleagues have managed to convey in this book the very essence of professional men and women working and existing together at sea, and pulling together for the good of the team and for the effective achievement of the mission aim.

In 1982, this was quite exceptional. In 2009, it is happening today and every other day, wherever the Royal Navy is needed as a force for good around the globe.

Commodore Carolyn Stait CBE RN
May 2009

Appendix Three

THE ROYAL NAVAL MEDICAL SERVICE AND QUEEN ALEXANDRA'S ROYAL NAVAL NURSING SERVICE TODAY

All QARNNS personnel, both officers and ratings, have served under The Naval Discipline Act since July 1977. Following affiliation to The Royal Navy in the eighties, QARNNS Nursing Officers switched to Royal Naval ranks in 1995, and QARNNS officially became part of The Royal Navy in March 2000. This is defined as "The Royal Navy's discrete (separate) Nursing Specialisation". QARNNS ratings now complete basic Naval Training at HMS *Raleigh* in Cornwall and, along with all other RN entry specialities, march in Naval Divisions, and wear "fore and aft" rig for drill and ceremonial occasions.

The QARNNS Patron today, as in 1982, remains HRH Princess Alexandra, the great-granddaughter of Queen Alexandra, the first President when QARNNS was founded in 1902.

The majority of QARNNS personnel serving today have been deployed to Iraq and/ or Afghanistan since operations commenced in 2003. At the time of writing, in early 2009, approximately 750 members of The Royal Naval Medical Service are serving in southern Afghanistan. This includes approximately 100 QARNNS personnel. The primary aims are running the Field Hospital at Camp Bastion, providing medical cover for all other British facilities, accompanying patrols on the ground, and manning the ambulance incident response teams. Injured civilians are also treated within this facility, which, as in 1982, comes under the auspices of The International Red Cross. From here, injured casualties can be "Aero-Medevaced" back to UK in appropriate Royal Air Force aircraft, accompanied by specialist RAF Teams, initially to RAF Brize Norton, and thence onward to The Royal Centre of Defence Medicine at Selly Oak Hospital in Birmingham, as described in Chapter Ten.

The deployments are based on six-month tours, which incorporate all elements of our Defence Medical Services including Reservists. In effect, the landlocked Field Hospital at Camp Bastion today is providing similar clinical facilities (albeit much improved and modernised in the intervening twenty-seven years) within tented structures in southern Afghanistan, as the floating Hospital Ship *Uganda* did in The South Atlantic Ocean in 1982.

On reading an internet contribution by QARNNS LNN Janine Whitley in 2008 I was struck by how similar her well-written summary of the current situation is, to many aspects referred to in more detail in this book. Camp Bastion is over 3,000 nautical miles from the sea, and yet the lack of fresh water for showering and sanitation seems to have changed little as the years have advanced!

Life in the British Services at sea, on land and in the air will ever be thus... the constant juggling between one's high professional ideals and aspirations; and the reality of day to day living, eating and indeed surviving with your colleagues in difficult, hostile, demanding and dangerous conditions. For professional military nurses, as with our civilian colleagues, the treatments, care, safety, welfare and wellbeing of our patients are always paramount. Nowhere is this demonstrated more clearly than in a war/trauma situation, where clinical skills have to run alongside speed, efficiency and accuracy, as well as a maintenance of morale for patients and staff alike, often in the most difficult and distressing circumstances. With our Tri-Service colleagues, Queen Alexandra's Royal Naval Nursing Service personnel seem to be demonstrating their skills as well today as when we were created in 1902.

With this Tri-Service Field Hospital operating today so far from the sea, ironically, twenty-seven years after The Falklands War, our adopted motto of: "HEAL NAVY" seems as apt today as it was all those years ago. Or, as injured Scots Guardsman and BLESMA member Robert "Ossie" Osborn wrote at the end of his contribution to this book: "When the Army's hurt – QARNNS Heal".

APPENDIX FOUR

EQUIVALENT QARNNS AND ROYAL NAVY RATES/RANKS IN 1982

QARNNS	ROYAL NAVY MEDICAL ASSISTANTS	ROYAL NAVY
	~ JUNIOR RATINGS ~	
Naval Nurse (NN)	Medical Assistant (MA)	Able Seaman (AB)
Senior Naval Nurse (SNN)	Leading Medical Assistant (LMA)	Leading Rate (LR)
	~ SENIOR RATINGS ~	
Assistant Head Naval Nurse (AHNN)	Medical Technician (MT)	Petty Officer (PO)
Head Naval Nurse (HNN)	Medical Technician One (MT1)	Chief Petty Officer (CPO)

QARNNS NURSING OFFICERS	NAVAL OFFICERS
Nursing Officer (NO)	Sub-Lieutenant (Sub Lt.)
Senior Nursing Officer (SNO)	Lieutenant (Lt.)
Superintending Nursing Officer (Supt. NO)	Lieutenant Commander (Lt.Cdr.)
Principal Nursing Officer (PNO or Matron)	Commander (Cdr.)
Chief Nursing Officer (CNO)	Captain (Capt.)
Matron-in-Chief	Commodore (Cdre.)
	Thence Flag Ranks:
	Rear-Admiral; Vice-Admiral;
	Admiral; Admiral of The Fleet.

GLOSSARY

Bergen	A military rucksack.
Bivvie	From "bivouac" – A portable military shelter/windbreak ashore.
BLESMA	British Limbless Ex-Service Men's Association.
BV	Volvo articulated vehicle that can travel over snow and rough terrain e.g. rock & peat bog. Can carry casualties.
CAP	Combat Air Patrol: A patrol flown by fighter aircraft.
CASEVAC/MEDEVAC	Casualty Evacuation/ Medical Evacuation.
CBFSAI	Commander of The British Forces and South Atlantic Islands. (Formerly Commander British Forces Falkland Islands CBFFI.)
CNO	Chief Nursing Officer (QARNNS).
CPO	Chief Petty Officer (Royal Navy Senior Rating, senior to Petty Officer).
CSSD	Central Sterile Supplies Department. (A department within a hospital that supplies sterile dressings and equipment for wards and departments.)
CVRT	Combat Vehicle Reconnaissance Tracked. In The Falklands War Scorpion and Scimitar light tanks manned by two troops of The Blues and Royals that moved with speed and efficiency across the rock peat terrain.

EOD	Explosive Ordnance Disposal (Bomb Disposal).
FAA	Fleet Air Arm. The Aviation element of The Royal Navy.
FH/DS/MDS	Field Hospital/Dressing Station/Main Dressing Station. Military medical facilities located some distance from fighting units e.g. Ajax Bay, Teal Inlet and Fitzroy.
HMHS	Her Majesty's Hospital Ship. The official title of The Hospital Ship *Uganda*.
HMS	Her Majesty's Ship – as in HMS *Coventry*.
HNN/AHNN	Head Naval Nurse/Assistant Head Naval Nurse QARNNS. Senior Ratings (see Appendix 4 Equivalent Ranks/Rates)
HQ/BHQ	Head Quarters/Brigade Head Quarters.
ICRC	International Committee of The Red Cross.
ICU/ITU	Intensive Care Unit/Intensive Therapy Unit.
LCU	Landing Craft Utility – a Landing Craft that can carry stores, trucks and men from ship to shore.
LNN/SNN	Leading Naval Nurse/Senior Naval Nurse (QARNNS Junior Rating).
LPD	Landing Platform Dock e.g. HMS *Intrepid*.
MA/LMA	Medical Assistant/Leading Medical Assistant: Royal Navy Junior Rating Paramedics trained to serve at sea and ashore. All male in 1982.
MOIC	Medical Officer In Charge.
NN	Naval Nurse (QARNNS Junior Rating).
NO	Nursing Officer (QARNNS) or Naval Officer (Royal Navy).

NP	Naval Party – a team of Royal Naval personnel. NP1830 was the official name for the Naval personnel selected to serve on board The Hospital Ship *Uganda*.
OT	Operating Theatres.
P&O	Pacific and Oriental Steam Navigation Company.
Para	Parachute Regiment: as in 2 Para, Second Battalion The Parachute Regiment; or 3 Para, Third Battalion The Parachute Regiment.
PMRAFNS	Princess Mary's Royal Air Force Nursing Service. Established in 1921.
PNO	Principal Nursing Officer (Matron) QARNNS.
Porthole	Small opening or window in side of a ship. Referred to as "a scuttle" in the Royal Navy.
PO	Petty Officer (Royal Navy Senior Rating).
QAIMNS	Queen Alexandra's Imperial Nursing Service. Established in 1902.
QARANC	Queen Alexandra's Royal Army Nursing Corps. Founded in 1949.
QARNNS	Queen Alexandra's Royal Naval Nursing Service. Founded in 1902.
RAF	Royal Air Force (can also refer to a Royal Air Force base e.g. RAF Lyneham).
RAMC	Royal Army Medical Corps.
RAP	Regimental Aid Post (located with fighting units).
RAS	Re-Fuelling At Sea (RAS-ing).

RCB	Red Cross Box (a defined Sea Area for Hospital Ships to work in). During The Falklands War Her Majesty's Hospital Ship *Uganda* was allocated numerous different RCBs as the conflict unfolded. To simplify this issue for the reader some RCB coordinates have been combined.
RFA	Royal Fleet Auxiliary.
RM	Royal Marine.
RN	Royal Navy.
RNH	Royal Naval Hospital: as in RNH Haslar.
RNMS	Royal Navy Medical Services.
RNR	Royal Naval Reserve.
SAMA82	The South Atlantic Medal Association. The (Service) Association for veterans of The 1982 Falklands War.
SAS	Special Air Service.
SBS	Special Boat Squadron.
SEN	State Enrolled Nurse.
SNO	Senior Nursing Officer (QARNNS) or Senior Naval Officer (Royal Navy).
SRN/RGN	State Registered Nurse/Registered General Nurse.
ST. DUNSTAN'S	National Charity for blind/partially sighted Ex-Servicemen and women.
STORE-ING	Taking on (board) Naval or Military stores.
STUFT	Ships Taken Up From Trade i.e. ships that have been requisitioned by the Ministry of Defence e.g. *QE2*, SS *Canberra*, SS *Uganda*.

Supt. NO	Superintending Nursing Officer (QARNNS).
TEZ	Total Exclusion Zone. In The Falklands War a circular sea area 400 nautical miles in diameter surrounding The Falkland Islands.
TSSU	Theatre Sterile Supply Unit (a department that cleans, processes and sterilises instruments, and all the essential sterile requirements for Operating Theatres in hospitals).
UK	United Kingdom.
VERTREP	Vertical Replenishment or transfer by helicopter.

SELECT BIBLIOGRAPHY

BOOKS

Clapp, Commodore Michael with Southby-Tailyour Ewen. *Amphibious Assault Falklands: The Battle of San Carlos Water*. Leo Cooper, 1996.

Frost, Major-General John. *2 Para Falklands The Battalion at War*. Sphere Books, 1983.

Hart Dyke, Captain David. *Four Weeks in May*. Atlantic Books, 2007.

Hastings, Sir Max. *Going to the Wars*. Macmillan, 2001.

Hunt, Sir Rex. *My Falkland Days*. David and Charles, 1992.

Jolly, Doctor R.C. *The Red and Green Life Machine*. Century Publishing, 1983.

McManners, Hugh. *Falklands Commando*. Harper Collins, 1984.

McManners, Hugh. *Forgotten Voices of the Falklands*. Ebury Press, 2007.

Rintoul, Doctor A.J. *The Unacceptable Face of War*. Published privately, 2002.

Southby-Tailyour, Ewen. *Falkland Islands Shores*. Conway Maritime Press, 1985.

Southby-Tailyour, Ewen. *Reasons in Writing*. Pen and Sword, 1993.

SS *Uganda* Trust. UGANDA – *The Story Of A Very Special Ship*. SS *Uganda* Trust, 1998.

Taylor, Captain C.M. *Nursing in the Senior Service 1902-2002*. Studio 6, 2002.

The Sunday Times Insight Team. *The Falklands War*. Sphere Books, 1982.

Thompson, Major-General Julian. *No Picnic*. Leo Cooper, 1985.

Tyrer, Nicola. *Sisters in Arms*. Weidenfeld and Nicolson, 2008.

PAPERS

Beeley, Doctor J.M. *Hospital Ship* Uganda – *At War in The South Atlantic*. Journal of The Royal Naval Medical Service, April 1983.

Bull, Doctor P.T. *Anaesthesia Ashore and Afloat during The Falklands War*. Journal of The Royal Naval Medical Service, August 1983.

Hope, Captain G.L. *Ere Their Story Die*. The Military Chest, 1983; Fix and Sound, 2007.

AUTHOR BIOGRAPHY

Nicci Pugh qualified as a State Registered Nurse in 1971. She immediately consolidated her training by completing a Post-Registration Course in Operating Theatre Technique at St. George's Hospital, Hyde Park Corner in London, and then worked for a year as a Staff Nurse in an Intensive Care Unit in a French-speaking hospital in Switzerland.

She was the youngest Theatre Sister to be appointed at The Royal Cornwall Hospital in 1975. She joined Queen Alexandra's Royal Naval Nursing Service as a Senior Nursing Officer on a five year short service Commission in 1980, and worked as an Operating Theatre Sister at The Royal Naval Hospitals Haslar, Gibraltar and Stonehouse.

In April 1982 she was selected with 39 other QARNNS nursing personnel to serve on board Her Majesty's Hospital Ship *Uganda* (The Hospital Ship *Uganda*) during the Falklands War. The QARNNS Nursing Officers and Naval Nurses were the only military females working within The Combat Zone during The Conflict, and the QARNNS Naval Nurses on board The Hospital Ship were the first female Royal Naval junior ratings in history to serve at sea.

In 2002 Nicci joined The South Atlantic Medal Association (SAMA82) and for some years helped with the process of helping veterans from 1982 make their much-needed return trips to The Falkland Islands.

In 2008 she organised The Inaugural Hospital Ship Reunion, which was held on board the P&O Cruises superliner *Aurora* in Southampton; 26 years earlier, to the date, Her Majesty's Hospital Ship *Uganda* had left from Gibraltar for the uncertainties of The South Atlantic. Attending the Reunion were former RN Doctors, QARNNS Nurses, Royal Marine stretcher-bearers, P&O personnel and former patients. The Event was an overwhelming success, and was the first time severely injured servicemen had been included in such a Function. This little book has been written at the request of the majority of attendees at that unique and meaningful Event, who have asked for one person to collate the information that may, otherwise, be lost in the mists of time as the years advance.

The book, written in a frank, thoughtful and sensitive way, seeks to cover the events of 1982 and The Falklands War from a Naval Nursing Sister's point of view. There are accounts from all levels who served on board The Hospital Ship: Royal Naval Surgeons and Doctors, QARNNS Nurses, Royal Marine stretcher-bearers and P&O personnel. Most importantly, there are accounts from the former patients themselves who were cared for and treated by the Royal Naval Doctors and QARNNS Nurses on board.

Nicci Pugh spent much of her childhood on board her family's houseboat, the 40' Thames Barge Yacht and Dunkirk Little Ship's veteran *Nancibelle*. Her father, Captain C.R.V. (Dick) Pugh CBE served in the Royal Navy from 1916 to 1950. In 1952 the family moved to Cornwall, where they ran a working dairy farm on the upper reaches of The Helford River. She could row, swim and sail by the age of five. She has always managed to combine her love of sailing, boats and the sea with her nursing career. She qualified from The Glenans sailing school in France in 1968, The Jersey Cruising School in 1979, and the Joint Services Sailing Centre as watch-keeper on Nicholson 55s in 1981. She completed her first of several subsequent transatlantic sailing passages in 1979, just before joining Queen Alexandra's Royal Naval Nursing Service in 1980. She has sailed more oceans, owned more boats, applied more coats of hull antifouling and belonged to more sailing clubs than she cares to remember. She belongs to The Royal Naval Sailing Association and keeps her own boat on The River Fal in Cornwall, which she describes as "still one of the most beautiful and changeable stretches of open water in the world".